MW01068221

TOY CARS

Nathan Spiteri

Toy Cars   Nathan Spiteri

FOR CHARLIE
FOR ALL SURVIVORS
FOR MYSELF
FOR EVERYONE

Toy Cars   Nathan Spiteri

Cover design by Jasmine Forecast.

Published by Three Little Birds Press
www.threelittlebirdspress.com

Dear Reader,

I am humbled that you are here. That you are choosing to be here.

Thank you.

Within these pages, within this memoir, are detailed experiences of my life.
Throughout my journey, I have experienced severe trauma, violence, sexual
abuse and addictions.

I feel it is my duty of care to you, to let you know that the experiences
within this memoir are graphic and detailed.

For some of you, this may be extremely difficult and may trigger your own
trauma response/reaction, past or repressed memories or the knowledge of
someone else's trauma.

Having said all of this, we heal together in community, as a global
community, together we can walk each other back home.

In this light, I am here with you every step of the way, I honour you and
your unique story.

My intention is for growth, healing, education, compassion, forgiveness,
peace and for love should you wish to go on this journey with me.

Together we rise.

Toy Cars   Nathan Spiteri

PREFACE

'Hurt People Hurt People.'

I was told this quote a few years ago and it has resonated within me ever since. It hit me hard and also triggered me because I understood it; for this was how I lived my life. I was deeply hurting, and all I was capable of doing was to hurt everyone around me; the ones I loved, in one way or another. I couldn't break the cycle. Late last year, Sally-Anne Ward, the publisher of this book, and someone who has become very dear to me, sent me a message after reading this very quote on one of my Instagram posts. Her response read:

'Healed People Heal People.'

Again, this message resonated within me, even more so, (not that I am or ever will be completely healed), but I am moving forward with my life, toward greater wholeness, evolving and entering a new chapter of who I am and what I am. I am learning that, in healing myself, I am healing others; and in healing others I am continuing to heal myself.

Since I was offered a book deal, people have asked me why I want to write something so honest, raw, intimate and vulnerable. This is a question I could not get out of my mind. It took many months for me to write this memoir, beginning in November 2019 in Sag Harbor, New York, before continuing on at my family house in Queanbeyan, Australia, over Christmas and into the New Year, and then finishing it in Brooklyn, New York in April 2020. Along the way I experienced the devastating 2019/20 Australian bushfires, where I was evacuated from my family beach house in Batemans Bay on the New South Wales south coast on New Year's Eve and almost forced by fire out of my family's home in Queanbeyan. I returned to New York in mid-February to a world struck down by the Coronavirus two weeks later. My father was diagnosed with a terminal blood disease and cancer and I witnessed the Black Lives Matter movement come to life in full force. Living through these traumatic events has really put life into perspective, showing me just how very small and powerless we are as humans in the world. It also revealed to me the enormous power and strength we all carry deep within; a strength that can change the world and make a difference at the same time.

I am writing this book in honour of the power and endurance of the human spirit and one's life journey toward greater wholeness. I am writing for the disempowered, the voiceless, the unheard and the not believed, so that, one day, they too might claim their power, find their voice, truly be heard, and finally be believed. Too many people in the world, men and women, boys and girls, go through their lives never able to share their stories; never able to heal, to grow and to find some closure. You may be one of them. If reading this book allows you to speak up, find your voice, be courageous, to get help and to find peace, then I believe it was all worth it.

From the very first moment I started on the journey of sharing my story – openly and publicly – I did it with the belief that if I can help one person, change just one life, stop one person from killing themselves, from abusing another child, or from going down the same road of being lost/trapped in a world of drugs, sex and violence as I did, then I will have done my job and I will know I did the right thing.

I wrote this book not only for sexual abuse survivors, but for all survivors of any kind of crisis and trauma, violence and abuse;

including people suffering through any form of mental health issue, addiction and PTSD. I see you; I see all of you and I am here with you.

As humans, we all need to be educated, from adults to children, parents to teenagers, about the signs of trauma, the signs of sexual abuse, and the ramifications and emotional impact that abuse has on the lives of innocent children and families. It is still a taboo subject and we need to start 'having the conversation' and not turn a blind eye to it, or sweep it under the carpet, ignoring the gravity of the situation.

We have one life to live to make a difference to ourselves, to the world and to each other; and, as one of many thousands, this is my story, my voice, my journey. This is my chance, my change and my contribution to make this world a better and more peaceful place.

When someone is abused, sexually, physically, mentally and emotionally, they don't just 'move on' with life. There are far reaching consequences, there are reactions, there is deep trauma and these life changing moments affect us all.

This book is how I survived and lived as a result of sexual abuse. This is my life. I may not be the perfect messenger, but I'll do my best to get the perfect message out there – I'll do my best to be the perfect voice.

The following story is not who I am, it is not my make-up. It might be the color of my pants, but it is not the whole of my outfit. It is a story of the 'first act' of my life, not the whole story, and it definitely doesn't define me. I still have so many more acts to go; still unwritten, undefined and unscripted. Everything that happened to me in my life has brought me to this moment, to writing this book, to sharing this message, to bringing life and shedding light on a subject that has been buried for so long.

I also wrote this book for my parents, my siblings and my entire family, so that they might finally understand who I was and who I now am, the person I have become and the story I am now able to share openly. I have put my whole life, my truth out there and it is scary as hell, but also exciting and life changing.

To my Mum and Dad, I love you. You have been the most generous, loving and forgiving parents anyone could ever ask for. I have become the man I am today because of who you are and all the support and love you gave me. Everything good I have inside of me, I have from you. Promise me, you will never blame yourself for anything that happened to me or for who I was. I was who I was to protect you and myself. I acted only out of love for you and my siblings. I am not a perfect person, I never will be, nor do I ever want to be. I would love you to see me for who I am today, not for who I was yesterday. See me for my achievements, for traveling this winding road, and for the man that I have now become.

All I ask is for you to be proud of me.

I have written this book for me: For the healing, growing and understanding I needed to find in myself, so I could truly realize who I am in this world. This writing journey has been ridiculously hard and painful, taking me to very dark and triggering places. It has also been unbelievably healing, therapeutic, uplifting and life-changing. The writing has opened my eyes to the darkness as well as the beauty there is in the world. It has opened many new doors for me, and closed many old and painful ones that no longer serve as useful.

Toy Cars   Nathan Spiteri

I have learned that through calmness and self-reflection comes clarity. I have taken a step back, allowed myself to breathe, to make mistakes, maintain calm, and finally find the peace, joy and love I have long desired.

In its essence as my friend, Mal taught me;

    "Everything is a reflection & nothing is as it seems."

Toy Cars   Nathan Spiteri

INTRODUCTION

I was made in Malta and born in Australia.

I was born February 3rd, 1978, in Canberra, Australia, the capital city. Most people think it's either Sydney or Melbourne. However, back in the day, Sydney and Melbourne were fighting over becoming the capital city of Australia and they gave it to Canberra, a little bush town in the middle, which is now referred to as the 'Bush Capital'.

My mother immigrated to Australia from Malta when she was one and a half years old on April Fool's Day, 1st April 1955, with her parents, her older sister and younger brother. My grandmother already had family in Australia, predominantly in Canberra. Following the second world war, where Malta was bombed heavily by the Germans and Italians, many Maltese moved to Australia for freedom, hope, a new beginning and a new life. Mum went back to Malta in her late teens for a cousin's wedding, where she met my father. They dated, mum went back and forth between Australia and Malta before finally settling back in Malta to be with my dad. They married and had my sister and, after a few years of living in Malta, mum missed her family and life in Australia and presented my dad with the dream and opportunity of a new life in Australia. They moved to Australia in November of 1977 and I was born four months later.

I grew up in Queanbeyan, New South Wales (NSW), a little town with a population of about 20,000 at the time. The town is situated on the

NSW border with the Australian Capital Territory, otherwise known as Canberra. Queanbeyan was a blue-collar town, mostly made up of middle-income earners. The majority of its population would travel into Canberra for work, mostly for the government or in the building industry. Queanbeyan had a few nicknames, 'Struggle Town', which comes from the iconic Australian band, The Choirboys, whose song 'Struggle Town' was written about Queanbeyan after one of the band member's father coined the name after visiting. Another nickname is 'City of Champions', named after the famous sports personalities that originated from the town. The name Queanbeyan actually hails from the Aboriginal word, Quinbean, meaning 'clear waters.'

Before Him

Chapter 1

One of my earliest memories was having a birthday party at Weston Park on Lake Burley Griffin in Canberra. It may have been my fifth or sixth birthday and my parents presented me with a Donald Duck cake. Being a summer baby, I remember it as a hot day and we were all swimming in the lake. I was with my parents, brother and sister. I think my grandparents and extended family may have been there also. In general, I was a quiet kid, even before it happened; I wasn't an extrovert by any stretch of the imagination. I was always a skinny little thing, scrappy, and a very fast runner. I loved being outdoors, playing sport; but I also loved my time inside alone too, playing with my toy cars and watching cartoons and movies on TV.

I remember my sister having a big birthday with lots of her school friends. She was born November 13th and is a little more than two years older than me. It was at our house, in the backyard, and she had a cake in the shape of a round swimming pool. It had chocolate biscuits around the edge; the inside was filled with jelly laying atop a delicious sponge cake, with little dolls swimming idly in the jelly. Crazy, the things you remember.

Another memory I have was the first time I got the cane at school. I was young, probably in Year One or Two. We were kids just playing a game; it may have been during P.E., and we had to crawl between the other students' legs. From what I remember all the girls were wearing skirts and every time I crawled under one, I would daringly look up. I was a curious little boy. I'm not sure if I got caught or if one of the girls caught me and turned me in, but I was sent to the principal's office where the Head Mistress pulled out a long, thin cane. She made me hold my hands out, palms up, as she whipped the cane down hard and fast onto the unsteady palms that I held out before her.

One of my happiest memories, still to this day, and the only time I really felt pure joy and freedom, was on our first family trip back to Malta. I think it was six months before it happened. My youngest brother had not been born yet, and I must have been about seven years old. We went to that beautiful island for three months, probably from June through August. I remember my sister Janice, brother Peter, and I were very happy because we were swapping the cold Canberra winter for the heat of the Mediterranean summer. But most importantly, we were missing three months of school.

Malta is a place like none other. It is located in the middle of the Mediterranean Sea, under Sicily, Italy and above Libya and Tunisia on the North African coast. It is literally a full stop on any world atlas or map. It is made up of three little islands, Malta being the largest and most populated, Gozo, second, with Comino nestled quietly between the two. Malta is literally a concrete island, there are not too many parks and trees around and the farmland is rough country, very rocky and solid, definitely not the easiest place to grow fruits and vegetables, but what they do grow has its own unique taste and is absolutely beautiful. The population today is close to five hundred thousand with most living on the island of Malta, followed by Gozo, and you can count on one hand the people living on Comino. The population almost education. He would often give us a history lesson on Malta, and drive us around the island to see all of the churches, catacombs, temples and museums that were a part of our family's history. We would definitely not have such a love and understanding for Malta if it weren't for him.

Our grandmother, Nanna Carmen, was the sweetest woman in the world; a gentle and warm heart with so much love to give. She doted over us kids, didn't care about the school work, but just wanted to see us happy. We were her only grandkids and she always made sure we had breakfast, lunch and dinner on the table, with plenty of snacks in between. They were married for over sixty years and they never spent a day apart. Nannu was ninety-seven years old when he died. We were all hoping he would make it to one hundred. I think Nanna died at ninety-two.

My Auntie Lina, my dad's sister, the eldest of the three kids, was a highly stressed and anxiety-ridden woman, but she was also the most loving Auntie with the biggest heart. I always feared that she cared and worried too much about everyone; she would fuss over us every minute of every day. She was about five-foot-tall; tiny to my eyes, but she had so much life inside of her. She had a lot of love to give, sometimes too much, and on occasion was a real pain in the arse. A piano teacher, highly regarded throughout the island, Auntie Lina never married; she lived for her parents, family and friends. She never moved out of the family home and she took care of my grandparents until the day each died. A beautiful woman inside and out, she died of cancer in early 2018, always trying to do anything for anyone.

Uncle Tony was dads' brother. He was the spitting image of my dad; they could have been twins. He moved to London in his early twenties and turned into a perfect English gentleman. Dashing, with a porcelain-like face, I often wondered if he had ever been out in the sun a day in his life. Dad, on the other hand, had a dark Mediterranean complexion.

Another distinction between the two is that Uncle Tony was a refined man with perfect manners and speech, whereas dad was more of a 'typical' Maltese man, a little rough around the edges. Uncle Tony spoke in a perfect English accent, while dad still has a little of the Maltese accent in him, now combined with an Australian flair.

My favorite person from my dad's family, and possibly my favorite person ever, was my great Uncle Ignatius, Nazu, as he was called, or 'Uncle Nuts' as us kids would call him. He was my grandmother's younger brother and he lived with them in the family home. He also never married nor had a relationship with a significant other. He told me that he was scared to be in a relationship thinking that he was going to get hurt or catch some disease. He literally lived in his bedroom, where he would only come out for food and to use the bathroom. He had a little piss bucket in the corner of his room that he would use during the day. We always knew when he had woken up in the morning, or from his afternoon siesta, because we would hear him peeing into his bucket. He would sit in his favorite chair, read his newspapers, listen to the news and his Maltese music on the radio and smoke his pipe and cigars. That was the entirety of his life.

Uncle Naz would always let me light and puff his pipe and cigar. I loved it and, to this day, the smell of a pipe brings me back to those quiet, innocent days back in Uncle Naz's room. Maybe it was because I was the first-born son, or maybe because he saw a bit of his younger self in me, he had a soft spot in his heart for me. We had a special connection; I knew I was his favorite, and I would spend hours with him in his room, Uncle Naz sitting in his chair and me lying on his bed talking about the family and life. He was always worried that one day I would catch AIDS or that I would get a girl pregnant. He once told me how he traveled abroad to Italy, and a man propositioned him in a public bathroom. Since that day, he said he was scared of all close relationships. I loved that man so much. Uncle Naz died in his late eighties. God bless him, his big heart, and his beautiful soul.

We must have good genes in the family because I had the chance to meet my great grandfather on my father's side, whom the family said I was exactly like. He was a skinny man with a finicky appetite; a trait I seem to have to this day. I also met my maternal great grandfather, a sweet old man with the spirit of my mum's father; and my maternal great grandmother, a cute, and sometimes crazy, old lady who could only hear us if we screamed. She lived to the ripe old age of ninety-nine.

My maternal grandfather, Nannu Charlie, was the patriarch of the Australian family. He came to Australia by boat with nothing, and built a successful plastering business in the building industry in Canberra. He was a hardworking man who didn't show much love or affection. Mum's brother, Uncle Ray, worked for him, running much of the details of the business. The youngest of three siblings, Uncle Ray was always the cool young uncle we wanted to hang with. I would go to work with them sometimes during school holidays and help out on site. Looking back, I imagine I was a bit of a pain at times; getting in the way and making more of a mess than they allowed themselves to admit. A tough old bastard, my grandfather was 'old school' European, with a personal credo that, since he worked all day and made the money, he didn't have to raise a finger when he got home. Thus, Nannu Charlie never involved himself in the cooking, cleaning or caretaking of the kids. I remember when I finished high school, I asked him if I could take over the business as he was planning to shut it down and retire. He shut down my request just as quick, adding firmly that all the grandchildren had to go out and get their own jobs and make their own money. He came from a different time with a different generational mindset. He seemed to have gotten grumpier and more impatient with age.

When he did finally retire, Nannu would sit in his chair at home watching his programs and sports on TV, not moving all day. On the off chance that he did go out, it was to muse over his little vegetable garden out back or to putter in his shed. I remember his work truck, so messy and piled so high with work tools and with the things he collected, that it was a wonder he never killed anyone on the road with falling debris. I remember being told a story about how his customers would pay him in cash, and he would drive around for months with envelopes filled with thousands of dollars, sometimes forgetting completely where the money was. He and my grandmother would fight a lot and, although he never truly showed it, he did have a great depth of love in him. He would be quietly proud when a new grandchild or great grandchild was born, and would often cry at Christmas and on my grandmother's birthday.

One of my earliest memories of Nannu Charlie was when I was a kid and he and his business partner were invited by a client to watch a Rugby League match in Sydney. It was a match between the Sydney Roosters and the South Sydney Rabbitohs, and he took me with him. We all piled into a van early in the morning, spent the day watching football in the corporate box, and drove home late that same night. I remember that was my first time in the city of Sydney, and I was mesmerized by its size and energy. I admired the tall buildings and told myself that I was going to live there one day. Even at a young age, I knew there was a big, bad world out there for me, and that the simple ways of Canberra could not hold me back.

Chapter 2

I spent a lot of my time with my mum's mother, my grandmother, as a child in Australia, Nanna Gina. She, too, was an amazing woman, beautiful with a big heart, who gave her whole life for her family. She didn't have an easy life but she was always full of love for us grandkids. We would spend every day before and after school with her, from kindergarten through to Year Two. Our school was a two-minute walk up the road from her house. We would get dropped off to her in the morning as mum and dad were on their way to work, and she would pick us up every afternoon at school and take us to her house. It wasn't just my siblings and I, but also my two cousins, Matt and Marissa, my Auntie Antionette's kids, she was my mum's older sister, a beautiful and loving auntie and person, who was always there for us and would do anything for us. We were very close to her as she lived next door; she was always either at our place or we were at hers.

I remember those sweet afternoons after school, when Nanna Gina would give us a bowl of cereal, either Weet-Bix, Coco Pops or Nutri Grain. She would make us eggs on toast or eggs with soldiers while we watched her favorite soap operas together. Once we were finished, we would go outside and play soccer, cricket, hide and seek, or simply run wild and free in her backyard protected by the shade of the trees and her watchful eyes. She was a talented cook and would make traditional Maltese soups, pasta and rabbit dishes. Rabbit is a national dish of Malta. I'll always remember her preparing the dish in front of us; skinning and cutting a whole rabbit up, with blood and guts going everywhere and preparing the dish in the traditional way. It always fascinated me. She is in her early nineties now, living with dementia in a home. She doesn't remember any of us anymore, doesn't speak and literally just sits all day staring into space, such a terrible and debilitating disease. I talk to her in Maltese when I visit her and I tease her sometimes, telling her how cute she looks. I sometimes get a smile out of her.

The first time I ever saw porn was at my grandparents' house. My Uncle Ray still lived with my grandparents at the time, it was one afternoon after school and he must have still been at work. All of us kids would sometimes pile into his room to watch cartoons or a kid's program on his television, if our grandmother was watching one of her shows. We saw this new machine called a 'video cassette recorder', a VCR; we put a video in the recorder and pressed the play button. At first, we didn't know what we were watching; it was zoomed in on either a sex scene or on someone giving oral, but then it zoomed out and we saw naked bodies and heard moaning and we turned it off straight away, laughing and screaming. We put it back on a few seconds later and watched a little more of it. I thought it was fascinating and it was possibly my first introduction to sex.

A memory that always stays with me is the day my dad picked me up from my grandparent's house after school. I was there alone with my grandmother. I went outside to meet him, my grandmother followed. My father walked over to me with a surprise gift; a shiny, new grey toy car. The back wheels didn't turn, they were jammed stuck, which made me love the car even more for its vulnerability and uniqueness. My grandmother invited him in for some afternoon tea and, while they went inside, I stayed on the front lawn playing with my new toy. I drove it on the railings of her front porch, up and down the light brown brick walls, and flew it through the cool afternoon air with my arms stretched outward, also throwing it high, ready to catch it as it landed into my waiting and safe hands.

Chapter 3

My family owns a beach house in Batehaven, Batemans Bay, about an hour and a half away from Canberra, a lovely haven for all of us to go for the Christmas holidays, as well as long hot summers. My grandfather was a bit of a crazy driver and brought a brand-new BMW and I would sometimes travel with him and my grandmother in the car to the coast, with my grandmother screaming at him to slow down. They were nonstop arguers; always going at each other. Maltese people tend to scream a lot at each other, even when they are just having a normal conversation. Sometimes twenty of us piled into that place, between the aunties, uncles and cousins, so it was always a loud, mad-house. As kids, we would spend all our days at the beach or learning how to swim, getting our bronze medallion at the local swimming pool with hundreds of other kids. We would ride our bikes around, play cricket or soccer in the front yard or on the beach, play putt putt golf in town and catch scores of lizards in the backyard. At night we would go to the carnival down the road and ride the rides or play the carnival games. It was a magical time and a magical place for any kid to grow up in and spend the summers.

I don't have many more memories before the event that changed everything, but from what I do remember, my parents were always loving and kind. Janice, Peter and I never wanted for anything when we were children. My dad was, and still is, a gentle, beautiful, soul. A sweet man who would do absolutely anything for us. He would literally stop what he was doing to pick us up, take us anywhere and do anything we asked. In this way he took after his mother. A quiet man with a big heart, he was apparently a handful and a bit of a trouble maker as a kid, and a lady's man before he met my mum. He was a big drinker and smoker who got into all sorts of mischief and was sent to boarding school for the discipline.

We would laugh at our dad growing up a lot, he was a funny man, even when he was trying not to be. We would tend to laugh more at him, than with him. Our friends all loved him and still do, he always had time for them, as they did him. My mother, too, was a loving parent who would do anything for her kids. She was the tougher parent though, the disciplinarian when we were growing up. She would be the one to hit us, give us the wooden spoon or the belt; and we would always run to dad and ask him to make her stop. In this way mum was just like her father, tough, but she was also an amazing cook and loving parent like her mother. I don't really remember getting much affection, hugs and kisses from either one of my parents growing up. I definitely wasn't one for affection anyway, even if they tried to offer it, though my brothers and sister definitely were.

I don't really have too many memories of my sister, Janice, before it happened. I do remember that, over the years, she was the one I would go to with any serious problem. I could never really talk to my parents about the serious stuff. Maybe it was a function of their generation, and of being of European descent, but it was hard for me to speak openly with them. I've laughed and cried with my sister, had lots of fights as well; one could say I was a difficult brother on occasion. At these times, Janice would kick my arse and force me to sit and think about what I was doing and where I had been. She is now a school teacher in Canberra. She has an amazing soul and a loving heart, although she still has a short temper for my challenging behaviors. She's been through hell over the past five years. Firstly, trying to get pregnant, before finally becoming so through IVF, and then losing her husband Charlie to a rare form of lymphoma when he was only fifty years old. She is the rock of my immediate family, the one we all go to when we need to talk about the hard stuff and ask for advice. She is the harbor that brings our family together; the shore of safety when we need it most. The educated one, the rational and strong one.

Peter is two years younger than me. I remember playing cricket, football and soccer with him in the backyard and out front in the cul-de-sac with the children from the neighborhood. We fought a little as kids, nothing crazy, a few punch ups, otherwise we got on quite well. He grew to be the sports star of the family, playing both rugby league and rugby union for the state during his teenage years and into his early twenties. He also played international rugby in Europe for Malta, becoming the country's first ever dual international in both rugby league and rugby union. He lives in Canberra and works for the government. He is married with two children, an eight-year-old girl and six-year-old boy. These kids are my life along with Janice's little boy who is four. Peter has done very well for himself; he has an amazing wife and a great family. He's tough, but also very sensitive; a big softie who would do anything for our family.

Karl is my youngest brother, eleven years younger than me. He came along right in the middle of it all. We're not sure if he was an accident or if he was planned. He lives up in paradise, in Byron Bay and works with animals and on the land as a Park Ranger. He's an ambitious and smart kid who has travelled and lived all over the world. He looks a lot like me, with tanned skin and darker features. We take after our father, whilst Janice is a mix of mum and dad. Peter however, is much fairer and takes after our mother.

As kids, I remember riding my bike to the local swimming pool to swim and play with family and friends. I would ride my bike to the various ovals and parks in town to play soccer, cricket and football with my cousin and his friends, my brother and sister and their friends. It was a different time, a little over thirty years ago, when there was no social media, Facebook, Instagram, Twitter, no mobile phones and only a handful of computers. During the summer, school holidays and on weekends, our parents would send us out to go play and tell us to just be home for dinner or before it gets dark. Growing up in a little town, just outside of Canberra, in the eighties and nineties was sweet, fun and safe. It was a different era, a different way of living and a more innocent way of thinking. It was a safe place, an easy place, where everyone knew each other and looked after one another. Life was so much simpler then.

Year Three, primary school started and I was off to what felt like big school. I was no longer at Sacred Heart School and was now at Marist Brothers Primary School across the Queanbeyan River. I had to catch a bus from around the corner of my street to the downtown bus interchange, then jump onto another bus to get to school. My class was in a little room above the gymnasium and was a combination of Year Three and Year Four students. It was in this class where I met my best friend, still to this day, Conan. Along with our other friends Ryan and Adam, Conan and I comprised a foursome and we were a tight little group. Conan and I were in Year Three, whilst Ryan and Adam were a year older. Ryan was a lady's man and the leader of our pack. He would bring playboy and penthouse magazines to school and we would flick through them, fantasizing about the ladies and their bodies. On the weekends we would hang out at Ryan's house. I remember him being my only friend with a pool, so I loved going there. We would look at more porn magazines, smoke cigarettes and drink alcohol that we stole from his parents.

I spoke with Conan recently and he told me that he remembers me being one of the cool kids back then; a fast runner, good at sport and liked by many of the girls. I really never saw myself as one of the cool kids. I hung out with them but I definitely wasn't one of them. Conan and I spent a lot of time together, I would stay at his place and he at mine. He had older friends who lived on his street who were into rock n' roll and heavy metal so he would always play this kind of music when we were together. His favorite band was Bon Jovi, and we continually listened to 'Living on A Prayer' and the entire 'Slippery When Wet' album. Other bands we listened to were Def Leppard, AC/DC, Kiss, Skid Row, Motley Crew, Guns N' Roses, Metallica and other classic eighties rock bands. I learned about most of my music and as much as I could about girls from Conan, Ryan and Adam.

I don't really remember too much about Year Three. I remember being in class above the gym, but I don't remember the work or how my grades were. I remember playing with micro machines and marbles during recess and lunch. Micro machines were like matchbox cars only on a smaller scale. We played a lot of 'British Bulldog'. In fact, I believe most of the whole school played it. In the game of British Bulldog, someone was always in the middle of an oval and the rest of the players were on one side. The players were charged with getting across to the other side without being caught. The person in the middle would call out someone's name and, if he caught that unlucky someone, they too would be thrown into the middle. However, if that player got to the other side safely, all the others would be required to run past him to the other side. I loved playing that game. I remember always making it to safety without getting caught. If only life was as easy as winning at British Bulldog.

With Him

Chapter 4

It was December of 1986, which means summer holidays were upon us. Up until now it had been a typical summer, very hot and, depending upon where you were in Australia, very dry or very humid. We finished school for the year around mid-December, usually two weeks before Christmas and we were headed to our beach house in Batemans Bay for the holidays. We jumped into the family car; the canary yellow 1983 Ford Falcon XE S pack. I loved that car, I thought it was the fastest car in the world and the best looking one too. It was a beast of a thing.

The car was packed to the brim, full of clothing, Christmas presents, toys and whatever else we could fit into it. We drove the one-and-a-half-hour journey to the coast, to be down there for a few weeks. I think half of Canberra and Queanbeyan would pack up their homes and head down to the South Coast for the holidays, so we were always guaranteed to run into a friend or two. Our house was always full this time of year, with our grandparents taking up one bedroom, mum and dad and my two sets of aunties and uncles in the remaining bedrooms. Janice, Peter and I, along with our cousins, would scramble for the fold-out beds and the couches. It was a fun house; a real family affair. They were great times. We had the Christmas tree up and decorated, with close to thirty presents resting impatiently underneath it. We spent most of our days at the beach and would sometimes be treated to the local swimming pool and an afternoon of playing putt putt golf. Most nights we cooked up a feast on the barbecue, usually consisting of a lot of meat and seafood, then us kids would go hang at the carnival for some fun. Lunch the next day was usually leftovers. We would buy a huge bundle of fish and chips, scallops, calamari and the odd Chiko roll, not my favorite thing but my brother and cousins loved it. A Chiko roll is an Aussie version of a deep-fried Chinese spring roll, but usually twice the size. It is an Aussie fast-food favorite. Every Saturday night we would go to Mass, followed by a night out at the Batemans Bay Soldiers Club for the best Chinese food in town. This was the place where Karl actually took his first steps as a baby. Other nights we would be at home, watching TV or renting videos from the local video store; one for us kids, and one for the adults.

Christmas Eve was always a fun day. Beach first, then a last-minute scramble for presents at the shopping center with mum and my aunties. We would always go to Christmas Mass, then head home to eat and to watch the Christmas Carols special on TV, 'Carols By Candlelight', with all the big Aussie celebrities and child favorites like Humphrey B. Bear. At nine o'clock, Santa would appear on the show and wave goodbye to everyone in the audience as he was off to deliver his presents. It was at that time that we would all have to go to bed. We always tried to stay up late into the night, too excited to sleep. Our parents would leave a glass of milk and biscuits for Santa and some carrots for the reindeer, that somehow would always be half eaten by the morning. Christmas morning was always a crazy one with wrapping paper being thrown everywhere and us kids comparing presents. This was usually done before breakfast and sometimes before our parents had even woken up. After all the presents were opened and breakfast was complete, we would play with all of our new presents and go to the beach and play with them some more. By the second week in January, we were normally back home with mum and dad needing to go to work. Us kids would stay home alone with Janice looking after us or we would go to our grandmother's place.

However, one January day Janice and I had planned to go to the local swimming pool to meet friends and enjoy the day. Peter stayed home with mum, it was either the weekend or mum had taken a day off work to stay home with us. During the summer I was literally in the sun all day. Being of Maltese descent, I would tan very easily and get very dark. Janice and I set off for the pool just after lunch. I rode my bike there. I don't remember if she did the same, if mum gave her a lift, or one of her friends picked her up. During the summer holidays, the Queanbeyan pool was the place to be, always full of kids and adults having a great time. There were two pools, the main one being an Olympic size fifty-meter swimming pool with a three-meter springboard and a one and half meter springboard at the deep end. The pool was surrounded completely by grass for people to sit, with BBQ's on one side and a kiddie pool with two little slides and a fountain spraying water on the other side. The pool was a fun place, a safe place where all the town folk would gather and spend summer days.

This was a day just like any other. Janice and I were at the pool, running around with our friends, jumping in and out of the cool water all day. Our cousin Matt may have even been there with us that day too, he was the same age as Janice. By mid-afternoon Janice had decided to leave with her friends, she asked; *"Are you ok at the pool by yourself?"* Of course I felt fine and said *"yes"* to her leaving. *I don't need my big sister with me, it's only a bike ride or walk home,* I thought to myself.

I had done the route many times before, both alone and with friends, and never had an issue. I spent the afternoon exhausting myself, running around, jumping in and out of the pool and having a great time. However, one by one my friends, and everybody else at the pool, were disappearing. I was left alone. It was near closing time; I think the pool closed at six o'clock in the evening. It was near empty except for maybe one or two people gathering their belongings and also leaving. I grabbed my things and headed to the male change rooms. Upon entering, I dropped my t-shirt behind me without knowing, and an average looking man, who could have been in his thirties or forties, picked it up and very nicely handed it to me. He followed me into the change room and I thought nothing of it.

The change rooms were near the main entrance of the pool. As you entered the pool, the female change room was to the right and the male change room to the left. It was a huge concrete room, cold and uninviting. There were benches around half of the room with hooks bolted into the wall to hang clothes or towels. The roof and walls were painted a sky-blue color and there were two or three big skylights that allowed in natural light. The other half of the change room was lined with toilets and showers. I placed my towel, t-shirt and sneakers on a bench. The Man sat on the bench opposite me, watching me as he slowly took off his clothes. I thought nothing of it, ignored him and jumped into the shower with my swimmers on. I loved jumping under a hot shower after I had been swimming all day.

He soon followed me in there, naked.

"I've been watching you all day and noticed that you were looking at me."

I ignored him as I was a shy kid and didn't really know what he was talking about.

I turned away from him, telling him;

"I've never seen you before."

He called me over to him.

Scared, I tried to leave the shower, but he grabbed me and shoved me into the corner.

He then said;

"...Don't lie to me...This is what you want, you're a very special boy...I like you very much and your parents told me to spend special time with you."

He was playing with himself, masturbating until he was hard, I didn't know what was happening or what he was doing. At that age I didn't know much about sex, homosexuality, rape or masturbation.
Again, I tried to get out of the shower but he shoved me back into the corner.

I struggled to break free from his grip, almost yelling at him;

"Leave me alone, I want to leave!"

I didn't scream for help.

Maybe I should have. I was scared for my safety; afraid that he might hurt me or get me into trouble with my parents.

He grabbed me and shoved my head against the wall. I was dazed, confused, possibly even concussed.
Once he let me go, I slumped to the floor. He placed me on my knees, demanding;

"Open your mouth."

I did. I was now scared and crying. He placed his penis in my mouth and I choked on it as he forced me to give him oral sex. I had no idea of what was happening or what I was doing. All I could do was feel his penis getting bigger and harder in my mouth and he was holding my head, guiding it back and forth. He suddenly picked me up and turned me around, shoving me again against the wall with the same force as before, making sure I wouldn't fight back. He pulled my shorts down to around my ankles and he brutally raped me.

The pain was unlike anything I'd ever felt. It was as if he was going to split me into two separate pieces. I felt myself about to faint from the pain, I couldn't handle it any longer. My body went numb, my brain switched off and I physically, emotionally and mentally felt myself leave my body. I don't know if I ever re-entered it. Any form of life and soul I had in me was torn out of me at that moment and I was quickly dying. Everything went black. I closed my eyes and just took it, for there was no way of getting out of there. He raped me hard; my hands were holding me against the wall, but they soon gave way under the pressure and the force of this man inside of me. I fell against the wall, unable to move and just surrendered myself to him. I saw myself from above, looking down as I was being raped, and my life had changed forever in that instant.

The young boy had disappeared and was never coming back.

After however long, it felt like an eternity but was possibly only a few seconds to one minute, I heard him moan and I felt his body shudder. He came. I don't know how long he raped me for or if anyone had come into the change rooms during that time. I fell to the floor when he was finished with me, unable to feel my body or any of my senses;

> *"...If you ever tell anyone I will kill you and kill your family.*
> *I know exactly where you live...this is what **you** wanted!"*

He casually left the shower, got dressed and came back in to see me. I was still sitting there, curled up in a ball in the corner, with blood streaming from my anus;

> *"Get up before someone sees you."*

I couldn't move.

He turned the shower off and helped me up. It's strange I say that he *'helped me up'* like he was doing me a favor.

He asked;

> *"Are you going to tell anyone?"*

> *"...no."*

I replied almost silently in the faintest whisper.

Again, he asked more adamantly;

> *"And why are you not going to tell anyone?"*

I stayed silent, he said it to me again;

> *"I will kill you and kill your family if you ever say anything to anyone. I will see you again soon."*

He was cool, calm and collected, like nothing had happened, like he had done it many times before. He talked to me like we knew each other, like we were friends and, sadly, I believed everything that he had just said to me. He left. He got me good. I was changed forever; I didn't want him to kill me or kill my family so I promised myself that I would never tell a soul for as long as I lived;

"Who was this man?...Would I really see him again?... He told me how special I was and that this is what I wanted. Was I special? Is this what I wanted?... Did mum and dad really tell him to spend time with me?"

I sat back down on the floor in the shower for a little while longer, before I heard someone walk into the change room and I jumped up. The pain was unbearable. I pulled my shorts up and slowly walked over to where my stuff was. I wiped myself down slowly, put my t-shirt on and slowly walked out. I must have been walking with some sort of limp. I felt the sun hit my body, it brought me back to some kind of life. I don't think I was scared anymore; I was just numb. I had a small lump on my head where he shoved me into the wall. I didn't know how to feel, what to think, where to be, what to do. I walked to where my bike was, it was early evening and the hot day was turning into a warm night. I don't remember how I got home, if I walked my bike, or I rode it. I know I was in searing pain and not sure if I was actually physically capable of riding.

I will never know if he was working with someone else and if he had someone keep watch to make sure we were alone. Many years later, I learned that there had been a history of sexual abuse going on at the pool. I also had people reach out to me after learning about my story that something similar had happened to them at the Queanbeyan pool. Who would have thought? It was such a fun loving, safe and family-orientated place to be. The person who did this to me was not a member of the Queanbeyan pool staff and never worked there.

That night, I had already separated myself from my family. I no longer belonged with them; maybe because I was trying to protect them. I

23

didn't know who I was anymore nor what I was doing. I couldn't stop thinking about this man. I was fascinated by him and what he did to me. There was no way I was going to tell anyone, I had to keep them safe. When you get threatened with your life as an eight-year-old kid, you believe it, you don't know anything else, especially in the eighties when times were so different and there were little to no resources, support and access to the help that we have available today. Back then, that's all I knew. I was in total shock and frightened for my life, but I couldn't show it. I was in deep pain but I couldn't show it. I remember fighting with my mum because I didn't want to shower that night, I was scared he was going to be in the bathroom, waiting for me in the shower, and that it was going to happen again. Mum won however. What my mum wanted, she got. In the shower, I stood under the water for an eternity, the hot water stinging the cuts in my anus. It burned so badly and was so very painful. It hurt for me to sit. It hurt for me to stand. It hurt to do anything. I noticed that my underpants had blood in them so, in an effort to make sure my parents wouldn't find out, I took them in the shower with me, trying in vain to wash the blood off. It didn't come off, so after I showered, I threw my undies away in the bin, making sure to bury them under some of the trash so they couldn't be found.

My family sat on the couch watching television, mum and dad with Janice and Peter. I sat alone on a separate couch, curled up in a ball, like I did in the shower when it first happened. I couldn't sit for too long in one position; I was in excruciating pain and kept having to move from side to side. I was ripped open and felt like I was constantly going to throw up, although I don't think I did. I had already disassociated myself from the family, keeping them at arm's length, wanting nothing to do with them. The more I kept them away, the more I was protecting them and less likely I would ever need to say anything. I kept thinking about this man;

Who was he and was what he told me actually true?... Did he know my family and where we lived?... Was I looking at him at the pool?... Is this what men do to special boys, to the boys they like, boys like me?... Was this normal, or was I actually special?... He told me he was going to see me soon. Where? When? How?... Did I need to go back to the pool for that to happen?... I didn't know where he lived, was he going to come to my house?

I had a million questions and thoughts running around in my little brain, unsure if they would ever be answered.

We lived in a big house, with a big backyard and front yard. There were three bedrooms upstairs, mum and dads' room with their own ensuite. Janice had her own room toward the front of the house and I shared a bedroom with Peter. Our bedroom was in the back corner of the house. We had two single beds with two little bedside draws on either side. The wall in front of the beds were cupboards for our clothes, toys, shoes and our precious junk. To the side of our beds was a chest of draws, running most of the length of our bedroom. They held more clothes, winter and summer, socks and undies, the usual stuff. Above the chest were bookshelves. One half of the bookshelves housed the complete set of Encyclopedia Britannica, which got me through many school assignments. There was no internet at that time so encyclopedias were indispensable, and I loved them. On the other side of the book shelves were regular books for us to read, trophies we had won playing sports, toy cars and other toys and figurines. Our room was always clean, we would definitely get in trouble if it wasn't, and we made our beds every morning before school. There was no getting away with anything back then when it came to keeping our room messy. There was another bathroom upstairs as was the kitchen and living area. The kitchen was predominantly red; red bench tops, red door handles, and red kitchen table chairs with a walnut brown background. Downstairs there was the laundry, a bathroom, a garage, lots of storage space and a huge rumpus/play room with a pool table and ping pong table, each separated by a wide-open space to play. For the rest of the school holidays, I spent most of my time there alone playing with my toy cars and other toys.

My dad worked for a steel company in the building industry as their sales rep, supplying mesh and footings for house and commercial building slabs, as well as pool and house fencing. He was the best in Canberra, even if I do say so myself. At one of his work Christmas parties, I received a present from Santa. It was a giant, yellow, plastic mat with city streets printed on it; buildings, churches, schools, road signs, literally everything you would find on a city map and I absolutely loved it. I spent hours playing with my toy cars on this mat; I never left the house. I became a recluse, spending all my time in the rumpus room or my bedroom playing with my cars. Every night without fail I would eat Neapolitan ice cream, chocolate, strawberry and vanilla ice cream with ice magic or chocolate syrup. Sometimes I would let the ice cream melt, stir it all together and drink it as a thick shake. Ice cream was my favorite. My favorite shows at that age were WWF wrestling and my favorite wrestlers were The Ultimate Warrior, Jake the Snake, Macho Man Randy Savage and The Undertaker. I also loved watching Fraggle Rock, The Muppet Show and Muppet Babies, too.

I never heard from or saw the Man for the rest of the holidays. *Had he forgotten about me? Was I actually going to see him again? Did he really know where I lived?* I never stopped thinking about him and I was always scared to think of what was going to happen next. I had continued to slowly push my family away. I remember at night time how my brother and sister would sit close to mum, sometimes even curled up in the crook of her arms for shelter and safety. I never did that, not once. Even when mum or dad would call me over to sit with them, or if they would try to cuddle or kiss me, I never would. I would push them off and run away. I would always sit by the side, or stay alone in a separate room, never kiss them or say goodnight. I would just go to bed.

School started not long after. I must have been starting Year Four. Marist Brothers had turned into St Gregory's Primary School and it went from an all-boys school to a co-ed program. The school still went to Year Six and I still took the same bus from around the corner of my house to the bus interchange, before jumping onto another bus to get to school. The interchange was always a fun place to meet friends before and after school, before going home and a good place to see a fight or two. Queanbeyan did kind of live up to its nickname of 'Struggle town', it was sometimes a rough little town with only two main streets, Monaro Street and Crawford Street. There were at least five or six pubs, the main shopping centre, Riverside Plaza and the RSL Bowling Club. A town with plenty of drunks and people who loved a fight or two. In many ways it was your typical small Aussie town. We were lucky, I guess, being so close to Canberra, a small city; but it had so much more than what Queanbeyan could offer, even with a little sophistication. As rough as Queanbeyan was, we all had a sense of pride being from there, and would always stick up for it and have a love for it.

Chapter 5

Mentally and emotionally, I was slowly becoming more closed off and spending time alone. I had gone into a shell to protect myself and my family. I was confused and scared about what had happened to me and asked myself many questions, usually always the same ones;

Was this a one off and was I ever going to see him again?... Was it normal for young boys to go through this and do we all go through it?... Should I ask one of my friends if it happened to him?

I promised myself I wouldn't say anything, so I kept it that way. I was starting to bury it inside of me like it never happened and pretended to be normal with friends and family. Maybe I was never going to see him again. I just had my ninth birthday. My birthday was always around the first week of school. I remember a few times it actually fell on the first day. What I don't remember is any of my actual birthdays from around that time, if I had a party or did anything with the family. I had completely wiped them from my memory.

I really don't remember how long the time was between when I first saw the Man to the next time and all the times after that. Sometimes it was days, weeks, even months. I was shut down and closed off and kept pushing all that happened to me deep inside. I don't remember much at all from those days, school, friends, family, life in general, it was all a blur. I do, however, remember my time with him, the violent and not so violent days. He would sometimes find me at the bus interchange, walking home from school, or in the park, he somehow knew where and how to find me and where I would be.

I remember the first time I saw him again. The Man took me to his house; he picked me up from the bus interchange. He casually walked up to me, I didn't see him until he was practically on top of me, he put his arm around me, said *"hello"* to my friends and walked away with me. They thought nothing of it. I recently spoke to Conan; he said he thought that the Man was a family member or family friend, it was all so casual and nice, so he never thought it was strange that I was walking away with him and I never made a fuss about it or tried to alert anyone.

On a normal day, I would get home from school by about four o'clock and my parents would return from work at five-thirty, so for the hour in between they had no idea what we were doing and thought that we were home doing our homework. Sometimes I would spend ten minutes with the Man and sometimes I was with him for up to an hour. We had a key hidden under the back stairs to let ourselves in and it was normal for us to be alone at home. We were always our parents' number one priority and they always worried for our safety.

His house was an older house, it was down near the Queanbeyan Park/Queanbeyan Pool area, on one of those side streets. His house was probably built in the sixties, a little shoebox of a house on a big block. He had big rose bushes out the front; there was a little porch in front as well, it was faced with deep red brick. The front yard was manicured quite nicely; however, the side and back were unkept and overgrown. He didn't have a garage so he would either park on the side of the road or on his block, just to the right of his house. The car was always exposed so it was easy for me to see if he was there or not. He took me inside hurriedly, as to not have anyone see us, I guess. I remember he would literally push me in the house and shut the door quickly behind him. When I entered, I would always stand to the left side of the entrance, both scared and somehow knowing what was going to happen.

His house was nothing fancy on the inside and it had a stale smell about it; there was no fresh air in the place, like he hadn't opened a window or door for months. There was also always a stench of dirty water emanating throughout the rooms. He would only keep me in the living room in the very beginning. To one side of this room, he had an old China cabinet with shelves, and on these shelves, he had some books, small little pieces of china and photos. Toward the middle of the room was an old three-seater couch and to the side of that was a single-seater with a television directly in front of it. It was an old brown leather couch, with small tears in the leather, so when I sat on it the ripped leather would sometimes hurt or cut into my legs. The house always seemed dark, curtains drawn, and little-to-no light ever turned on. He always locked the front door behind him and would sit on the couch. I wouldn't follow. I would stay by the front door, looking straight down, never at him, looking for a way to get out.

He would call me over;

"...come and sit next to me."

If I wouldn't, he would come to me, aggressively grabbing me from behind and shoving me to the couch. That is when the grooming, manipulation and lies began. Looking back at it now, he was a master at it all. He would never ask me how I was or what was going on with me or my life. He would never ask about my family, school, friends, nothing. He didn't want to know anything about me.

He would get straight into it, saying;

"This is all your fault. You wanted this and you were looking at me at the pool."

I always replied the same way every time he said that to me;

"..I didn't look at you, I've never seen you before and I don't know who you are."

I always think about that;

Did I actually see him at the pool that day?... Was I looking at him in some way or glance past him and we caught eyes?

I will forever answer these questions with;

No. I didn't see him, I didn't know him, I wasn't looking at him that day at the pool.

He would continue with the lies and the manipulation;

"You're a liar. Your parents and I hate liars and they already love your sister and brother so much more than you."

He moved closer to me, sitting right next to me, placing his hand on my leg. If I tried to shake my leg to get his hand off me, he would squeeze it tight, till it hurt, and I gave in to him.

He would say;

"I love you."

He would repeatedly tell me every time he saw me;

"...If you tell anyone... I will kill you and your family... Your parents won't believe you and neither will your siblings... If you ever say anything, they will all hate you."

He ingrained this into my head. He was a master manipulator and, as a kid, I believed every word of it.

When we would sit on the couch, he would take his clothes off and sit naked beside me, then grab my hand and put it on his penis, guiding my hand up and down, as to stroke his penis. Then he would make me masturbate him. I rarely looked at him or at what I was doing, I would look straight down and off to the side, trying to think of anything else. I could feel his penis get hard in my hand and he would just sit back and enjoy it. I can still hear the moan in my head, it sounded like an inward moan, as if he was moaning to himself, if that makes any sense. I wish I could make the noise for you so you could understand.

When he was hard, he would make me stop and grab the back of my head, forcing it down into his crotch. I would fight it, try and pick my head up but he was too strong and forceful. He would smell down there sometimes, making me dry retch on it. The smell, his penis, the whole situation broke me. I fucking remember that smell now and want to throw up just thinking about it. It was a musky, sweaty smell, I couldn't get away from it and I could never forget it. The Man telling me; *"I really like this. You are really good at doing this."* More than anything I hated giving him oral, I remember crying and fighting to get away from him. I would scream, I would do anything to get away from him but he was too big and too strong and I was powerless to do anything. If I made too much noise or fought too hard, he would give me a good punch or slap across the face or up the side of the head. Looking back at it now, I should have bitten the fucking thing off!

He was violent towards me;

"Stand in front of me and take your clothes off."

He would say this whilst he sat on the couch, playing with himself. There I would stand, in front of him, not saying a word, terrified, and I wouldn't take my clothes off. He would ask again and, if I still refused, he would again slap me across the face, but at the same time tell me;

"I really love you and I'm the only one who does. This is what your parents want, and I hope that you love me too."

Eventually, I would take my clothes off as slowly as I could, knowing what was to come and maybe in the hope that someone would bang down that door and rescue me. No one ever did! He would make me stand in front of him and make me play with myself, the same way he was. Once he had enough of that, he would throw me on the couch and have sex with me. I would fight it at first, maybe it was the pain I was fighting against, and not him, but after a few seconds, it was like the first time in the change rooms at the swimming pool that day; I would just go numb to the whole experience and leave my body. I felt like he was chipping away at my soul, killing me, piece by piece, thrust by thrust, a little more every time, destroying the innocent child that was me before all of this. For some reason I would always end up facing the old china cabinet to the side which had the photo on it. This photo would call out to me every time I was at his house and in this position, and I couldn't take my eyes off of it. It was a photo of the Man with a little girl, and I felt her eyes just stare at me all the time, just as I would stare at her. He had a big smile on his face, she didn't. *Was he doing the same to her as he was to me?... Who was she?... Was she one of the special kids, like I was?* When he was done, he would stand up and leave me naked on the couch. He would get dressed and, once he was, he would give me a towel to clean myself up, then throw my clothes at me to get dressed. I was exhausted, beaten up and ripped to shreds, like I had just gone ten rounds with Mike Tyson. I would get dressed as quickly as I could, so he wouldn't be able to do it again and so I could get out of there as quickly as I could. When I was dressed and just before leaving his house, there would be more talk from him;

"I spoke to your parents and they told me that you are a miserable little boy and they don't like you anymore... You have to continue living with them but they don't want you to speak to them... I love you and I am going to take care of you and make you happy... Now remember, I will kill you and your family if you ever say anything... This is our special little secret because this only happens to special little boys."

Each time I would leave his house I left more confused than the time before. Not exactly sure what was happening to me or who I now was;

Am I really that special?... If so, why is he hitting, slapping and hurting me the way he is?... Why is he causing me so much pain and making me bleed?... Does he really love me and do my parents really hate me and want nothing to do with me?

However, in fear for our lives, I continued to say nothing.

As time went on, I began to feel less love for my parents, Janice and Peter. I would push them away without them knowing it, talk to them less, share less about myself, about school and whatever else was going on in my life. When I was home, I would sit in my bedroom or in the rumpus room downstairs playing with my cars or marbles and watch television somewhere away from the family. I would think to myself; *Do mum and dad really hate me like the Man said? Do they not love me anymore? They never say it to me, so I guess they don't love me.* Looking back now, I realize that they were saying it, but I was so closed off and so shut down that I never heard it. My frightened thoughts would continue, as if on a repetitive loop;

Do they think I'm a bad little boy?... Do Janice and Peter not like me too? Do they think I'm a liar?... I'm not playing with them as much as I normally would, so I guess the Man must be right.

I kept questioning everything I was thinking and believing, feeling more and more confused with every passing day.

Peter and I were starting to fight with each other more. I remember we would be playing a game inside and all of a sudden, I would be chasing him around the house, punching him and screaming, for no obvious reason at all. We would play cricket, soccer or rugby in the backyard and I would try to hurt him. I would hit him harder, kick the ball at him purposely, making sure to hit him and, if we were playing cricket, I would throw the ball or the bat at him. I wasn't a sore loser or a wildly competitive boy, I just wanted to hurt him, to see him cry. I was happy to lose, I really didn't give a fuck. It was starting to be ingrained in me that I deserved to lose, I deserved to be unhappy. Self-sabotage and self-destruction were already starting to take root at such a young age. With Janice, I was never as bad; I was mean to her and would fight and sometimes punch her, but more than anything, I was just becoming further and further detached from her.

In primary school, I kept a low profile, I wouldn't bring any attention to myself, I did my school work and acted like any other kid. My favorite part of primary school was P.E. (Physical Education). Playing sports at a young age was an escape for me. I was a fast runner, one of the quickest in the state for my age and I loved playing any kind of sport, and excelled at most of it. It was a way for me to be a kid once again and feel some kind of freedom and connection to other children my age. I was able to play; to be good at something, and not have to worry about what was going on in my head or in my life.

The more time I spent alone, the more I liked it, and the more I felt that I wasn't deserving of love and happiness. I felt that, through all of the Man's lies, his power games, that maybe he was telling me the truth, that he *did* love me and that no one else did or could. Maybe this was the normal thing, that I was special and I was lucky to be with him. My head was a fucking mess, I was a fucking mess. *Why would he hurt me; make me cry and be violent towards me?* None of it felt good or natural; but being with him was starting to become 'normal' and I felt lost for feeling these things. On occasion, I would think about that little girl in the photo again; was she one of his special friends? Every time I would go to his house, no matter where I stood or sat in that room, I would always find her and she would always find me, always staring back at me with that same expression on her face, sad; not wanting to be there.

Chapter 6

It's 1988, I was ten and mum was heavily pregnant with Karl, my youngest brother, which was great because the family was worried about mum and her pregnancy and less about me. I got a bit of a free pass for a while. My family, along with my Auntie Antoinette, my Uncle Joe and their two kids, Matt and Marissa, went on a little family vacation to the Gold Coast and Brisbane for World Expo '88. We jumped in a van together and drove up the New South Wales north coast for 24 hours. First stop was Goulburn, a little industrial town known for Goulburn jail, the highest maximum-security prison in Australia. Obviously, we weren't there for the jail, we stopped to see The Big Merino, the world's largest sculpture of a concrete constructed sheep at fifty feet tall, and we had some morning tea and I probably had a meat pie or sausage roll, my two favorites. From there we drove all the way through to Coffs Harbor and we got to see The Big Banana, a thirteen by five-meter banana, set on a banana plantation and theme park. Yes, Australia is full of these big, weird and wonderful sculptures in a lot of the little country towns. We drove through to Tenterfield, a little town in northeastern New South Wales, just south of the Queensland border where we spent the night. It was the worst little hotel ever. There was a huge Huntsman Spider living on the ceiling of our room, probably the size of an adult hand. I don't remember if dad got rid of it or we just left the spider there. Peter and I shared a single bed. I remember how every bed had sheets that were dirty and torn. Then halfway through the night, Peter wet the bed. He will kill me for saying this, but he wet the bed a lot as a kid. We slept in our normal clothes, not our pajamas, just in case we had to get up and leave in the middle of the night because the place was so dodgy and disgusting. It's funny how you remember the craziest things, and that which you want to remember, you can't!

The next day we made it to the Gold Coast and stayed at a fun little resort with a large pool and a slide going into the pool. All of us kids spent a lot of time playing in that pool. We went to the major theme parks in the area, Wet N' Wild, Dreamworld and SeaWorld; we rode on all the rides and roller coasters, saw the animals and sea creatures and spent a full day at Expo '88. Mum had a little fold out chair with her and would need to sit and rest as we walked around so much. I remember going to the different country's exhibitions, particularly China for some reason. I think it was the biggest one there. This is one of the happier memories that I remember from childhood, one of the only ones that I remember. On this trip I felt care free, without any troubles, almost forgetting what was going on and waiting for me back home.

Six days after my birthday, my youngest brother, Karl, arrived, on the ninth of February. I remember going to the hospital and sitting in the waiting area with Janice, Peter and my grandmother may have been there too. Dad finally came out to tell us that we had a new baby brother. We were all so excited to see him. When we finally did get to see him, he was sleeping under a bright light; he was suffering from jaundice, a medical condition that causes yellowing of the skin, arising from excess of the pigment bilirubin and typically caused by obstruction of the bile duct. He was a cute little thing, hairy, and was the biggest of all four kids when he was born. Mum was doing well after the birth. It was her fourth caesarean, or c-section as it is otherwise known. She had problems giving birth to Janice and couldn't have a natural birth with the rest of us. Janice, Peter and myself all had a chance to hold him, for a minute or two, before putting him back under his little tanning light. Mum and 'bub' were in hospital for a few days and, when they finally came home, everyone's attention was again on him. Janice was playing big sister as well as playing mum, Peter was doting on his little brother, and I had a chance to be invisible for a while. I was the last thing on my family's mind and they were the last thing on mine. They were in my life, but I did all that I could to keep them out of it. I had put up a wall and didn't know where I belonged or to whom I belonged. I was of the belief that my family didn't love me anymore and that as much as I was keeping my life from them, they were also doing the same with me. They were keeping me with them out of necessity, I told myself. They didn't believe anything I said and they no longer liked me. I believed that, as much as I was lying to them about who I am and what I want, they were lying to me about their love and happiness toward and for me. It gave me a chance to be alone, sit in my room or disappear downstairs out of sight. Watching television, playing with my cars or being outside riding my bike was all I wanted to do.

Though years had passed, I was the same skinny little kid and the abuse was still happening. It was still violent and very abusive sexually, physically and more so mentally and emotionally. It was becoming a more common occurrence. The Man knew where to find me, the days and times, where I would be and what I would be doing. I almost expected him and would sometimes wonder where he was if he wasn't there. I found myself riding my bike down to where he lived. I wouldn't go up to his door and knock on it. I would sit across the road, hide behind a tree or a parked car, waiting for him to get home or peer outside his window, catch a glimpse of me and call me in. Sometimes I would wait for hours, riding my bike up and down the street in the hopes that he might see me. On occasion he would; at other times I would feel rejected and make the lonely bike ride home. When he did see me, he would hurriedly wave me over and quickly push me into his house. He hated me just showing up this way and he would certainly let me know it. He would close the door behind him; I would move myself to the side of the door as usual. He looked out the window to make sure no one was watching or noticed that anything was up before shutting the curtains. He stormed over to me, grabbed me by the neck and shoved me up against the wall, sometimes picking me up off the floor. He was an angry man and could work up a temper from one to a hundred in the blink of an eye.

> *"What the fuck are you doing here?!*
> *Does anyone know that you're here?!"*

I didn't know what I was doing there and why I wanted to be there with him. I couldn't answer that question. I would struggle to find my breath, find my feet and would fight with all I had in me for him to let me go. Eventually, he would let go and calmed himself down, explaining to me;

> *"I can't have you just show up like this... You will get into very big*
> *trouble with the police if anyone ever finds out and you will go*
> *straight to jail... I will never be able to see you again, and I'm sure*
> *you don't want that."*

It was always me getting into trouble with the police and going to jail, never him. A second later he would say;

> *"You are such a beautiful boy. I love you so much."*

He would move me over to the couch, asking again;

> *"Does anyone know where you are? Does anyone know where you*
> *were going or what you are doing? Have you told anyone that you*
> *are here with me?"*

I always replied the same way;

"...no!"

This was the truth. I never told a soul where I was, who I was with or what I was doing. Never! He repeatedly said;

"I love you."

I would never reply and would look away. I didn't know what love was or even how to do it. He would sit there waiting for me to reply but I would sit there in silence. He would squeeze my leg tight and I would move it around to try and get his hand off.

"Ouch...You're hurting me!"

He didn't care though, telling me to say it;

"Tell me that you love me."

I wouldn't. That's when he would slap me across the face or give me a tap up the side of the head depending on the mood he was in, and then he would apologize;

"I'm sorry, you are so special to me, you are my favorite little boy and this is what everyone wants."

He would move my face so that we were looking at each other.

"I love you."

He would wait for a reply. I finally said it back to him;

"I love you too."

41

I'm not sure if it was out of fear or if I actually did love him. He would place his hand on my leg, before moving it to my crotch where he would play with my penis from outside my pants and put my hand onto his penis. Eventually he would get me naked, whilst getting himself naked too, play with my naked body, kiss me on the lips, my chest and work his way down to my penis, giving me oral until I got hard. And I did get hard. I hated where I was and what was being done to me, but I didn't want to be anywhere else. He would soon turn the situation around and make me give him oral. I still couldn't stand the smell and the taste, no matter how long it had been happening. The older he got, the worse it got; the sex was still as brutal and violent as it was in the beginning and the pain was always there, still the same - unbearable and just as excruciating as when it first happened. It was still happening on the couch, the Man throwing me around and with me looking at the photo of that little girl, who, no matter where I was in that room, would always be staring at me without a smile on her face, feeling the same way about him as I did.

I once asked him;

"Who is the little girl in the picture?"

He looked at me for some time, he didn't show any emotion before finally telling me *"mind your business."* I guess I would never know. When he was done with me, I would get dressed as quickly as I could and not that it counts for anything, but he would ask *" Did you enjoy it? Did you have fun?"* I would never answer him or give him that satisfaction. He would then continue on with the manipulation, grooming and the lies;

"You are so beautiful - we are meant to be together…
This is what you wanted, what you have always wanted…

42

Don't forget you picked me up at the pool that day... You make me very happy and I know I make you very happy... Your family doesn't love you and they won't believe you if you say anything... You are such a special little boy because I'm giving you all this attention... I love you very much."

When I heard these things over and over again for years and at such a young age, I believed them. I believed him and as a result my feelings towards him were growing. Once I left his house, I would ride my bike home, see my family and pretend like life was normal and nothing out of the ordinary was happening, while at the same time slowly pushing them further away. I was the world's greatest little actor.

My dad loved his cigarettes, his beer and his whisky when I was a kid and he still loves his whisky and beer to this day. He would smoke Blue Rothmans, at least a packet a day, if not more. When I could, I would steal his packets and smoke his cigarettes, drink his beer and whisky. I would smoke and drink as often as I could and it was becoming a habit, doing it when I was in pain and not in a good place, when I was confused or hating myself. Depression had already set in deeply. I couldn't be around anyone or talk to them. I hated myself and who I was. As a relief, and to escape reality, I would take huge puffs from his cigarettes, cough up a lung, get high for a few minutes, and feel my troubles melt away. I'd drink the small middy size bottles of VB, Victoria Bitter, one of Australia's well-known beers, or drink whatever whisky I could get my hands on. I'd usually get drunk on a mouthful or two, or at least I would feel tipsy. I loved the feeling; it would stop me from thinking bad thoughts; thoughts like I don't deserve to be happy or see my family happy. I would always feel like I was on the outside, even though I never really was. I was always a part of everything the family did, I was always involved, however, I just thought it was out of necessity because they were my family. In truth, I constantly wondered if they really liked me or even wanted me there.

My dad went to see a doctor one day for a checkup, he wasn't feeling too well. The doctor told him that he needed to stop smoking otherwise he was going to get very sick. He quit cold turkey the next day and that was the end of my regular smoking habit, that was until I could steal a cigarette or a packet from someone or from a shop somewhere. I would steal a lot as a kid, I stole whatever I could get my hands on. I stole from my friends at school, money from my parents, food, drinks, magazines, books from shops, newsagencies or supermarkets. It's not that I actually needed any of this stuff, it was more that I needed to do it for my own satisfaction. I needed to feel the rush and I was beginning to not care what or who I hurt.

It was the seventh of May, Peter's birthday, and the extended family were over. I remember I was sitting in my parents' bedroom watching television, while everyone else was in the living room and kitchen, eating, connecting and enjoying the night. I kept hearing Janice, Peter, Matt and Marissa laughing and having fun and I kept running back and forth between the living room and my parents' bedroom. I wanted to know what they were doing, even somehow involved, but I always ended up back in my parents' bedroom alone. I felt more comfortable there. Mum finally came into the bedroom and told me to *"get in the kitchen to play with the other kids"* and turned the television off. When mum said to do something, I never argued with her.

I sat at the kitchen table just watching the kids interact. I ate some lollies and Janice brought out one of her new games, 'Hungry Hippo'. She set it up on the kitchen table, a game for four players, and she played it with Peter, Matt and Marissa while I watched from the side. They were happy, laughing and screaming at each other with enjoyment, having a great time. I could never really relate to that, and only felt like I didn't fit in. I didn't know how to enjoy myself that way or be happy like that. Janice finally asked if I wanted to play. I did want to feel what they were feeling, to be happy like they were, so I played the game with them. After a few games, I really got into it and was having fun, but I kept losing. Peter and Matt were very competitive, they still are to this day actually and compete against each other all the time, like big kids. I kept losing and Peter and Matt were teasing me, as kids do, so I grabbed the game and slammed it down on the table and the balls went flying everywhere. Janice got angry and yelled at me, whilst Peter ran to mum and told on me. Mum came over with anger in her voice and I had to go sit over near her. At that time, I probably preferred that.

It was time to finally sing Happy Birthday and to cut the cake. Everyone gathered around the kitchen table; the kids all surrounded the cake and I stood off to the side. Dad told me to *"go stand with the other kids,"* but I didn't. The family started to sing and my dad put his arm around me with love and I shrugged it off. The kids were smiling, singing as were the adults, but I showed no emotion and didn't care to be there. Any attempt of affection from my parents, Janice, Peter or my extended family for that matter, were met with a cold shoulder and I couldn't run away quick enough, wanting nothing to do with them.

Winter had arrived, I would have been eleven years old and my relationship with the Man had evolved into something different; it had progressed into something I had never felt before. He picked me up from the bus interchange one day and we drove back to his house. He parked in the driveway and we walked into his house casually; he wasn't hiding me from the world and there was no hurry to get me inside the house. He wasn't angry or worried that someone might see us together, or so I thought in my little brain. When inside, he had his arm around me, just like my dad tried to do, and I didn't shrug it off this time. He walked me over to the couch. I felt comfortable with him and with his arm around me. We sat there and talked, he called me by my name. He never normally did that, actually he never called me by any name, he would normally just say;

"...come here... sit down... do this... do that."

He was finally engaging more personally;

"How are you doing at school?... Do you have many friends?... What games do you like to play? I saw you playing soccer on the weekend."

I was so shocked as I never told him I was playing soccer. It would have been easy for him to find out, as our games were announced in the local paper. I was a very good little player, a very fast little runner and I scored lots of goals, so it would have been easy for anyone to find out when and where I was playing. I never saw him at the ground and I don't know how many games he went to. He actually started to offer me food; chips and lollies, and also cordial or water, Coca Cola and Sprite, and would share them with me. He was being extra nice to me to the point where he said;

"You are the best little player on the soccer field and you look very cute in your uniform... I have a present to give you for being the best player on the team."

He got up and went to his cabinet and came back to me with a little toy car, a little tow truck. It was shiny and bright red, it looked new and the wheels turned perfectly. He said;

"You deserve this because you are my favorite little boy."

Hearing this I wondered *"how many other boys were there?"* He gave it to me and I sat there with it in my hand, I loved it but didn't play with it in front of him at first. I never said anything in return and he asked me;

"What do you say?"

I sheepishly answered;

"Thank you."

He followed that up with;

"What else do you say?"

I knew what he was getting at and to avoid being hit or slapped, I said it;

"I love you."

This always put a smile on his face and he told me;

"I love you too."

He put his hand on my leg and talked to me some more. At this time, I was feeling more comfortable with him and started to push the truck ever so softly up and down the arm of the couch. He put his arm around me again and played with my hair, which I absolutely hated, and still do to this day. I hate anyone playing with my hair or with my face. I looked for the little girl in the photo but she was gone, he got rid of her. I didn't dare ask where she was. He stood up and got me up with him. Again, he put his arm around me and walked me into his bedroom. I'd never been into his bedroom before; I had never really been into any other room besides the bathroom to use the toilet. His bedroom was minimal with just one bedside table and nothing else, except for some clothes on the floor, folded in the corner. He sat with me on the edge of his bed and we talked some more. Even the sex was gentler and more affectionate, more loving and, when we were done, he handed me my clothes and made sure that I was ok whilst I got dressed, before starting again with the grooming and manipulation. Soon after he then went on to say the same things as he always did; threats against my family, threatening me being taken away by the police and telling me yet again that this is what I wanted.

If I didn't have my bike, he would drive me back down town, to the bus interchange, or somewhere closer to home so I didn't have to walk all the way. He would never take me all the way home in case someone from my family saw us together. He treated me with love and compassion sometimes, or what I *thought* was love and compassion.

Thinking about this now, verbalizing it in writing, it all feels so fucked up and wrong… love and compassion; I wanted it from him, needed it from him and didn't want it from anyone else, but as I said earlier, that was all I knew. We had grown into something more than a man and a young boy who was scared for his life; who would stand to the side of the door when he first entered the house waiting to be raped, physically and mentally abused. I was no longer the little boy who was being choked, punched and manhandled. He had finally taken an interest in me, an interest in my life and who I was as a person. I often thought that;

Maybe everything he's always told me about my family was actually true... They didn't treat me with this much love, give me gifts, even ask about what's going on in my life... Maybe they do all hate me and think I'm a liar.

He was right, maybe they do want all of this and so does the Man and now, so do I. My mind would go in circles...

Is this what my life is supposed to be like?... Am I supposed to feel
love for the Man?... Am I supposed to care for him more than I do my
parents, brothers and sister?... He tells me that he loves me, he tells
me that we will be together... If I ever say anything I will get into big
trouble with the police and he will never see me again.

I didn't want that to happen. When there is so much manipulation, it's
hard to see what the truth really is. My parents really were the sweetest
people in the world, maybe a little naive, but they had so much love
for all of us children. They believed that we lived in a safe and easy
town and that this shit would never happen in my family, or our town
for that matter. They were both so busy working full time jobs and
raising four children. I continuously pushed them away, kept them at
arm's length and never communicated with them; and this is what I
wanted. I wanted to be with him more than my own family. I wanted
to love him more than my own family. I would ride my bike to his
place more than ever, wait for him to get home, look for him at my
soccer games, at the bus interchange, downtown when I was with
friends or shopping with my mum. I would look for him wherever I
was, although I never once saw him. It was always on his terms - when
and where he wanted to see me. Even during the summer, I would go
back to the pool hoping to see him there. I never did though. I was
becoming more and more confused about my place in the world. These
constant thoughts were inescapable;

Who am I?... Where do I belong and who do I belong with?... Is he
with other boys?... Does he have other favorites?... Does he hurt
them like he hurts me?... Does he love them like he loves me?... Give
them gifts?... Go to their sporting events?

School was going along fine, the years were passing by, it was 1989, I
was in Year Six. My grades were good, I had friends, I *acted* like a
normal kid. I was definitely more on the shy and quiet side, I had the

odd girlfriend through Primary School; well, we called each other boyfriend and girlfriend, even though we never held hands, never really spoke or actually hung out. I was always attracted to girls... was that wrong considering my relationship with the Man? I loved him (well I thought I loved him), thought I knew what love was, but I really had no idea. I had my mates at school, my male friends, but I never felt the same way about any of them or any other boys as I did the Man. I was not attracted to any of them, just the girls and I would see my mum and dad together, all the grown-up ladies and men together around town. Television was all 'straight', although my family was good friends with a gay couple and we would sometimes hang with them. I was always fascinated by them. I always wondered if they started out as *'special boys'* like me and if this was who I was supposed to be; that maybe I was a *'chosen one'*. Here I was with this old man who was physically, mentally and emotionally abusive towards me. He hurt me very much, made me bleed and cry, did all sorts of things to me that no child should ever experience, but somehow, he made me want to see him, he made me want to spend time with him and want to love him. As much as I hated the sex, giving and receiving oral from him, I wanted it too. It broke me and yet it gave me life. What does that even mean? How do I explain that? I was a young boy who had to let go of his innocence, let go of his childhood, to grow up and become an adult to get through and survive those years. I didn't even know how to act like or even be a child anymore. However, I wasn't an adult either... I was in no man's land; completely lost, it was all becoming foreign to me.

I did all the *normal* things a kid would do; I played with my friends, went to school, stayed around my brothers and sister, my cousins and my parents. I went to my friend's birthday parties, played games, played with toys. I *acted* like a normal kid, but none of it was normal, none of it felt normal, genuine or real. It was all for show, it was fake so I could get away without anyone ever knowing *'the real me'*.

Conversely, my relationship with the Man felt real, more genuine and normal, like that was where I belonged. Being with him was turning into my safe place.

Let me be clear; as much as I *thought* I loved the Man, I hated him. Even when our relationship *'evolved'*, if you can even call it a relationship, it grew into something more than violence and sex. There was constant overwhelming confusion; I was still frightened for my life and didn't want to be there. I didn't know the version of him that I was going to get from day to day, someone who showed me love or someone who was going to beat the fuck out of me, throw me around the room, choke me out and make me pee my pants. But this was also somehow what I wanted, or I should say what I needed, because it was who I was now. This is what felt real to me. He had entrenched himself deep into my head, and deep into my body, and there was no getting him out of it. He was now the one I believed, the one I trusted and the one I loved.

Through the whole relationship, from beginning to end, when he supposedly loved me and wanted to be with me, it was all still rape of an innocent child; manipulative, coercive, violent, abusive and wrong. He never made love to me, there was never any love. It was all a lie, a game of power to him, he groomed me, manipulated me, took advantage of me every way he could and he knew how to do it very well and I fell for it all.

On occasion, we wouldn't have sex, but he would make me give him oral for what seemed like an eternity until he came. I hated this more than anything. I would sometimes dry retch and almost throw up from the smell of his penis and the motion. I'm not sure how often he actually cleaned it, or even washed himself for that matter. Over time, the smell got worse, not just his penis, but also his body odor. I can't explain it, it was a dirty, sweaty, pungent smell. Rarely was it clean

51

and without an odor. When I would try to stop or move away, he would aggressively shove my head back down there to start all over again as well as to start the manipulation and lies. I had no idea what I was doing, so he would always hold the back of my head and shove it in and out, fast and slow, hard and soft. I always knew when he was about to cum because I could feel his penis start to pulsate and get harder. He would always direct my head in a harder and faster motion and when he was going to reach orgasm, he would hold my head still, then thrust into my mouth. I would usually choke on it, I would spit it out, dry retch and throw up. One time I threw up onto his legs and his feet. He complained a little and went into the bathroom and cleaned himself up. Fuck him, it was the least that he deserved. Again, I really should have bitten that thing off.

I remember the first time I got a hard on away from him, in a normal adolescent situation. I was at home and the movie 'Class' was on TV. It was a movie made in 1983, starring Jacqueline Bisset, Rob Lowe and Andrew McCarthy. It was about a young, innocent, country boy named Jonathan (Andrew McCarthy), who got into an exclusive prep school and roomed with a rich, popular, handsome guy named Skip (Rob Lowe). Skip helped Jonathan to lose his virginity by sending him out for a big night on the town, this is where he meets Ellen (Jacqueline Bisset), a beautiful, older woman who seduces him into having sex with her. Jonathan soon realizes that this woman was actually Skip's mother and tries to end the relationship, but ends up having an affair with her, only for Skip to catch them and you can guess the rest. It's funny, after everything I've shared about myself so far, this is what I'm most embarrassed about. In one scene, Ellen and Jonathan begin to have sex in an elevator and, as that was happening, I was happening. I was aroused by watching the two of them go at it. I got hard and was thinking, what the fuck is this, is this supposed to happen? Here I am getting turned on by the Man in real life, but I am also getting turned on by these two people on screen, and it felt natural and good. At the end of the scene, I got up and ran out of the room, I didn't know how to be. Thank you, Jacqueline Bisset, you sexy thing!

Chapter 7

As time went on, it was just a continuation of isolation as I spent more time alone, alienating myself from everyone, either in my bedroom, my parents' room, or downstairs in the rumpus room and my parents would just leave me to do my thing. One particular day, it must have been a weekend or the summer holidays as it was hot outside and both my parents were home. I was in the rumpus room, playing with my toy cars. I had about thirty odd cars of all different shapes and sizes, colors and conditions. They were spread out on the 'city' mat, but I was always drawn to the grey car my father gave me with the broken wheels, and the tow truck that the Man had given me. Whilst playing my mother came down and asked me what I was doing, I told her I was playing with my cars; she then told me to go outside and play with all the other kids from our neighborhood. There were probably ten kids outside playing; it was a weekly occurrence. I told her that I didn't want to go out, that I preferred playing inside with my cars instead. I distinctly remember mum saying that I never wanted to go out to play and that I always wanted to be on my own. She followed that up by saying; *"As long as you're happy."* She would always say that. I told her that I was happy and she walked out leaving me to play with my cars.

After a short while, I became inquisitive about the kids outside and what they were doing, thinking about Janice and Peter having fun with them all, so I ran upstairs with the tow truck in hand, past my parents who were watching TV in the living room. I ran into Janice's bedroom to look out the window but couldn't see them very well, so I ran into the lounge room (the 'special' room) with the antique furniture that we weren't allowed to sit on or play with. The windows and balcony to this room looked out onto the cul-de-sac. I stood at that window for what seemed like an eternity, watching them play. I didn't have any particular feeling about it, still not wanting to go outside and play or feeling like I was missing out. I just watched them out there, chasing after each other and having fun. It felt weird to see them all together, running around, having a great time. My father walked over to me and put his arm around me again, I again shrugged it off. He told me to go outside to play with the other kids, but I told him *"no!"* He saw me holding the tow truck and asked me if it was new, telling me that he liked it. I didn't answer and ran back downstairs, shutting the door behind me.

I continued to play with my cars, pretending that they were alive and real, having them talk to each other. I parked the cars and lined them up on the mat and drove the car my dad gave me past them so they could talk to it, but they were really talking to me. I was the broken grey car that my father gave me. They would say things like *"You suck, your wheels are broken and don't turn... you're a loser and no one wants to play with you... you're an ugly color and no one wants to be your friend."* This went on for hours; and I realize now that I was reenacting the trauma of my real life in this symbolic fashion. Eventually I stopped the car in front of the ones that teased me, then drove off to the other side of the mat where I was, once again, alone. I then drove the strong tow truck over to the grey car and it would show it love and compassion, telling the grey car that it loved it and that it would fix it up. I hooked the broken car onto the hitch of the tow truck and drove the two cars together into the mechanic's shop where someone could fix the broken wheels. But in this game, the wheels couldn't be fixed, so I compulsively, and violently drove the broken car along the city streets of the mat. Eventually I reached the parked cars, smashing into all of the ones that teased it (me), making them crash all over the place, and launching them all over the room. I then picked up the broken car with the broken wheels and threw it against the brick wall, as hard as I could, trying to break it even more, screaming out, *"I hate you!"* whilst holding the tow truck in my other hand as tightly as I could. Finally, I gathered all the cars I had thrown, besides the broken one, brought them back to the mat, played with them and let them each have a turn getting towed around the streets from the strong tow truck. I left the broken car where I threw it, and did not play with it again.

I wonder what my parents were thinking when I was acting this way. Should they have noticed something? Should they have realised that there was a change in me from being the kid who played with other kids on the street, having fun with my friends, with Janice and Peter, to now rarely wanting to spend time with anyone at all? I'm sure they were thinking that I was a quiet kid, an introvert who liked to be alone. I figured they thought I was just growing into myself, into who I really was; a shy and quiet child who didn't like affection or sharing anything about himself with others.

I started high school; I was a big boy now. It would have been toward the end of January or beginning of February, close to my birthday, possibly even on my birthday. I would have just turned twelve years old. I was in Year Seven at St Edmund's College, in Canberra, or 'Eddies' as we called it. It was one of the bigger high schools in Canberra, a Catholic School and a very big rugby union school, one of the best in the country. It went from Year Four, primary school, all the way to the end of high school, Year Twelve. It was about a fifteen-minute bus ride from Queanbeyan and a few of my friends from primary school migrated with me too. I think my first tutor was Mr. Sinclair, a nice guy. Every morning following the first period we would report to our tutor group; there were usually about fifteen boys in a group. I imagine this was a way for the teachers to check in and see who was at school and who was missing.

A few weeks after school began, we had our swimming carnival, at the Australian Institute of Sport, the same pool where Australia's very best athletes, the Olympians, train and swim. I was in Rice House, a green colored house. I don't think I had any of my friends with me in that house. I wasn't the best swimmer and never really cared for the swimming carnival. I believe I competed in only one race and didn't do very well at that. A few weeks later, we had our Athletics Carnival, which I loved. I competed in almost all the track and field events. The athletics carnival was one of my favorite days at school. I won the one, two and four hundred-meter sprints for my age group, breaking the school record in the four hundred. I was really proud of that. I felt special, a different kind of special to what I usually felt, for once I felt liked by some of my fellow students and the teachers who were paying extra attention to me. It was not the same kind of attention the Man would show me. They knew my name, who I was and even joked around with me because I was a good runner. I never really experienced that before. I made the athletics team and we had training twice per week after school, for the upcoming athletics season where we would compete with all the other schools in Canberra. I won some races, placed in some and lost the others. I did enjoy my athletics, taking days off school, competing against other schools and making new friends.

My parents always taught me and my siblings the value of a dollar and of hard work, nothing came for free and we were made to work for everything that we wanted. I really appreciate this lesson, as today I understand the value of a dollar. I was probably around twelve or thirteen years old when I started doing the paper run in my local area with Janice. She started doing it with her friend, and then later took over the route. I started helping Janice, before taking over from her when she got another job in a pharmacy. The paper run was every Monday, Wednesday and Friday and I'd do it after school. If I remember correctly, my route was about fifty houses close to where I lived. The office and printing house for the paper, called The Queanbeyan Age, was across the road from the bus interchange, so after school, Janice and I would collect the fifty odd papers and either walk the route, ride our bikes, ask our dad to drive us around or drop us off and later pick us up when we were done.

Our route wasn't too far from the Queanbeyan swimming pool actually, just above from Queanbeyan park and just below Queanbeyan High School. I don't remember how much I made doing the paper run but it was probably around thirty dollars per week. We would make the most amount of money on a Monday as most people would pay for the full week on that day. It wasn't huge money, but for a youngster doing his first job, it was great. I would hate doing it through the winter months, when it was cold or wet, but it kept me fit and busy. On the route I would sometimes steal money, not usually from my customers, but from the houses next door or up the road who were getting the milk delivered. I would steal their milk money, which was usually between two to five dollars, that was sitting outside in the little yellow envelope, hidden only for the milkman to find. Sometimes I would find a five dollar note in the envelope and I would think to myself how much money that was. One time there was a ten dollar note. I guess someone owed money for a lot of milk, and I thought I was the richest kid in town. I wasn't too pleased with myself whilst doing it; I did know right from wrong, but I didn't really care.

Janice, Peter and I had a 'Dollarmites' account with the Commonwealth Bank. This was a special account for kids, and every week we would bank most of our earnings. We were allowed to keep some of it for spending money. We didn't just make money from doing the paper run, we would also get pocket money and make money from washing the cars, cleaning the house, mowing the lawn, picking the weeds or other household chores. I actually enjoyed doing the work as I found it very therapeutic and, for a couple of hours or however long the chore took to do, I was able to let go of everything that was happening in my life and be a normal kid who didn't think about those darker things. Mum taught me how to wash and iron clothes and how to wash the floors from a young age which I also really enjoyed doing. To this very day I find these things to be therapeutic, cathartic and somewhat enjoyable. There were days, however, that I hated doing any kind of work and all I could think of was the Man; what he was doing to me and how I felt about him and my family. There were days and weeks when I couldn't get him out of my head; he would be all I thought about. He was taking over my life, consuming me, and all I could think of was when I was next going to see him, knowing too well what he was going to do to me. As much as I hated it and him, I was scared for my life, I loved him and wanted to be with him. I also knew I was going to be in pain for several days after it, yet I wanted it and I needed it. I was trapped in a cycle of confusion.

The last time I saw the Man was at his house. He was very paranoid and suspicious toward me, more than usual. He repeatedly asked me if anyone knew anything and if I'd ever told anyone. He was acting strange. He was aggressive in his behavior, in the way he treated me physically and in his words. He had brought out a bunch of board games to play with me, but we never actually played them. I sat on the couch, he had the television on, he never had the television on, I don't remember what show it was.

He demanded;

"Take your clothes off."

I didn't. I didn't feel safe and comfortable being there. He demanded more aggressively;

"... take your clothes off!"

59

Again, I didn't. I wanted to leave.

"... I'm scared, can I leave?"

He didn't let me, he became very angry with me and then turned it all around onto me;

"I am very upset, you have upset me because you want to leave... I love you very much, you are very important to me... I am sorry for getting angry at you, something happened at work."

He **never** apologized for anything.

I have no idea what he even did for work, it was pretty much the first time he ever spoke about himself, his job, or anything about his life.

"... would you like some ice cream?"

I loved ice cream as a kid, I ate it almost every night. I had some and he sat in closer to me, putting his arm around me.

"Look at you turning into a big boy now... into a handsome young man."

He then got naked in front of me, which I was so accustomed to that I didn't much flinch anymore.

"Take your clothes off."

He said this with an icy calmness. I did as he said. I didn't want him to get aggressive with me.

He made me play with him. I could never look at him when I did it, I would sit there or be in whatever position he had put me into and I would always look off to the side. I didn't like the feel of it and touching it because I knew what was going to happen, which was so weird because I hated it and enjoyed it both at the same time.

This time he didn't take me into his bedroom; we stayed on the couch and he aggressively turned me around. I would normally be on all fours or have my chest up against the back of the couch. He raped me violently, he raped me hard, he made me cry. I had my hands on the top of the couch, holding on for support, but they started shaking and soon gave way under the force and pressure of his pounding and his weight on me. I could feel his big body against mine, his sweat dripping onto me. That was the most disgusting thing to me.

I had become so used to him penetrating and raping me, the smell of it and feeling of it all, but feeling his sweat drip...drip...drip...drip...onto my body is what I found to be the worst part. That, and his musky smell. Hearing him breathe heavily, pant and moan turned all of my insides. That's what felt dirty to me, while the other, infinitely more vile actions, didn't even feel dirty anymore.

Over the years he had become unhealthier; his belly had grown bigger, his hair receded, he'd let himself go. I looked for the photo of the little girl but she was long gone, and I felt more alone now than all the other times I had been with him. I just stared at the cabinet where the photo had been and took the punishment; it was different this time. He hadn't been this forceful for a very long time, his aggressive actions felt like they did on the very first day, back in the change room, at the pool, where it all started. It was as if he was absolutely determined to hurt me, like he didn't love me. *Would he do this to someone that he really loved?* I guess we had come full circle.

Maybe he knew it was the last time he was going to see me. I will never know. When he was done, he got off me and just sat on the couch breathing heavily, staring blankly. He didn't say a word. I sat there, I couldn't move, my body numb and in pain, I was shaking. I felt paralyzed, I could not speak. I was breathing heavily, trying to get my breath back, trying to feel, trying to return to my body, to feel alive again. Once I was capable of moving, I felt a torrent of shame wash over me. I felt like I had disappointed him, that I had let him down. I was angry at myself. I felt like I deserved to be violently abused that hard and, in that way. I deserved the pain and suffering. I told myself;

"This is where I belong. These are the feelings I should be feeling inside and out."

I was moving more than ever towards the belief that I was worthless and undeserving of love and happiness from anyone. The deep shame and self-sabotage that would take over my entire life in the coming years was already taking root, penetrating into my body and into my psyche. The way I felt about people, relationships, myself, my body and my entire life had all changed.

I got out of that place as quickly as I could. We didn't say a word to each other.

We would never look at each other ever again.

Chapter 8

School itself was fine, I guess. I had the same core group of friends with whom I went to primary school, I also made a bunch of new friends. Overall, we had a good year group all the way through high school. We all got along well and there were not too many fights or issues among us. It was compulsory for us to play a sport at school, I chose Soccer given I had played for most of my childhood. We had a decent team, winning more games than we lost. Year Seven through Nine is a bit of a blur to me, nothing memorable really happened; it seemed to go by fast, and I can't remember too much of it. When I was in Year Eight, one of the boys in my year killed himself. I didn't know him well; we weren't in the same friendship group or in any classes together. Looking back on it now, I wonder why he did it;

What was he going through?... What had he been through?... Was he sexually abused as a child as well?... Could he not talk to anyone?... Did he not have support around him?... Did he feel shame?... Was it still happening?... And was he scared for his life and thought this was the only way out?... He was so young. We both were.

Most of my friends had girlfriends or were talking to girls, kissing them, discovering the female body, but I wanted nothing to do with them. I would mostly talk to the girls at the bus interchange who I already knew from primary school or from Girls Grammar, Merici College or from St Clare's College, three all-girls high schools. St Clare's was directly across the road from Eddies. We would often travel on the bus with them, to and from school; see them during lunch breaks. It was pretty much a given that Eddies boys would date girls from St Clare's. I was a decent looking kid growing up; I always had a girl or two interested in me, wanting to be my girlfriend or go out with me, but I would always shut it down early, wanting nothing to do with them in *that* way. It was the last thing I thought about and I didn't know how to act on it. I was a bit of an introvert around them and kept to myself, letting my friends take the lead and have all the fun. I found girls and women to be beautiful and feminine, but also thought that everyone felt this way about them; that this was just a normal thing to feel, but that doesn't mean we need to *be* with them. I was used to having sex with a grown man and my friends were just starting to kiss and fool around with these young girls. I felt so much more superior, *special* and more experienced than they were. I had been having sex for five years already; and had been in *that* relationship with him. They were just starting to talk about it.

Sometime during Year Eight, I realized clearly that I hadn't seen or heard from the Man in a while. I was missing him, missing my time with him, wondering where he was. I desperately wanted to see him; *Why hadn't he been to find me at the bus interchange, around town or come to watch me play soccer?*

I'd sometimes ride my bike down past his house, sit out front, across the street, and hide behind parked cars or trees lining the street. At this stage in my relationship with my family, I was only talking to them out of necessity, not sharing anything about myself with them, about school or about anything that was going on in my life. Sometimes I would sit across the street from his place for what felt like hours, but in reality, it was probably only minutes. Once or twice people from the neighborhood would ask me if I was okay, or if I needed any help. I would tell them that I was waiting for my friend to get home, or I would just jump on my bike and ride off. I would never tell them who I was waiting for. I couldn't say anything specific, afraid and nervous that someone, anyone, would find out about my relationship with him.

After months and months of waiting outside his house, I finally saw a car parked out front. It wasn't his car, but there was movement inside the house; *Had he bought a new car that I didn't know about?* I sat across the street, opposite his home, hiding behind a tree, trying to catch a glimpse of something or someone.

There was definitely someone walking around inside, though I wasn't sure who. I could see shadows behind the curtains and I finally built up enough courage to go and knock on the door, knowing full well that this could end very badly for me. I didn't care though; I hadn't seen him in months and I was determined to do so or at least find out what was going on.

I picked my bike up and walked it across the road, ditching it in his front yard. I walked up to the front door, stood there breathing nervously, and finally knocked. I heard footsteps running around inside, finally the door opened. It wasn't the Man but a lady who I had never seen before. She looked like a sweet lady, definitely a pretty lady. I only really remember her long blonde hair and her warm smile; she looked like someone who had a lot of love to give. I remember she answered the door;

"Hello young man, can I help you?"

I just stood there frozen, like a deer in headlights, definitely not expecting to see her and not knowing what to say or do. I thought I was at the wrong house, maybe even on the wrong street.

She asked again;

"... can I help you?"

I finally gathered the strength to say;

"I am looking for the Man who lives here."

She looked at me with concern;

"Why are you looking for him?"

At that very moment, the most amazing thing happened. I heard another set of footprints coming to the front door and I thought they were those of the Man. But they were not. Standing behind the woman was **that** little girl from the photo. I was taken aback; I couldn't take my eyes off of her. In that moment she was the most beautiful thing I had ever seen. She had long red hair, a gentle smile, and her beautiful green eyes were staring straight at me, just like they did all those times I saw her in the photo. She was shorter than me, she hid behind her mother's legs, holding on as if for dear life, watching me with great thought, as though enquiring who this young boy was and why he was at the front door. We were locked into each other's gaze.

The lady asked again;

"...why are you looking for him?"

I did not answer. I was transfixed on the eyes of the young girl, I wanted to speak to her so badly and ask her so many questions;

How did she know the Man and was she special like I was?... Did he do to her what he did to me?... Did he love her like he loved me?... Did he give her gifts, tell her that her mum doesn't love her and that he's the only one whom she can love?

The lady then asked me another question; a question that still haunts me today;

"Is he a friend of yours?"

I think about that question today like I thought about it back then, with great confusion and an inability to answer.

It took me a while to respond, but when I did, I said,

"...yes!"

The lady kept trying to shield her daughter by pushing her further back inside the doorway. Maybe she could see the way I was staring at the girl and how consumed I was by her.

The lady then told me something that didn't really sink in nor did it hit me for quite a while;

"The Man is gone, he doesn't live here anymore and you will never see him again."

That was the moment I took my eyes off of the girl and looked up at the lady. She wasn't angry at me; she looked at me with great sorrow and pain in her eyes. I felt as if she wanted to hold me, to give me a big hug and to protect me, letting me know that everything was going to be okay, like she was doing for her little girl. I think she knew what the situation was, between the Man and I, although she never directly said it or asked. There was one last question that tied it all together;

"How do you know my husband?"

I turned and ran to retrieve my bike as soon as she asked me. I rode off as fast as I could, not looking back to see if she was following me. I don't remember if I rode directly home or if I rode around the neighborhood, going over in my head what just happened; *What had just happened?!*

This is a memory that will live with me for eternity; the vision of the Man's wife and daughter, curious and afraid, loving and ashamed, all at the same time. I think of them often, even to this very day. I especially think of the little girl in the photo who kept me company during those very violent days, during all of the days, even when I wasn't at the Man's house.

Was it me that her mother was protecting her from that day at the front door?... Could she see that her husband had already gotten to me?... Did the lady know what the Man was doing to me and possibly to other little boys?

The girl seemed so pure and innocent, unaware of who I was or what the Man had done to me. I feel conflicted about whether I would actually even want to meet them today. Part of me feels that if I knew where she was today, I would love to meet her, to speak to her and find out more about her, her mother and the Man. There are so many questions I want to ask her. I would love to tell her that for years she was my guardian angel; that she kept me alive throughout my entire relationship with her father; and that if she wasn't there to keep me company, to watch over me and protect me, I would be dead today.

I never saw the lady or that little girl again.

After Him

Chapter 9

For months following the day I met his wife, I was in a daze, still trying to work out what had actually happened, and if it really did even happen. And his daughter, well, I couldn't stop thinking about her.

Who was this woman to tell me that he was gone and that I would never see the Man again?... Where was he?... What actually happened to him?... Did he love her as much as he loved me or did he love me more than he loved her?... Why was she allowed to see him and I couldn't?

I didn't actually know if she was seeing him or not, if she was even allowed to see him or if the Man was actually still in their lives. I was in a constant loop as to whether he actually did leave town; if he was in trouble with the police, or if something bad had happened to him. As much as I was upset, I was angry. I was angry with him, with my family, with his family, with the world. *How the fuck could he abandon me like this?* More importantly, I was probably most angry with myself.

How the hell could I just let him disappear out of my life like this?... How could he not tell me where he was or why he left?... What did I do wrong?... What more could I have done?... Was I not nice enough

to him?... Did I not show him enough love and affection as he did
me?... Or treat him as good as he treated me?

These were the honest, yet fucked up, things I was thinking. I felt like
I was truly alone. I felt like I had no one. I couldn't get away from the
same repetitive thoughts. At this point in my life, I wanted nothing to
do with my family.

I constantly told myself that I didn't want them, and that they definitely
didn't want me. I told myself that they thought everything about me
was wrong, that they would prefer for me to be with the Man; they
didn't love me, didn't want me, hated me even. I told myself that they
saw me as a liar and would never believe anything I ever told them. I
thought that Janice and Peter hated me and Karl was too young to know
what was going on. Thank God we had Karl because he took a lot of
attention away from the rest of us kids; mum and dad put most of their
time on him as we were getting older and capable of taking care of
ourselves. I do know that my parents loved us all equally; that they
were there and would have done anything for all of us. I just couldn't
see any of it clearly; and if I did, I could never acknowledge it.

My identity was lost;

Who was I?... What was I?... Where did I belong?... Where was my
place in the world?... Now what do I do?... How do I survive?...
Nobody likes me or wants to be with me!

I had my friends, I had my family and everyone who loved me around
me, but I was brainwashed and under the power of a man who hurt me.
I didn't know it at the time. I couldn't see it. I knew my family so well
but at the same time they felt so foreign to me, like strangers I didn't
care to know and who didn't care to know me either. I had grown from
an innocent eight-year-old boy into a lonely man overnight, just to

70

survive. I had so much self-anger and self-hatred; I believed I deserved failure and to live in shame. My biggest problem was that I kept it all inside, pushed it so far deep down so that I could keep up with my life. I pretended I was a normal kid, like nothing had ever happened to me. I remained a quiet introvert and kept to myself. I had friends at school and friends outside of school; I still played soccer and did athletics on the weekend, but I was forever changed, forever broken, a shadow of my former self. I was a victim who lived a secret life, a double life, lying to myself and lying to everybody about who I really was and what I had been through, but it couldn't be any other way. I still had to protect my family. I didn't want to see any harm come to them even though the Man was gone. I couldn't tell anyone, nor could I go to the police, because this was all my fault and I deserved this. I still feared that if I went to the police I would have been sent to jail and then I definitely wouldn't be able to see him again or my family. I still had hope that he might come back, that he wasn't gone forever.

When I was thirteen, my parents sent Janice and I over to England and Malta for what would have been about two months to be with family. It was our summer holidays in Australia and winter in Europe, and we got to miss the last few weeks of school. About a week before going Janice had emergency surgery to get her appendix out; we weren't sure whether we would make it over, but luckily, we did. First stop was Cobham, in Surrey, England, with dad's brother, Uncle Tony, whom I'd finally met for the first time. He had a beautiful old farmhouse on a few acres with horses and stables. It was such a warm and welcoming home. We had a great time in England, visited London on numerous occasions, went to all of the tourist spots, and I also met a bunch of new cousins that were all around our age. We hung out with them a lot, had sleepovers at their houses, went shopping together and played games. It was then that I found my love for Tottenham Hotspur Football Club. The family all supported them, so Spurs were forced onto me. C'mon you Spurs!

I will always remember that trip because a day or two after arriving in England, Freddie Mercury, the lead singer for Queen died. We would listen to Queen a lot as kids, an amazing band, one of the best there ever was or will be. We were in England for about one week, then we were off to Malta, where we stayed with our grandparents, our Auntie Lina, and Uncle Naz. Christmas in Malta is a beautiful time of year; it's not very cold like the rest of Europe. All of the streets are lit, everyone is out eating, shopping and celebrating the festive season. Christmas Day was always a big occasion, my grandparents' house was the focal point for the extended family, cousins, aunties and uncles and friends who would float in and out of our house all day. Well-wishers came by giving presents, dropping off food and drink, getting drunk and having a great time. Getting out of Australia was always a good thing for me when I was young, as it took my mind off of everything and I almost got to forget about the Man for that short time. He was always there with me in my head but being out of Queanbeyan made life so much easier for me. Out of sight, out of mind. We spent a great deal of time with our cousins Edna and Karen. They are our age and lived across the street from our grandparents, and we spent time going to cafes, restaurants, bars and nightclubs. I'm not really sure if there was an age restriction in Malta back then when it came to drinking and going out, I still don't think there is one now to be honest.

I mostly loved spending time with Uncle Naz. I would sit in his chair in the corner of his room, right beside his piss bucket, and he would lie down in bed or sit up while we talked for hours about everything, until he needed his afternoon sleep. I would always play with his huge belly, tapping it like it was a drum, and having fun with him. He made me laugh more than any other person I knew. Our grandfather would still test us on our times tables and our spelling; and our grandmother continued to dote on us, feed us and give us anything we needed. And yes, Auntie Lina still fussed and worried over us. Malta is a very catholic country; my grandparents said the rosary every morning and

72

night and went to church almost every day, it felt like that anyway and we had to go with them most of the time. Religion, and the catholic faith in particular, were a big thing for my family, and every year my grandparents in Malta would mail us kids back in Australia presents. My sister and brothers would always receive clothing and toys, whereas I, for a few years, always received statues and figurines of Jesus and the Saints. As the first-born grandson in the family, I think my grandparents desperately wanted me to become a priest. I think I would have failed miserably as one, as I probably would have tried to sleep with all of the nuns. I will always have the fondest memories of Malta as a young kid. They were some of the happiest and most carefree times in my life.

The next two years back in Australia were pretty quiet. I was thirteen, and I kept to myself, still hiding away from the world and still trying to make sense of all that had happened to me. I was more lost than ever; I felt like a stranger in my own skin, my own house and with my own family. I felt dirty, ashamed and not worthy of love. School was fine, I was doing my work, passing my tests and grades, and keeping out of trouble. I had the same core group of friends from the previous few years; they were all good guys. I would sometimes hang out with friends, other kids from the neighborhood or children of my parent's friends. All of it felt a little difficult, often I would prefer to isolate and be alone. I tried to keep up appearances, act like a normal kid, pretend to be happy. All I really wanted to do was to sit at home in my room or to watch television and movies away from everyone.

Television was turning into a life-saver for me; a chance to escape reality, to get lost in the world of make believe, with fictional people and made-up stories. By this age the *toy cars* were packed into a box, and the mat on which I used to play was put away. Peter didn't have much of an interest in them. He was very much an extrovert, playing sport and excelling at it, out with friends and doing 'normal' kid stuff.

Although on occasion I would sometimes get the cars out and play with them with Karl, he was getting older and was only into cars for a short period. I would still give most of my attention to the car that the Man gave me, holding onto it with affection. It was literally the only item I had that he ever gave me. There were plenty of memories there, memories I would never forget, but I started to suppress them and push them down even further deep inside of me.

I was getting along fine with Janice and Peter. Karl was only three years old, a cute kid. I loved him. It was a very different love compared to the rest of the family as he came around at a much later date and when I was deep into my relationship with the Man. I was happy to have him around. I looked at him differently than I did the others. He was much younger than the rest of us. There was an eight-year gap between Peter and Karl, so he was still a baby to me. I felt a responsibility to protect him and to ensure that nothing bad would ever happen to him, like it did to me. I fought with Peter a lot, and I'm not really sure if he looked up to me. I was his big brother, two years older, and we shared a bedroom together for most of our childhood. We spent time together, playing in the backyard and on the street with friends and neighborhood kids. Peter was a good kid, very friendly, affectionate and loving toward everyone. I don't think I had an affectionate bone in my body at that age, I hated being touched by anyone, receiving presents, or having any love shown my way. I didn't care for love and affection from my parents, whenever they tried to kiss or cuddle me, I would run away from it. If I saw them kiss and cuddle my siblings, I would leave the room. I didn't want to see it nor be a part of it, as I was sure I was next in line. It made me feel uncomfortable.

Even though my parents were very loving and caring, I do remember them not always being affectionate people, as there was no kiss or hug goodnight, and sometimes not even a goodnight wish. I'm not sure if there was much affection going around the house or maybe it was just me; I didn't see it and didn't want to see it, I ran away from it every chance I had. I think Peter was the most affectionate one of us all. He was always cuddled up with mum from what I remember.

As time went on, I would find myself still riding my bike or walking past the Man's house. The house was always closed up, dark; no one was to be seen. The front yard had been totally neglected; the grass had grown wild and the plants were either dying or dead if not wildly overgrown. I still and often wondered where the Man had disappeared to and where his wife and daughter were. Just like the old days, I would sit across from his house, waiting for him to peer outside the window or pull his car into the driveway, hoping for him to open his front door slightly and usher me into his house quickly so no one would notice anything. On occasion and knowing no one was at the house, I would go to his front door and knock on it. No one ever answered. I would try to sneak a peek into his house through the windows, but the curtains did their job and I could never really see anything. At the bus interchange, before and after school, I would look out for him but he was never there, never waiting for me, never sitting in his car or anonymously walking past. On the weekends, playing soccer, I looked for him too. Literally, wherever I was, I tried to find him. Looking back on it now, I'm not sure if it was out of a hope that he would be there, or out of a fear that he would be angry at me, having not seen him in a while and him thinking I've told my family or the police what had happened. I realized soon after this that I really would never see him again, that he was actually gone and was never going to return to the house.

I continued to distance myself from people. I was starting to resent and hate the Man more and more, also feeling the same about myself, feeling deep shame, having large bouts of depression and blaming myself for **everything**. I would lose my temper and fight with my family and strangers, putting more and more blame onto myself for him disappearing from my life. I had repetitive and compulsive thoughts. W*hat did I do wrong?... What did I say wrong?... Was I not there enough or too much?* I must have been walking around like a zombie, oblivious to my surroundings and to the real world around me.

I was becoming more sexual with myself, masturbating all the time, playing with myself, thinking about him, about sex with him. One time over the summer holidays, I was about fourteen, the family was down at Batemans Bay and I was at the local swimming pool with my siblings and cousins. It was a typical, hot, summer day and everyone was in the pool. I got out to use the toilet in the change room and there was a gentleman in there; he looked like my Man, probably of a similar age, and I couldn't stop looking at him. I think he had just gotten to the pool; he was dry and changing into his swimmers. I felt intense anger towards this stranger. I wanted to hit him, to scream, but I was nervous and scared, my heart pounding a million beats per minute. It all seemed so familiar and almost normal. I was so confused and didn't really know what was going on, but at the same time I wanted him to rape me, to have sex with me. I went to the toilet, took off my swimmers and jumped into the shower, leaving the door open. He walked past to use the toilet, looked in, but kept going. I was standing under the water looking out, waiting patiently. He walked back past a short time later, looked in again, but he didn't stop, he didn't walk in and wanted nothing to do with me. I probably looked like a drowned rat standing under the shower. I don't remember if I was playing with myself in front of him or if I had an erection.

As soon as he went back to get changed, I jumped out of the shower and went into the changing area, naked, with shorts in hand. I slowly put my shorts back on, looking at him, but he left the change rooms soon after, not giving me any attention at all. When he left, I quickly got dressed and ran back to where Janice, Peter and my cousins were.

I don't remember if my parents were there at the time or if they just dropped us off for a few hours like they usually did. That poor guy; what must have he been thinking? Here was this young boy trying to seduce him and get attention from an older man. I was lucky he didn't report me to anyone. Crazy. I remember thinking to myself;

This is what's supposed to happen to me... Maybe this man will want to be with me and give me attention.

I wanted it. I needed it. It was all I knew and I missed it. At this stage, I knew it wasn't normal or right; adults weren't supposed to fuck and have *special* relationships with children. All of my friends at school were engaging more with girls, had girlfriends and were talking about kissing and experimenting with them; maybe one or two of them had even had sex by now. I saw my sister and her friends with their boyfriends, I heard them talking about boys. I knew right from wrong in my head, but I didn't understand it. I couldn't comprehend it. I only knew what I wanted and what I was longing for. Up to this point in my life, abusive sex with men was all I knew, so for me it was all I wanted, and I needed to have more of it. But how, where and when? I still wasn't interested in girls and never hung out enough with them at school or in a group environment with friends. I thought they were beautiful and I enjoyed looking at them and sometimes even talking about them with my friends, even though I wasn't interested in them sexually. I was friendly towards them, and was never rude or insulting.

I remember how friends would talk about the nights they went to house parties and there were girls there. They would talk about how they would make out with them in the hot tub. They would tell me that they would go to the cinema with girls and finger them whilst watching a movie. I remember them telling me about it and how amazing it was, but I didn't care as it did nothing for me. If anything, it felt weird, unnatural and foreign.

As my sexual desires, curiosity and total confusion of where I belonged, grew, I saw myself alone more and more. My friends were hanging downtown in Queanbeyan or out in Civic, the city center of Canberra. They were meeting more girls, making more friends and becoming more social. I was going the other way, becoming more of a recluse, sexually frustrated and turning into a sexual deviant.

Chapter 10

I'd heard about Fyshwick before, a suburb in Canberra. I'd heard that it was full of brothels and sex shops. I'd driven through it with my parents on hundreds of occasions. It is the industrial part of Canberra and one can drive through it in order to get to and from Queanbeyan to Canberra. People used to say that Fyshwick was the sex and firework capital of Australia; the only place in the country (at the time) where both were legal. I was fifteen, I had received a new BMX bike for Christmas and I was riding it everywhere. It was black and red and the coolest BMX in town at the time, well I thought so, anyway! Fyshwick was a twenty-minute bike ride from my house and I was riding there more and more, but it wasn't for fireworks or fitness. The first few times I would ride through Fyshwick learning where the brothels and sex shops were. I never went inside them; I just rode past or would sit across the road, looking to see who would go in and out. I was good at doing that. Finally, I summoned enough internal courage and started going inside the sex shops. I would walk in as quickly as I could, hoping the person working there wouldn't see me and that I wouldn't draw attention to myself, although I probably drew more attention to myself by rushing in and hiding once in there. I knew I was underage and not allowed in, but it was the early nineties, and these were dirty little sex shops in little old Canberra, and no one seemed to blink an eye. I was not really sure what I was looking for or what I was doing there, these shops were full of porn videos of whatever you were into. They also sold dildos and strap-ons, fake vaginas, lingerie, bongs, pipes, cock rings, piercings, blow up dolls; any and all things related to sex.

Some of the shops had video booths where you could put in a dollar or two, and watch up to ten different videos and jerk off. Some of these booths had glory holes. The videos were all mixed; some straight, some lesbian and gay. I would flick through them all, sometimes stopping at straight porn, sometimes at the lesbian videos, but finding myself watching the gay porn more than the others. I discovered that I needed the videos to contain hard and dirty sex; if there was a couple making love, I wasn't interested. I'd masturbate to the videos but would find myself feeling shame and disgust as soon as I'd finish, and then needed to get out of the shop as quickly as I could. It wasn't the first time I'd seen porn; the first time was at my grandparent's place, in my uncles' room, for literally twenty seconds with my sibling and cousins. However, the first time I really watched porn was probably a few years prior, when I found a VHS porn video that my dad had hidden in his little walk-in closet. I was probably stealing coins from his huge money box and somehow stumbled upon the video. I waited for the moment when no one was home and put the video on. It was straight porn and I was fascinated by it. It was weird, I thought the women were sexy but still had no real desire to be with any of them. I watched it a few times, masturbated to it and thought it was amazing. When the video mysteriously disappeared, I had hoped that another one would show up in its place, but none ever did.

The clientele at these sex shops were mostly men, middle aged and horny young guys looking to buy porn. There were a number of couples coming in together, looking to buy toys, and sometimes I saw women there alone. There were probably between five to ten sex shops (at the time) in Fyshwick and I'd been to most of them, and I definitely got kicked out of a few of them for being underage. I knew the stores that I would be safe in, where the worker would actually say hi and ask if I was looking for anything in particular. There was never a question of my age.

I soon discovered that two of these sex shops had a secret door that men were walking in and out of; never any women, only men. One of the doors was locked from behind the counter and the shop assistant had to buzz you in. The other shop wasn't that way and you could walk in and out as you pleased. My first time going into the *secret* room, I waited for a man to walk out and I snuck in before the door shut. I entered a dark hallway that led to different rooms, like a maze, not knowing where I was going. I heard moaning as I walked down the hallway, finding myself deeper inside the maze. This secret room had a certain smell to it, a mixture of sweat, men, sex, cum and poppers. As I walked further in, I saw a TV with gay porn playing; I kept going and I noticed a little theatre room with a projector playing gay porn. There were two men in there, one was giving the other a blow job. I was fascinated by what I saw; I'd never seen anything like it or been anywhere like this place before. I kept walking, keeping my head down so no one could see my face. I didn't want to look at anyone either. There were private sex rooms, televisions on the walls with glory holes, a sex swing, and a room that was pitch black. I was in a gay cruise lounge where anything goes. Men of all ages, shapes and sizes would wander in and out of the lounge, some of them with clothes on, others naked, some dressed in leather, or whatever they were into.

I kept walking, doing a lap until I discovered a secret sex cave with probably between five to ten men inside. I stood in a corner, away from everyone, unsure if I wanted to be seen. I was taking in my surroundings, coming to grips with where I was and all of the emotions coming over me; excitement, curiosity, disgust, anger and fear. I felt strangely comfortable in this place and at the same time oddly out of place and I didn't want to be there. I didn't want to look at anyone, I didn't want to touch anyone or want anyone to touch me, but I was compelled to stay. I needed to be there; my heart was pounding at a million beats per minute. I thought it was going to jump out of my chest and run away without me. I was nervous as hell as a man approached me. I kept my head down, I didn't want him to look in my eyes and I definitely didn't want to look at him. I wanted to run away but I was frozen still; I couldn't move and I didn't want to. Part of me was scared that he might recognize me, know who I was and know my family. All of these scenarios were coursing through my mind as to how he might know who I was.

He said hello to me; I kept my head down and gave the faintest of smiles. I didn't talk back. He reached for my crotch, feeling for my penis. The room was dark, he started rubbing me up and down; I put my head into my arms before pushing his hand off. He asked what I liked; I didn't answer. He then asked what I wanted and I walked away. He didn't follow, he just stood there, rejected. I walked out of the cruise lounge as quickly as I could and into a little booth in the sex shop, inserted two dollars and started jerking off. I don't remember what kind of porn I was watching, I don't think it really mattered at that point anyway, I was horny, I was ready to explode, as much as a fifteen-year-old kid could. A few seconds later I heard movement in the booth next to me and could see an eye looking at me through the glory hole, definitely a surprise and not what I was expecting. I kept jerking off, a few seconds later this person put one finger through the glory hole, waved me over and said *"I want to suck you."* My heart was racing, still not sure where I was and what situation I had even got myself into. I couldn't believe what I had discovered and what I was experiencing. I put my penis through the glory hole, waited for a second or two, then suddenly felt a hand on me, I was being jerked off. *"Was this really happening?"* A second or two later, I felt a warm and moist sensation; I was being sucked off. I put my arms against the wall dividing me and the stranger on the other side, and I closed my eyes. I could hear the porn playing in the background so I opened my eyes and watched the TV, imagining I was in a porn movie, doing whatever it was that was going on at the time. I could feel myself getting closer to orgasm; I thrusted myself forward and as deep as I could into this stranger's mouth, like the Man would do to me. I came. An enormous wave of emotion washed over me, I was feeling shame, anger and disgust towards myself and the stranger on the other side of the wall. I needed to get out of there as soon as I could. I knew that these emotions came about through all of the grooming and the manipulation the Man had ingrained all through me. I felt like I was the dirtiest person in the world; like I didn't deserve to feel any kind of joy or pleasure from the experience I just had.

The Man groomed me into feeling like a piece of shit; worthless and unable to care. Anger and disgust towards myself and towards him welled up from deep inside, and I began re-questioning why he had abandoned me. *Why had he left me this way, emotionally and mentally?* I wanted to ask him so many questions; I wanted him to hurt me again, to rape me again. I missed it. I wanted it and again I felt I needed it. At the very same time, I was still wanting to protect my family from anything and everything I was going through. I punched the wall hard; it was aimed at the Man, the stranger on the other side of the wall, and also at myself. I had so much hatred toward myself. I quickly stepped back, got some tissues and wiped myself clean, leaving a few clean tissues in my undies so there was no post-cum spillage in them so that my parents wouldn't have a clue when they were washing them. I pulled my undies and pants up as quickly as I could. In the meantime, the stranger had put his penis through the glory hole for me to return the favor; *No fucking way am I going to suck your dick!* I thought to myself. I left that room, not touching him at all and walked out of that sex shop as fast as I could. As soon as I exited, I ran to where I had chained up my BMX and was off as fast as I could possibly peddle.

For the entire bike ride home, this was all I could think about. My mind was all over the place. I was lucky I didn't hit anything or fall off my bike. I was excited to have discovered this sordid place but at the same time I was petrified that it even existed. I needed this place and I remember already thinking how I couldn't wait to go back there, while at the same time thinking I can never go back. It was, however, too late for that. I was already addicted.

Who were these guys?... Would the Man be there and would I finally see him?... Who was the old guy rubbing me up?... How long has that place been there?... What is going on?

It turned me on, but I wanted nothing to do with him. I needed to go back as soon as I could, but I couldn't go back for fear that someone would see me. I had ambivalence and shame spinning within me simultaneously. There was absolutely no way I could return to this place, and yet, I knew that it was the beginning of a whole new dangerous addiction.

For the next few weeks, that secret place was all I could think about, whether I was at school, home, with family or with friends. I could not get this place out of my mind and I needed to get back there as soon as I could. In the meantime, I had started a new part-time job. Every afternoon after school, from four to six o'clock, I worked at the local Amcal Chemist on Monaro Street, the main street of Queanbeyan. I was making four dollars and eighty cents per hour doing ten hours each week. To me it was like making one million dollars, I felt so rich. Janice was working there as well, she got me the job. I worked mostly in the office and storeroom at the back, running around town going to the local clinics, picking up prescriptions for the elderly and bringing them back to the chemist to be filled and delivered. I really enjoyed the job; it was easy and I was making money. I would walk to a few of the elderly homes close to the chemist, delivering their medication. I came to know some of the elderly people well, sitting and chatting with them, taking as much time as I could so I didn't have to go back to work.

Toy Cars   Nathan Spiteri

Every afternoon without fail I would have my mint chocolate Freddo
Frog and a few jelly beans from an open packet that the girls were
snacking on. This job was my real introduction to women and the first
time I truly started interacting and getting close to them. Alongside the
girls, there were two male pharmacists, Mr. Mitchell, the owner, a very
sweet and generous guy, but also very serious. We couldn't mess
around so much while he was there, he was always on top of us making
sure we were doing our jobs. Then there was Rod, an old army veteran
of the Vietnam War. He would tell us stories of the army and would
try to instill army discipline into us; he was hard but fun. We never
really took him too seriously.

I was the only other male working there at the time. The rest were girls,
around my sister's age and older; some were married, some were
single. I found that it was easy to talk to them; they were gentle, kind,
trusting, loving towards me, and they were all so beautiful. I was
everyone's 'little brother' and that's where I learned how girls behaved.
It was here that I discovered that I felt more comfortable hanging with
females over males, beside my closest male friends who I'd known
forever. I learned that I definitely found it easier to talk to these
women, to trust them and let them into my world. It was at this Chemist
that I discovered I could (possibly) be affectionate, loving and sexually
attracted to them. I think the Chemist had a reputation back then for
hiring all the cute girls in town, and I got to work with all of them. The
girls would talk about sex, relationships, boys, getting their periods in
front of me. They got new boyfriends, broke up with them, got
engaged, married and divorced, all right in front of me. I learned what
women liked and didn't like; wanted and didn't want. I learned how to
treat a woman and how to talk to a woman. I did not realize it then, but
they taught me well. Though I was learning about the wonderful
mysteries of women, my addiction to the Man was pulling from inside
of me.

85

Every day at the Chemist it was either Elton John or Bette Midler playing and I had a love/hate relationship with most of their songs and almost knew all the words. Everyone working would quietly sing the songs to themselves as the afternoon went by.

About six months after I started work there, one of my oldest friends, Joe, began working there as well. We grew up playing soccer together and were also in the same year at school. His older sister and two of his cousins also worked at the chemist; it was a real family affair and we all got on so well. He and I would go to the local 'Fish and Chips' shop next door almost every afternoon and order a few potato scallops each, the workers began to know us well that they would always give us an extra scallop or two and some hot chips. On special days, we'd treat ourselves to a hamburger with the lot. Joe was a year older than me and already had his driver's license, so his job was to deliver medication all around Queanbeyan.

The very next chance I got, I was back on my BMX, riding out to Fyshwick. It was usually on weekends as I was now working Monday to Friday at the Chemist after school. I probably told my parents I was going for a bike ride or going to visit friends somewhere. It was usually mid-afternoon and they couldn't get in contact to see where I was, this was before I had a mobile phone. I would ride that bike as hard and as fast as I could, on the bike path, alongside Canberra Avenue, looking out for the crazy magpies that would swoop down and have a go at my head. They were only protecting their territory and trying to protect their young chicks in Spring. Luckily, I had my trusted 'Stack Hat' on to protect me. I was probably more scared of these birds than what I was about to walk into.

I finally reached the sex shop, chained my bike and stack hat to a fence around the corner, and sprinted to the shop, stealthily so no one saw me enter. Once inside, I would wait near the door for someone to exit and I would sneak in. Sometimes the door wasn't actually closed properly and just sitting there, ajar, so I could easily just walk in. Inside the cruise lounge, I kept my head down so no one could see, or recognize, my face. My heart was again pumping at a crazy pace, ready to bust out of my chest. The adrenalin inside of me was going wild. I walked around, checking out my surroundings and the guys who were inside. Subconsciously, I was looking for the Man, but he was never there. I wouldn't talk to anyone and kept to myself, standing again in the same dark corner as I did the previous time I was there. Some of the guys would see me and walk past; I guess not everyone was attracted to young, skinny, teenage boys. Like the first time, a guy approached me and tried to get something started. I brushed him off more than once and he finally walked away. It was at this moment I discovered that I had some power in this place. I could dictate the terms for who and what I wanted, when I wanted it and how I wanted it. I was no longer going to be thrown around the room, slapped, beaten, choked or raped. Looking back, I realize that at fifteen, I was actually still being raped by these older guys, in that, I was not consenting with all of me. They never asked my age, and I never told them. I walked through the lounge, seeing who was around and what action was going on. I could hear two guys having sex in one of the little private rooms. These rooms normally consisted of a mattress, a container full of condoms and packets of lube, a box of tissue paper and a little trash can. I really didn't know what I was doing with so much conflict within me and if I still wanted to be there, I just knew I had to be there, that I needed this.

Another guy came over to me, on the younger side, average build and look. He felt for my penis outside of my pants. I kept my head down and looked to the side, never making eye contact with him. He put his hand down my pants and started to jerk me off. I was scared, angry, hated this guy but didn't want him to stop either. He walked me into one of the private rooms, pulled his pants down, started playing with himself. Getting hard, he put my hand onto his penis and directed me to jerk him off. He tried to pull my head down so I would suck him. I pushed his hand off and didn't move. He then got down onto his knees and started giving me oral sex. I felt such deep pain and agony as he was doing it, burying my face into my arms, not only to hide my face but also to hide the pain I was in. He wasn't physically hurting me at all; I was emotionally and mentally detesting where I was, what was happening and what I was doing. I hated this guy but I was already trapped and addicted to it. Sexually, it was all I knew and all I wanted.

He saw me with my head in my arms and asked *"are you ok?"* I just grabbed his head and made him continue giving more oral. I was close to orgasm and again I grabbed his head and thrusted hard and deep into his throat. I came. As soon as I was done, I lost my mind and needed to get out of there as fast as possible. I was shaking, pulled up my pants, heart beating like crazy and I still couldn't look at him or talk to him. I wanted absolutely nothing to do with him ever again. Something about it all felt like when the Man would rape me. I felt myself physically leave my body, I had checked out and wasn't there, I was a shell of my former self. He was still on his knees, jerking himself off at the time. He stood and again tried to make me give him oral sex. I was in such an angry state, hating myself, that I shoved him as hard as I could. He tripped back and fell onto the mattress. He stood up, and then instinctively, I punched him in the face, not that my little fifteen-year-old punch did any damage. I got out of there as quickly as I could. Once outside, I made sure no one was watching as I desperately ran to my bike, unchained it and rode as fast as my little legs could go for the twenty-five-minute ride home. I looked back from time to time to ensure no one was following me. The truth is despite feeling pain and anguish, disgust and hatred, I knew that I would be back there again.

Daphne, one of the girls from the Chemist, was having her twenty-first birthday. She lived down the road from us. I think she was the first girl

I ever had a real crush on; she was such a beautiful girl, with her blonde hair and blue eyes. All of the girls from work were there. I went with one of my best mates, Bernie. I got really drunk that night from Vodka Cruisers and Bacardi Breezers. These were the cool drinks back then. Best part of the night was having my photo taken with Daphne and her best friend, Grace, who was equally as beautiful. They were on either side of me, kissing me on my cheek. I loved that photo and had it framed and placed it proudly on my bedside table. Bernie and I left that party later that night and walked to his house. On the way there, I threw up, the first time I threw up from alcohol. Not the best feeling.

We were close to graduating Year Ten. School was fine, I didn't care much for it, although I was still a decent student. My friends and I got into the usual mischief; we would skip class now and then. One time in Food Science class, Bernie and I threw eggs out of the window onto students playing down below. When we were caught, we said we were throwing the eggs to each other to use but they accidentally fell out the window. We thought that was a great excuse and that we'd get away with it, but we ended up in afternoon detention. I received detention a few times for acting up in class, cheating on a test or doing something ridiculous and stupid with friends. Most of them had girlfriends and, even though I was developing a love for women, I still didn't care to date or be romantic with them. Anything sexual for me was still with guys. Sports and athletics were an escape for me and I was starting to go to the gym more. The gym was in Queanbeyan and called Odd Bods, and that was starting to become a place where I would spend a lot of my time. I would either ride my bike there or I would go with Matt, my cousin. It was a good way for me to release my frustration, confusion and anger. I enjoyed lifting weights as well as the odd spin and body pump class. I would work out with Matt and his friends. Being two years older than me, he already had his driver's license and the fact that he lived next door was always convenient. Our Year Ten graduation party (Formal) was upon us. I bought a dark green microfiber suit and asked Elizabeth, a friend of mine, to go with me. Elizabeth went to school at St Clare's across the road and her mum worked at the Chemist with me, so we knew each other quite well. I don't remember much about that night, or not sure how much time I actually spent with her. I definitely didn't kiss her. I don't remember where it was, or what we did. I don't even remember if we got drunk or went to a party afterwards.

Soon summer holiday was upon us, which was great as I could be by myself for a large part of it. I got straight back on my bike and rode out to Fyshwick and this time my visit was different. I went into the sex shop and found my way inside the cruise lounge. My mixed and complex feelings for this place hadn't changed, I hated it yet still needed it all at the same time. I was inside walking around and again found myself standing in my usual corner, out of the way and hiding my face. A guy came up to me, he was aggressive, very forceful, he led me into a private room. He pulled my pants down and tried to take my top off but I wouldn't let him. My heart was again beating at a crazy pace. He got naked and threw me around the room. I felt like a rag doll, being put in all these positions. He was aggressively directing me here and there, and I followed. He tried to kiss me; I turned my face away. He tried again and this time I pushed him off. He gave me oral sex; again, I buried my face, hiding myself away in disgust and self-hatred. I felt like a piece of shit, like I didn't deserve any pleasure; I didn't deserve anything and I should be dead. He stood up over me and shoved his groin in my face. That smell of the Man came flooding back to me in an instant, my head jolted back and I felt sick. He shoved his penis in my mouth and like the Man, he grabbed my head and held it there while he thrusted back and forth with pride and aggression. I let myself go and felt like I was back with the Man. I had again lost my power, falling back into old ways and gave myself over to him. I didn't try to get out of there, resist, nor push him off. Just like all the times before, I was addicted to feeling these feelings from being so conditioned into needing to experience them and the sensations they brought up in me. I felt a distorted kind of comfort in it all. He turned me over, I tried turning back around. I knew what was going to happen but he was bigger and stronger than me and before I knew it, I was back over on my stomach and he shoved his finger in my arse. I jumped, I guess that was his way of lubing me up before ramming his dick in me. I don't even know if he was wearing a condom.

The pain was excruciating, it was the first time I'd had sex since the last time I was with the Man, which was about four years before. I was on my hands and knees, looking straight ahead, lifeless. I didn't want to be there, I didn't want this guy to touch me, but again I didn't want him to stop either. I wanted him to keep doing everything he was doing to me. I was imagining the Man, not this guy. As he was fucking me, the rage was building, I was incessantly thinking of the Man; *Why did he abandon me?... Where the fuck is he?!... Fuck him.* The aggressive sex this stranger was consuming through using me was all too familiar and yet, I wanted more of it. I hated him, I hated myself and just like when I was a kid, I felt myself leave my body. I didn't want to be there. I was watching it all from above as this guy fucked me. The torture was real, physically and mentally. The guy was moaning and asking me; *"...How is it?... Do you want more?"* Listening to him say these words brought me back from wherever I had disappeared to. I came back into my body with the shame erupting within, bringing with it the growing reality of how unworthy I was, how I did not deserve happiness and love. My rage towards the man grew in every moment, *Why the fuck am I here with this guy and not with the Man?* At the same time, I desperately wanted him to fuck me more. I hated this feeling, I couldn't look at this guy, I couldn't touch him, I definitely did not feel any affection or love from him. It was the most disgusting thing in the world and I felt like a piece of shit, however I was addicted and needed it badly. I was hard, I was enjoying it and I came.

91

Once that had happened, I immediately needed to get him off of me so I could get the fuck out of there. I tried to push him off, I tried to get up, but he pushed me back down and held me there, he kept fucking me saying he was close. Again, I tried to get up but he pushed me down. He came. He then let go, got himself off me, and sat by my side. I got up in a fit of rage, pulled my pants up, turned to him as he sat there, ever so proud and satisfied with himself, and I punched him as hard as I could two to three times. I kicked him. He fell back from the blows. Again, I'm not sure if I hurt him or if he was in shock by the attack. I was a young, skinny kid of average height, so I couldn't do too much damage. I got out of there as quickly as I could and ran to my bike. I was shaking and felt like I was going to faint. I composed myself and made sure no one had come out of the sex shop to look for me. No one did. Maybe I did hurt this guy, I was hoping that I did. Maybe he was in shock, or maybe he felt guilty for holding me down and fucking me when I'd had enough and was trying to get up. I didn't know and I didn't want to know. I jumped on my bike and peddled like the wind.

For the bike ride home, that evening and for the next few weeks after the incident, I felt exhilarated, the adrenalin was still pumping through my veins and I felt alive for the first time in a very long while. I thought about the guy I had hit and also about the Man. It wasn't this guy I was hitting, subconsciously it was the Man. I thought about him and how much I hated him, not for what he did to me but more for abandoning me, leaving me lost, hopeless and without anyone.

We were on summer holidays, it was a few days before Christmas, I was sitting at home with Janice, she had just graduated from high school. It was mid-morning. Peter may have been out with friends somewhere or with Karl at our grandmother's house. I remember it was only Janice and I at home. She was on the phone with one of her friends when I collapsed onto the floor in the most unbearable pain. It was a totally different kind of pain to being raped, but the same level of agony. I was holding my testicles, something was wrong. *"Get off the phone and call dad, something is wrong with me."* She told me to stop being an idiot; that I'd probably accidentally hit them or just knocked them against something. The pain was getting worse, I started crying and yelled out to her again. I remember swearing, *"get off the fucking phone and call dad."* She did as I asked and Dad came home as soon as he could and took me to the clinic down the road. I was taken in to see the doctor right away, he checked me out, I was given pain killers and sent straight to Woden Hospital in Canberra as the situation was urgent; he called ahead and let them know that I was on my way.

The pain killers were kicking in and the doctor at the hospital took me straight in for X-Rays and an ultrasound. We discovered that my testicles had twisted. The doctor said it is the worst pain a man could ever endure, other than a heart attack. It felt like I was being kicked in the testicles one hundred times over. The doctor said it could be caused through vigorous activity, a minor injury, a blow to the testicles or sometimes during sleep. Mine was brought on by vigorous activity or a blow to the area. I remember feeling hints of pain for a few weeks before, but had little knowledge as to how it actually occurred and what was going on. I needed surgery immediately because if the testicles were to lose too much blood supply they could die, rendering me infertile. I was given more pain killers, given a space to rest in, and then needed to wait for a few hours for the surgeon and the operating theatre to become available. The last thing I remember before going under anesthesia was a nurse wheeling a tray into the theatre; the tray had knives and scissors on it, my last thought was they were going to chop everything off, leaving me with nothing.

I woke a few hours later, in an enormous amount of pain, but with testicles and penis still attached. I was told that one testicle had died. I

93

had a scrotum full of clips and pins, but was still left with the chance to have kids of my own. I was in the hospital for two or three nights and discharged on Christmas Eve. I needed to use a walking stick and I moved about like I'd just shat my pants. I walked as slowly as I could, feet wide apart, waddling from side to side. We had the extended family over to our house on Christmas Day and I received a present from my 'Secret Santa' that was wrapped with a bow that had two Christmas tree ball-ornaments hanging from it. Everyone thought it was funny and had a good laugh at my expense. I must admit it was pretty funny and I had a good laugh too, although the pain was excruciating.

It was the beginning of February and I started Year Eleven at school, still walking slowly from my operation. I had just turned sixteen and was able to get my driver's license. I was a year younger than most of the boys in my grade and most of my friends were already on their L-Plates. L-plates were given to learner drivers, which meant one could only drive with a fully licensed passenger. P-Plates come one year later, and they permit solo driving at a maximum speed of eighty kilometers per hour. After a year on P-plates, you move onto your full license. Bernie and I went to the motor registry, took the test together and the Gods were looking down on us that day as we both passed. I could finally drive, with a licensed driver; it was better than nothing.

Not long after, I bought my first car with the money I had saved from working at the Chemist and from delivering the paper. The car was a white 1982 Toyota Corolla. I loved that car. It was the first thing I owned for myself. I would wash and vacuum the inside of it every weekend. Mum and dad took me out for my first few lessons. Mum was tough; she had a bit of a temper, so I preferred to go with dad. My Uncle Joe took me driving a lot too; we would drive together around the neighborhood and in car parks once or twice per week. He taught me the basics on how to take care of my car; showing me how to change the tires, brake pads, headlights and rear brake lights when the light bulbs blew, replace the oil, check the water and coolant. My days of peddling my BMX bike were finally over.

The last two years of high school passed by uneventfully. I was skipping a few classes per week with my two best friends Conan and Shane. We would frequent the local 'take-away' down the road and order hot chips, sit in the park and eat them. On the days we attended classes, we would amuse ourselves pulling typical teenage pranks. I remember a time in either Religion or Social Science class when Bernie purposely missed an exam. The following day he was made to take the exam in an empty room next door. I sat near the exit of our classroom, so as Bernie walked out to take the test, he slipped it into my hands. I answered all of the questions for him. When class was over, Bernie walked back into class, picked up the finished product and handed it in to the teacher. He passed with flying colors.

Bernie, Conan, and Gianni (my oldest friend who I have known since kindergarten) and I would all hang out during the summer months. We would tell our parents that we were going to sleep at each other's houses and end up wherever we did. Some nights we would just wander the streets until sunrise. On quite a few nights, we would steal our parents' cars and go 'joy riding' around town and sometimes into Canberra. On garbage night in Canberra, everyone had their bins out front for collection the next morning. The four of us would drive past the bins, grab onto them and drive off, eventually letting them go so they would roll down the street, causing chaos and spraying garbage everywhere as they fell. Looking back now I realize that it was such a stupid thing to do, but back then, we didn't think about the effects and mess we were creating.

One night we were out driving in both Conan and Bernie's cars, and we stopped at Bernie's house at four in the morning to put the keys back so that his parents wouldn't realize that we took the car out the night before. Conan was waiting in his car and I followed Bernie into his house. We had just walked into the kitchen when his mum called out, asking if it was him. Frozen, Bernie replied to his mum, saying that he had forgotten his toiletries and that he had come back for his toothbrush. He was clearly caught and I ran out of there as quickly as I could, back to Conan in the waiting car and left that place in a real hurry. Other mischief we created included seeking revenge on people who had mistreated us. I had friends that would frequently DJ at a local disco downtown, and sometimes the organizers wouldn't pay them for their work. On one of those nights, we drove down to the club under the cover of darkness, broke in, stole their alcohol, DJ equipment, speakers, and whatever else we could fit into the car. We also took whatever money we could find.

I have memories of less mischievous times as well. A particularly significant memory of those days was meeting a girl at the bus interchange one afternoon. She went to a Queanbeyan school and her name was Audrey. Her friend came up to me and told me that Audrey liked me and later introduced us. At this stage I was starting to show a little more interest in girls who weren't from the Chemist; I was feeling more comfortable around them, and I was intrigued. Audrey was a cute girl with sandy blonde hair and blue eyes. A week or so after we met, I got together with her. She lived on the other side of Canberra Avenue near the Queanbeyan Racecourse. We were walking through the tunnel that runs under Canberra Avenue and she grabbed my hand, which felt awkward and unnatural to me to begin with, as I still hated affection and being touched by someone. She kissed me; I was nervous and thought to myself; *What the fuck just happened?* I didn't know what to do or even how to do it, but I grabbed her and kissed her back. I don't quite remember how I felt about it all but I do remember getting an erection; so, I guess it was good and I liked it. I don't think I saw her again after that as she reconnected with her ex-boyfriend. I'm guessing

I must have been a terrible kisser to send her running straight right back to her ex!

Once or twice per year through Years Eleven and Twelve we would have a school disco with the girls across the road at St. Clare's. I never really went to any of them as I was involved in other things like riding my bike to Fyshwick and doing what I was doing out there. A stupid school disco with girls was the last thing on my mind. My good friends would go to underage parties at various clubs around Canberra and Queanbeyan, but I wasn't interested in going to any of those places either. Conan recently told me that I would always use the excuse that my mother wouldn't let me, which couldn't have been further from the truth. Mum would always let me and my siblings go out most times when we asked; within reason of course. Truth is, I never had any interest in hanging out with girls or in meeting girls that I didn't know, care for or had an interest in being with.

I finally decided to go to a school disco. I danced with one of the girls from St Clare's for most of the night. I don't remember her name, but she was tall, super cute and had brown hair. We made out for most of the night and I was starting to get the hang of this 'girl kissing thing'; not sure if I was any good at it, but practice makes perfect they say. I didn't make out with many other girls for the rest of high school.

School was flying by and I didn't have any idea what I wanted to do after I graduated. We were allowed to do work experience twice per year. Work experience involved going to a work environment without pay, for a week, in a career that you could be interested in pursuing once you finished school. I enjoyed cooking and hospitality so I went to a hotel and worked for a week doing everything from administration, helping out in the kitchen and bar, restaurant and dining, to changing the sheets and cleaning rooms. The second place I went was the Canberra Airport. I loved planes and wanted to be a pilot. I could easily

97

sit at the airport all day watching planes take off and land. Still to this day I find it therapeutic and relaxing. I fell in love with planes from traveling to Europe a few times as a kid. My dad also loves airplanes; he collects model planes and must have close to fifty. They were set up in the rumpus room where I used to play as a youngster. Sometimes I would sit and stare at them or even play with them a little, even though none of us were allowed to. I would imagine that I was actually in the plane going to faraway lands; disappearing and never coming back home. I always felt the same way when I saw a plane flying overhead in the sky. I just wanted to be on it and I didn't much care for its destination. *Just get me out of here,* I thought to myself.

At the airport, I worked with mechanics in a little hanger by the main terminal, fixing and washing small, private and charter planes. I went flying a few times per day in them, circling Canberra from above. I was given control of the planes and flew them for a few minutes. I helped with take-off and landing and on one occasion; the pilot took the plane up pretty high and stalled it purposely so we could nose dive for a few seconds. It was an amazing rush; so fucking scary and exciting at the same time. *I could do this, I could be a pilot,* I told myself. But when I learned the number of hours required and the money needed to become a pilot, my dream was quickly dashed. I had very poor eyesight anyway; I wore glasses as early as Year Six. I was far-sighted and my eyes have been slowly deteriorating ever since. If school knew what I was doing, they would never have signed off on it or allowed me to go flying for work experience.

Life at home was cruising along. I would still spend most of my free time alone watching TV or movies. Dad bought a billiard table, we had a ping pong table as well, and I was going to the gym as often as I could. Having moved on from playing with my cars, I was now playing a lot of billiards alone. I was also putting one side of the ping pong table up and playing against myself. Sometimes I played with Peter or

Janice. It was something I found calming, but sometimes very frustrating.

Karl was growing up fast and would have been in primary school and Peter was a sports star playing state rugby union and league, so mum and dad were busy with them most weeknights and weekends. Janice was studying corporate travel, still working at the Chemist and dating boys, so she was busy living her best life. I got my P-plates and finally had my freedom; I was able to jump in a car and escape, which only meant trouble for me. I was able to go to Fyshwick freely. I would drive my car to school sometimes (instead of taking the bus) then drive to the Chemist for work. I was going to Fyshwick sporadically, sometimes once or twice per week, and other times once per month or every few months. It was always on my mind though, but I was either too busy or just trying to stay away. When I did go, everything was planned. I always parked my car around the corner, in an alleyway or down the road; never in front or close to the place, just like when I rode my bike. I would always run and sneak in, trying to make sure no one driving or walking past would see me. Sometimes I would just go to the sex shops, jump in a booth, watch porn, get off or get sucked off in the process; and other times I would go into the cruise lounges and do my thing. It was always the same inside the cruise lounge. I would keep to myself; head down, never looked anyone in the eyes and I'd always turn away. Sometimes there were two people in there, other times there were twenty. I would never engage with these guys; I would only say the bare minimum to get by. I wanted absolutely nothing to do with them. I was in there to get what I needed, then I was out straight away.

Whenever I was with a guy, I always felt and did the same series of predictable things; bury my head into my arms, be disgusted, then rage within myself, get into self-sabotage mode and tell myself repeatedly;

"I deserve to be raped... I deserve all this pain and hurt... I am a piece of shit, worthy of nothing... This is who I am and this is where I belong mentally, physically and emotionally."

My behavior was now becoming habitual. I would let these guys have their way with me and as soon as they were done, I would become violent by punching and kicking them, sometimes stealing their wallets, ripping off the chains from around their neck. At other times I would just get up and run out. The times where I would steal their wallets or jewelry, I would just take their cash and throw the rest of their stuff away. I didn't want anything but the cash. Being a skinny kid, a lot of the times I would be overpowered by them; I would be hit and beaten, and I think subconsciously I must have wanted this to happen. I wanted to feel the same feeling as I did with the Man. I was trying to recreate *that* pain, I wanted these guys to hurt me, to hit me back and to rape me. On more than one occasion, when I became violent with them, they would then easily overpower me, push me back down, rape and fuck me even harder than the time before, and I found that I got off on it. I would let them do it, not that I really had a choice in the matter at that point. Once done, they would clean themselves up and leave the room. I would just lay there for what seemed like an eternity, beaten and bruised, unable to move and completely lost inside my own head. This destructive cycle went on for years, well into my twenties, and I didn't know how to stop it. To be truthful, I don't know if I wanted to.

Chapter 11

I was still working at the Chemist. Joe had left and I was doing all the same chores, except now I was also driving delivering medication all around Queanbeyan. I felt like a total *'Jekyll and Hyde'*; one day cruising lounges, having underage sex and beating up men, and the very next day I was driving around town offering support and delivering medication to the sick and elderly. For the most part, they were very sweet and lovely people and I came to know a lot of them quite well. I would sit and listen as they shared their life stories. There was an elderly woman who was once a champion ballroom dancer and, every time I delivered her medicine, she would teach me a dance step or two. I never stole from any of these people and; never harmed them in any way. I didn't have that in me. They had nothing to do with *that* other life. Sometimes it was a fun and interesting job but I was slowly getting tired of it and was ready to move on. I stayed working there until the end of high school.

Janice and I befriended a lady to whom I would deliver medication regularly. Janice knew her as she would visit the chemist on occasion. Janice made the mistake of sharing her mobile number with the lady and visiting her once or twice; the woman didn't have any family or friends so she would call Janice a lot. When I delivered medication to her, she would beg me not to leave; she longed for the company. We were both put in a hard situation as the lady was very sweet but also very needy. One time she called Janice telling her that she was going to slit her wrists and kill herself. Janice called 000 and the police and ambulance went to check on her. They were too late to stop her, she had slit her wrists before they arrived; but luckily, she survived. We went with mum to see her in hospital and she gave us her house keys, asking us to pick up some essentials. We went to her house and found what appeared to be a murder scene. Blood was everywhere; on the walls and floor, in her bedroom, in her bed; and in the bathroom the tub was overflowing with dark red-colored water. She had filled the bath, slit her wrists in her bed, and made her way into the bath to die. Mum came with us to make sure we were fine; Janice cried and was deeply affected by what she saw. Mum being a tough woman was ok with what she saw. I, on the other hand, was totally fine; I walked through the house and felt nothing, I was emotionally dead. It didn't have an impact on me at all. We returned to the hospital to give her the things she'd wanted, then walked out of her room. We never saw nor heard from her again.

High school was coming to an end. I passed without any real issue and I topped accredited English for the year. I enjoyed writing essays and assignments, but never imagined that I could write or even be a writer until much later in life. We had our end of school formal, most of the boys had girlfriends, but I still didn't have much interaction with them, except for making out with a girl or two. I knew a lot of girls; I was friendly with them but never pursued a relationship with any of them. I invited Katie, a Queanbeyan girl and family friend, to the Formal. We were in the same year at school. Just like my Year Ten Formal, I didn't spend much time with her. Instead, I got very drunk and spent the night making out with one of my friend's dates. His date was a Queanbeyan girl as well, and I had actually met her when I delivered medication to her grandmother months earlier. It was a surprise to see her at the Formal, she was a sweet girl and we had fun.

After graduating, I started to get more social with friends; going out to bars and nightclubs and acting like a *normal* seventeen-year-old boy would. My friend made me a fake ID card, so I used that until I legally became an adult and turned eighteen. I was playing sport and becoming a lot more active at the gym, a place where I was able to just be myself.

I would take whatever I was feeling out on the weights, the boxing bag or in a fitness class. One of my friends from school wanted to take boxing lessons and he asked me to go with him as he knew of my love for fitness. We went out to the Police and Community Youth Club (PCYC) in Erindale, a suburb of Canberra.

PCYC was a not-for-profit organization that delivered a broad range of youth and community programs and activities in partnership with the police youth and crime prevention command. My friend only lasted about two weeks and took off to join the army, but I stayed on. I felt a sense of community and family there, training with these guys, learning about discipline and how to box. There were probably about ten boys in the group and we would train for three hours every Monday, Wednesday and Friday. I had never felt more fit in my life; the discipline, fitness and strength needed to keep up was unlike anything I had ever experienced. I found that getting into a ring and sparring for three minutes was so much harder than I had expected. I absolutely take my hat off to professional boxers, they are beyond human, they are machines, unbelievable athletes. I'm left-handed so I was a southpaw, leading with my right hand. I was training and sparring with amateur boxers. Some were training for the Olympics and Commonwealth Games, and others were simply there to learn. They were amazing athletes and would beat me up around the ring on more than one occasion as we sparred. I loved being in the ring with them, learning from them, getting hit by them. I walked out of that ring many times with a black eye, bloodied nose and fully winded from body shots. I stayed on and trained at PCYC for a little over a year until I got a stress fracture on the bottom of my foot from dancing around the ring on the balls of my feet. I was never going to be a champion, but boxing gave me the skills and confidence that I needed to be able to protect myself in a fight.

I was becoming more confident and starting to meet a lot of girls out; it was easier to talk to them, and I would try to make out with whomever I could. I was making up for lost time. Conan got a job laying cables in Sydney for cable television, and Shane and I would drive up to Sydney as often as we could to spend the weekend with him. We were going out, getting ridiculously drunk, chasing every girl that moved, getting rejected time and again. Sometimes we got lucky. We were young and free.

Back in Canberra and on a night out with friends, I met a girl at the Private Bin, Canberra's biggest nightclub at the time, and was making out with her for most of the night. She was a few years older than me and told me she had a boyfriend. I didn't care at all; I was into her. As the night wore on, I got more drunk and invited her back to my house. My parents had gone away for the weekend with Peter and Karl, and Janice had since moved out. I had the place to myself. She didn't come over that night as she couldn't leave her girlfriends, she gave me her number and told me she would come the following day.

The following day rolled around and I called her, gave her my address, and she came over. It was late afternoon when she arrived. She said she had plans with her boyfriend that evening. I was nervous; I'd only ever kissed a girl but was ready to have sex with one. I was hoping that's why she came over. We went into my parents' bedroom, the only room with a double bed. The first thing I did was fold the bed cover down, so as not to get it dirty. My mum would have been proud of me for trying to keep it clean; then she would have beaten the shit out of me for doing it on her bed. The girl got naked first and I couldn't take my eyes off her body. It was unlike anything I had ever seen. I found the female body to be so beautiful. I touched her everywhere, played with her breasts, kissed them. I was ready to explode. I put my fingers inside of her; it felt weird but so beautiful and natural. She was warm and wet. She then grabbed my hand and put my fingers in my mouth so I could taste her. I'm not sure if she knew at that time that I'd never had sex with a girl before nor done anything like this. She got me naked, complimented me on my body, which gave me a little more confidence, and went down on me. I caught myself putting my head into my arms, just the same way I did when I was with all the guys. I started thinking about the Man. I had to get him out of my head so I opened my eyes and looked at the girl. I pulled her close to me; we kissed and I went down on her. It got my mind off of everything else and I was back to enjoying the experience with her. I could have stayed down there for days, not that I really knew what I was doing or looking for. I loved her taste; loved the female body and it was starting to feel natural to be with a woman.

She pushed me off and called me up to her face so we could kiss some more. Then she stood up, went into her bag, pulled out a condom, unwrapped it and put it on me. I was hard and ready to experience this new feeling and new experience. She got back onto the bed and positioned me on top of her. Maybe she knew this was my first time by the way I was acting. I was trying to be super cool, like I knew what I was doing, like I'd done this a thousand times before. I'm sure she knew better. She grabbed hold of my penis and put it inside of her and suddenly I was having sex with a girl. This was my first time. It felt foreign and weird but it also felt amazing. Obviously, it was unlike anything I'd ever felt before. I liked it… and it was literally over in ten seconds! I was in and then I was out and in and out a few more times before I lost control of myself. I was so embarrassed and apologized many times for being so quick. She was sweet, said it was fine and asked me if it was my first time. I told her *"no"* and she asked again. I admitted it was and asked how she knew; she said she could tell by the way my body was shaking and from my inexperience. She got dressed, told me never to call her again; that it was never going to happen again because she had a boyfriend. I was more than happy with that situation and she left. I cleaned my parents' bed; it was over so fast that I didn't have a chance to make a mess on it anyway.

Afterward, I didn't know how to feel. It was exciting and felt amazing but it also felt weird and empty at the same time. It didn't fulfill me like sex with a male did. I knew I wanted to have more sex with women and wanted to be with women, but I didn't feel alive. I didn't feel the energy that I felt with guys. Maybe it was the type of sex I was having with men; rough, dirty and hard, it was all that I was used to. I needed to be kinder to myself; it was my first time with a woman; I was inexperienced and had no idea of what I was doing.

As the day went on, I felt those all too familiar waves of shame, anger and self-sabotage come over me. I was so severely in my head;

I don't deserve to be with this girl or any other girl... I don't deserve to feel love, to feel any joy or happiness from having sex with a female for the first time... I deserve to be alone, to have bad things happen to me, to be in a dark place and to be nothing... I am nothing!

I started drinking a few beers and followed that up with one of my dad's bottles of scotch. He had so many bottles he wouldn't notice if one was missing. A huge rush of depression engulfed me and this was happening more and more. I was done, broken and lost and in a very bad place. I wanted it all to be over. I didn't know what to do with these feelings so I drove myself to Fyshwick; the only place I knew where I fit in best. I was massively over the legal and safe drink/driving limit, but as always, I didn't care. It was a weird feeling; I just had sex with a girl, and I should have been over the moon with happiness, jumping for joy and calling all of my friends to brag. But for the past nine years (from eight through to seventeen years old) all I'd done was have abusive, violent and dirty sex with men.

I had continuously let men rape me and abuse me. It was there where I felt comfortable, and it was all that I wanted. I went into the cruise lounge feeling completely defeated. I could have been anyone's, I didn't care. I wanted these guys to fuck me hard, to rape me, to beat me up, to give me AIDS and just let me die. I didn't want my revenge this time, I didn't want to beat anyone up, I just wanted to feel that same series of feelings that I always felt. I wanted to be hurt physically, mentally and to feel like the worthless piece of shit that I was; like trash and feel that my life didn't matter. I don't even remember who the guy was, what he looked like or how old he was. I do remember that he was married. I will never forget that he had a wedding ring on his finger. I asked if his wife knew that he was there and he told me to shut my mouth and had his way with me. I was a rag doll being tossed from side to side, I didn't care anymore. He could have done whatever the fuck he wanted with me and he did. It seemed to have gone on forever and I just lay there, moving into whatever position he wanted me, taking it all. I wasn't enjoying it, I was hating it, I wasn't hard, yet I needed it. I needed it to fuel some kind of life in me, even though it was killing whatever life I had left in me.

He came, he got up and left. I didn't say a word to him and he didn't say a word either. We both knew what we were there for and it was done. After he left, I didn't move until an older guy came into the room. I let him suck me off until I came, I couldn't have felt any lower or any more like this was all I deserved in life. I pushed him off, I got dressed and walked out of there, head down, so slow and completely defeated. This time, I didn't even care who saw me and what they thought of me. It felt like I had sobered right up but I'm sure I was still way too drunk to be driving home. I hated myself so much and just wanted to die, I wanted to disappear and never come back. All of these very dark feelings were starting to become much more of a common feature for me. I finally made it home, continued to drink until I passed out on the couch with the television blasting. I probably passed out around eight or nine o'clock at night, it wasn't late, and I remember waking up in the early hours of the morning and put myself to bed.

Chapter 12

I continued to work at the Chemist over the summer months whilst I was deciding on what I wanted to study or whether I should find a full-time job. That was when Gabriela started working at the Chemist. She was the same age as me, born three months later in May. She was a beautiful girl, of Australian and Chinese descent. She was unlike anyone I had ever met; we had an instant connection and started talking and flirting straightaway. I asked her out after a few weeks and, for our first date, we hung out at her uncle's house who was away on summer holidays. It was a lavish home with a pool in the backyard. We sat by the pool and got to know each other better. It wasn't the fanciest or most romantic first date, but it was easy and it was perfect, plus we were still only seventeen. We kissed and I was in my first relationship. I had my first ever girlfriend. I wasn't quite sure how I felt about the whole situation or what to do a lot of the time, but I knew that I liked her and thought; *It could be fun, how hard could it really be?... All of my friends have girlfriends and are having fun, so why not me?* It felt like the normal thing to do and I was hoping it would make me forget about all the other things I was doing. I was starting to go down a slippery slope with everything I was getting myself into, and this was a much-needed distraction.

Before I went up to Gabriela's house to meet her family, she warned me a little about them; told me what I needed to know, like most partners do. She lived on the other side of Queanbeyan, up near Karabar Shopping Center. She had an older brother; he was the same age as Janice and her younger sister was the same age as Peter. She told me that her father used to be a senior member of a Motorcycle

Gang and there would likely be a few motorbikes and old members hanging out in the garage with him. True to her word, we turned up the first time and there were a few motorbikes and old gang members hanging out front with her father. Needless to say, I was a little nervous, though I had no reason to be. They were the most welcoming and friendly guys, scary looking though, and her father was a man of few words. *"If you ever hurt Gabriela, you will never be seen again"* one of her father's friends said, and I believed him! They also told me, *"If* you *ever want to get rid of someone, you should tell us and this person will disappear forever, never to be found again."* That was good to know - if only I had met them a few years earlier! I could have definitely taken them up on their offer a few times since.

I loved Gabriela's mum; we got along great, she was loving and welcoming. A beautiful but tough woman who had been through her own shit, she had a big heart that emanated love and loyalty for her family. She was also a great cook who would always serve amazing meals. The two dishes I loved the most were an Abalone dish and a Chinese Pork dish with noodles and bok-choy. Abalone are not very well known; they are a type of single-shelled herbivorous marine mollusk. Their body is large and fleshy and attaches itself to reefs or rocks using suction. Their shells are rough, flat and ear shaped. Gabriela's mum was funny; she would tell everyone what's what, and was just a very real woman.

One of the very first conversations I ever had with her was when she sat Gabriela and I down and told us that she knew that we were going to have sex and would prefer us to do it in the safety of her house, in Gabriela's room instead of the back seat of a car in a dark alley somewhere or in a dirty hotel. She told us to be safe and to respect each other. That's the kind of conversation I would like to have with my children one day, if I ever have any. Gabriela's brother was also a man of few words, exactly like his dad, whereas her younger sister was friendly and easy to get along with. They were a loving, tough, very loyal family; a family of fighters who wouldn't take shit from anyone and would definitely let you know if they didn't like you. I will always have a lot of love and respect for them.

My eighteenth birthday had arrived and I had a joint party with a friend of mine from school. It was his eighteenth birthday as well and he was also called Nathan. We were now legally allowed to drink and to go out, even though we had been doing it for years already. We hired a party bus that drove us around Canberra, going through the main hotspots in town, Manuka, Kingston and we ended the night in Civic. There were about twenty boys from school with us. I don't remember too much of the night, except for the fact that I got very drunk, probably threw up, and that Gabriela came to meet us once we got off the bus.

It was time for me to quit the Chemist. Mum got me a one-month contract working with her in the public service at the Attorney-General's Department in Barton, a suburb of Canberra. Barton is part of the Parliamentary Triangle, a ceremonial precinct containing some of Australia's most significant buildings. The apices of the Parliamentary Triangle are the Parliament House, (our equivalent of the White House in America), the Defence Headquarters at Russell and City Hill, representing the civilian part of Canberra. It was a good job to have whilst deciding on my future. I wasn't working directly with mum; I was working in the finance section with a group of about ten people. I paid bills, sent out invoices and did the mail every day. I would get the office car on a daily basis and collect checks and money from the Department of Finance and the Reserve Bank of Australia. It was basic and mundane work but it was easy and the money was great. Best of all, I liked the people I worked with; they were a mixed group of men and women in their twenties through to their forties who liked to drink and be social outside of work. Every second Friday at lunch we would go to the ACT Rugby Union Club (RUC Club), around the corner and have drinks, hopefully win the meat raffle and play on the poker machines before going back to work. The one-month contract turned into a three-month contract, which turned into another three-month contract, before I became a permanent employee of the Attorney-General's Department. My future seemed all sorted for me. Every couple of weeks we would go out to dinner and then to a bar and get wasted. They were a great bunch of people to drink and party with.

Things with Gabriela were great; I was feeling more comfortable with her every day. We would spend as much time together as possible and I was getting more comfortable having sex with a female. Our relationship and my work were welcome distractions from everything else going on in my life and I had no desire to go to Fyshwick or to act out. I didn't really know much about relationships, so I just followed her lead and went with it. We usually spent every Friday through Sunday night together and I would visit her at her house once or twice during the week. She rarely came over to my place; I felt much more comfortable and freer at her house, spending time with her family. I would sleep at her place most weekends. She never slept at mine and would not have been allowed to, as my parents were strict about things like that. Most Friday nights we would go to Woden Plaza or the Canberra Center, check out the shops, have dinner, maybe see a movie and go back to her place. Saturday nights we would go out and, since she liked to drink just as much as I did, we had a lot of fun when we went out. Sometimes I would have to hold her back or calm her down from getting into a fight or hitting someone who said the wrong thing or looked at her in the wrong way. Gabriela loved to fight and wasn't afraid of anyone; she definitely had a temper. We got into a few fights with people she disliked or with people that did wrong by her. This was all part of the excitement of being with her. She was loyal, loving toward her friends and family, and quite protective of their honor.

I started to play Rugby Union for the Queanbeyan Whites on the wing and I was pretty good. I had plenty of pace, scored lots of tries and was the goal kicker because of all of my years playing soccer; I knew how to kick well. It was my first year of playing rugby; I never played at school, even though we were a huge rugby playing school. In my first year at the club, I was awarded 'Most Promising Player'. I never expected it and I received a huge trophy that I was able to keep for a year, and a smaller trophy that was mine to keep forever. I was playing for the Colts' team, under eighteens and also played a few games in first grade by the end of the season. I really enjoyed my time playing for the Colts, most of the boys were friends from school, were great players and there were also a few other Queanbeyan boys that I already knew. We had a strong team and made the semifinals that season. Every Saturday night we went to the clubhouse and drank ourselves silly; there were always a few girls down there who would flirt with me and I would with them, too. If Gabriela was there, I definitely wouldn't be flirting and was always on my best behavior. The older boys at the club gave me the nickname, 'El Masri,' after Hazem El Masri, a Lebanese Australian who played on the wing for Canterbury-Bankstown Bulldogs in the National Rugby League competition. I was given that name because of my European ethnicity, just like El Masri. I may have been the only Southern European player, or 'wog' as I was called, at the club. Wog is a slang word, used as an ethnic or racial slur, directed at Italians, Greeks, Spanish, Maltese, or Lebanese; in other words, Southern European people, people with a darker complexion, dark hair and eyes. It was a derogatory term, but having been called a wog my whole childhood, I got used to it, most wogs did. I didn't take it personally or take offense to it, but I definitely know people who did.

My nickname growing up was 'Spit' for obvious reasons. I was called that throughout my whole school life and still to this day by my closest and oldest friends in Australia. There was a running joke for a while between my friends; I was called 'Spit' Peter was called 'Swallows' and Karl was called 'Gargles.' Luckily it didn't stick, for their sakes anyway.

Gabriela and I had a great relationship; it was easy with her, we had our ups and downs and occasional fights, but who didn't? Yes, she had a temper and, because I was so closed-off and had my own rage inside, we would sometimes go from "zero to one hundred" in a heartbeat. There were times we would both be on our lunch breaks; she would meet me and we would get into a public yelling match in the middle of the street. We couldn't help ourselves and sometimes didn't know when to stop. I absolutely adored her; we were best friends and every time we'd go shopping; I would try to buy her something. I bought her a watch, a ring, or whatever else I knew that she liked or wanted. I wanted to spoil her; to make her happy. But if she (or anyone) ever bought anything for me, I couldn't handle it and didn't know how to act or how to receive the kind gesture. I hated it; I never wanted anything from anyone.

Maybe deep down I knew that my over-effort at making this relationship work was a way to cover up what was going on in my private world. Our first year together was great, we travelled, spent time in Sydney together or down the coast. Sex was great and I was finally lasting longer than ten seconds! We had wonderful chemistry. It was always an adventure with Gabriela; I never knew what was going to come out of her mouth, the shit she would say sometimes. She made me laugh a lot. Like me, she was lost in her effort to find a career. She enrolled in beauty school to become a beautician. She would always practice on me, giving me facials, showing me how to cleanse, tone and moisturize. I owe my daily facial routine to her.

Gabriela and I talked a lot about growing up, work, children and being different from the thirty-year old's we knew. Thirty felt so old when we were eighteen. Gabriela wanted to be married with a family, a

114

house and all the trappings by the time she was thirty. I had a yearning for more in life; I knew I no longer wanted to stay in Queanbeyan, or even in Canberra. Too much history was there for me. I was starting to feel resentment towards the place, and slowly, I felt resentment toward Gabriela growing as well.

I was slowly starting to distance myself from her and keeping everything to myself; I was never a good communicator and obviously never shared anything from my past with her. Now suddenly, I was not sharing anything about my present. I could trust her with my life; she was the most loyal girl I knew, but I was slowly closing down, putting up a wall and gradually pushing her away. We were starting to fight more and, whilst I always tried to stay calm, once tempers flared, I would go at her just as hard as she would go at me.

I hadn't been to the cruise lounge or any of the sex shops since we'd met; I probably stayed away for about two years. I stayed loyal to her and I tried not to think about my past; until one time when she got a new job at a different chemist, this time in Fyshwick of all places. I dropped her off at work one Sunday afternoon; it was actually just around the corner from one of the sex shops I used to frequent. I hadn't thought about the place at all until I drove her to work and, suddenly, lots of emotions started to churn. My heart started to beat faster and I felt nausea rise within me. I had promised myself to not go there; to not even drive past the place. I dropped her off, kissed her goodbye, but I couldn't help myself. There were so many other ways I could have driven home, but I couldn't stop myself. Like the sound of drums beating in my head, growing louder as I drew closer, I was being pulled in. I drove past and thought, *yes, okay, I've done it, that was easy, I can go home now until it's time to pick her up!* Only I couldn't drive home.

I stopped around the corner and sat there for about ten minutes thinking of the many reasons why I should not go in; getting angry and frustrated with myself. I really liked Gabriela and the last thing I wanted to do was to hurt her, cheat and fuck around on her. It all came rushing back to me; I couldn't drop the feeling that this is what I deserved; that I was a failure. The sabotage grew ever wilder, as it inevitably always did. I was becoming angrier with myself, not for doing this to Gabriela, but for loathing the person I was inside.

I drove back past, made sure the place was quiet and parked my car around the corner, same as always, so no one could find it. I ran in, making sure I wasn't seen. I was on a mission; *in and out, head down, next victim, let's do this.* I felt like I was about to 'fall off the wagon', so to speak; like a drunk who hadn't had an alcoholic drink in two years and was now going to have a sneaky one. In all honesty, these feelings never left me, I was never free from them, being with a girl and in a relationship never made me shake them off. It never left, I still needed and wanted it, as much as I was acting like I didn't. Like I was normal and had overcome and forgotten about my past. Inside, I found my guy, kept my head down and stood close to him. He came over and we went into a booth. I never touched him, I didn't look at him or show any affection towards him. Nothing had changed, as always, my head fell into my arms. I felt overwhelming disgust at the act and also at myself. It had been a few years so the emotions were hitting me harder and with extreme clarity. Emotions like hatred, rage, self-pity and anger awakened like a sleeping giant within me. We did what we did, I dressed quickly, he was still naked, and, without warrant, I hit him a few times. The poor guy had no idea what was happening and he fell to the floor. I got out of there as quickly as possible.

Once outside, I ran as hard and fast as I could to my car, got inside and sped off. I felt such deep sorrow, anger and disappointment, but loneliness more than anything. I realised that this was who I was. I couldn't explain it; I couldn't explain to myself why I was still acting out; the sex, the violence, the cycle. I couldn't explain the fact that I was addicted to these feelings, all over again and this is what hurt me the most. Like a hamster on his wheel, going round and round in circles, I was unable to get off this crazy ride. I never thought of the mental, psychological and physical pain I was inflicting upon others or upon myself, and I didn't really care. I needed this. Fuck you all.

Chapter 13

It was time to upgrade my car to something a little cooler and faster. Gabriela and I kept driving past a car yard in Queanbeyan where there was a grey 1991 Ford Laser TX3 sitting out front. It was a two-door sports coupe and it looked perfect to me. I arranged to take it out on a test drive; it drove very well, but before buying it, I took it to my uncle next door who was a mechanic to give it the once over. I got his tick of approval. Mum and Dad were overseas at the time and I called and told them I wanted to buy it, they told me to wait until they came home. I didn't do as they said, and I bought the car. It cost me five thousand dollars. The car served me well, I kept it for a few years before the engine literally blew up. I sold it for five hundred dollars to Karl's friend's father who was a mechanic; he put a new engine in it and gave it to his son to drive.

Gabriela and I were on and off, breaking up and getting back together. Looking back there was a lot of tension and high drama in our relationship and all around us. Sometimes, it can be easy to overlook the signs and signals that happen when things are out of alignment. Things are always reflected from every direction, where life and relationships feel complicated like a constant grind of hard work.

We were still spending a lot of time with one another, but I had already switched off in my head, and she probably had as well. I knew I couldn't be in this relationship any longer. I didn't love her although I told her that I did; I didn't know how to love and, honestly, I didn't know what love was. I said it to make her happy. I really wanted to make her happy; she deserved it, but I couldn't give her what she wanted. I no longer wanted to pretend, mislead and then resent her. During one of our break-ups, I was out with my friends from work, (usually a group of up to ten of us). It was a Friday night and we went for dinner; probably Hogs Breath Cafe in the city. They had great steaks and we went there quite often; we drank plenty of alcohol and eventually ended up at a bar somewhere. It was late and time to go home. One of the ladies lived near me and we took a taxi to the main street together, went for another drink at one of the pubs and started making out. She would have been about ten years older than I was and had a teenage son. We decided to walk to the Queanbeyan Park and had sex on the picnic table that sat right behind the police station. We were laughing more than we were fucking; luckily, we weren't caught or heard and arrested. There were a couple of people who walked past and cheered us on. She and I had sex a few more times; it was fun, easy, no strings attached. I think I had a crush on all of those ladies I worked with in the Finance Section; I thought they were all beautiful in their own special way. More than anything else, they were genuine, caring, fun people who worked hard but played harder. I got on well with all of them and cared for them as well.

I had my best mates from school and all my rugby friends in my life, but I could have dropped all of them. I loved them, I cared for them and yet somehow, I could have just as easily never seen them again. I still wanted to be alone and away from everyone. I hated myself. I was drinking a lot; there were days I would sit at home alone drinking until I passed out. Along with the gym, alcohol was a total escape for me. I finally had my own bedroom; Janice had moved out and Peter moved into her room. My room was downstairs so I could be completely alone and away from everyone. I would sit downstairs alone, watch tv and the mental torture would begin. I hated myself and also felt sorry for myself at the same time. I loved watching movies and would do so all day. Television was another way for me to escape the thousand conversations going on in my head; it allowed me to live through other characters, live a different life where I could love, laugh, feel pain, sorrow and loss through someone else. Without film and TV, my mind wouldn't stop; it would race a million miles per hour. My head would be screaming all the time. I was constantly drowning in the good, the bad, the ugly, the violent, of it all. It was also hard for me to concentrate on one thing; to actually sit and listen without zoning out.

I had organized a weekend away with Gabriela. I don't really remember where we were going. It might have been up to Sydney or to my family beach house in Batemans Bay. We were going to leave on Friday and return Sunday evening. She was at home waiting for me to pick her up. That afternoon, Conan and Shane rang me and told me we were going to Sydney instead for a boy's weekend. It was an easy decision. The boys picked me up and we drove to Gabriela's house. She came out to see me and I told her that I wasn't going away with her; she wasn't happy and tore me to shreds, deservedly so. I think she also had a go at Conan and Shane; they weren't too worried though. We broke up that day for good.

Looking back now, I realize how wrong I was in the ways I acted and treated her at times, however, I wasn't happy and neither was Gabriela. We were young and wanted different things in life. I was miserable inside; no one would have made me happy. I was becoming an expert at lying and faking my way through life, pretending that everything was good and I was fine. No one suspected a thing, or so I thought. The truth is many of them caught me in my lies, knew that I was full of shit, thought I was a dick and actually called me out on it. Gabriela today remains one of my closest friends. She will always have a special place in my heart; my first relationship, my first girlfriend, and someone that I will always have a lot of love and time for.

Family life was fine, it just felt like we were coexisting with each other. I kept out of the details of their lives and they kept out of mine. Mum and dad were happy that I was working in the public service, making money and they thought that I was keeping myself out of trouble. In their eyes I now just needed to meet someone, get married, buy a house, have babies and live happily ever after. At that time, I couldn't think of anything worse.

I was enjoying my time alone; most days I wanted to go to bed and never wake up, disappear into a black hole to never find my way out. I was having these thoughts more and more and it was the only thing that brought me peace. I was descending even further into darkness. I found myself going to swingers' parties; I went to about five of them, alone or with a friend. I was becoming addicted to sex as much as I was to alcohol. I remember the first time I went to a swingers' party; it was at a random house in Canberra. I was naked with just a towel around my waist and I was invited into a bedroom by a woman. A few minutes later her husband walked in and I jumped up, worried I was doing something wrong. He just sat in the corner and jerked off as I fucked his wife.

Chapter 14

I had turned twenty-one and needed to get out of Canberra; everything was starting to build up and completely suffocate me. I bought myself a trip overseas to Ireland with Shane; he was of Irish descent and had a lot of family over there. We left in February, a few days after my birthday, flew to Belfast, dropped our bags off at Shane's cousin's house and went straight out to party. We spent most of our time with his cousin Celine (she was actually from Canberra and was living in Ireland) and her friend Orla. When we were out I got separated from my friends and ended up spending the night with a group of strangers back at their house, we stayed up all night drinking and smoking marijuana. This was back in 1999 and there was still some tension between Northern Ireland and Ireland. I remember seeing the barriers and the barbed wire, army and armed guards everywhere. I don't know how, but I made my way back to Shane and his cousin's house early the next morning. They told me how crazy I was and that I needed to be more careful as Belfast was still a very dangerous place; especially for someone who didn't know his way around. I loved the grit and soul of this city. To me the danger in the streets of Belfast was familiar and welcoming. It was an amazing city, my favorite in Ireland.

The next night changed my life forever.

We all went to a rave in a warehouse somewhere in Belfast; my very first one. We had organized to take ecstasy. This was the first time I was going to take drugs. The place was packed, there were several huge rooms playing different forms of techno, deep house and electronic music. We had a few drinks before taking ecstasy and it probably took about thirty minutes to kick in; but when it did, I was hooked. I began to dance wildly and with abandon. One image I will always remember was a video of John Travolta in Saturday Night Fever, brushing his hair over and over again on a huge projector; it was on a constant loop and it was the coolest thing I'd ever seen. Taking that pill started something in me; it gave birth to a whole new range of feelings I'd never felt before; feelings of freedom; of truly being in *ecstasy*, without a care in the world. This was something that I'd never felt before. It allowed me to forget about all of my problems, escape reality and gave me a deep sense of belonging. For the very first time, *ever,* it allowed me to get completely out of my head; to feel like I didn't have a head at all, to be honest. Everything about me felt light; my thoughts, my body and even my demons. I felt huge amounts of love for everyone around me and, for the first time in my life, *I felt willing to receive it.* I wanted to be close to people, to talk to them, to interact with them and get to know them better. I danced and danced and danced and *I was free.* I didn't care who I was, what I was, nor where I was. Shane told me that, at one point, I was dancing like a maniac, losing myself in the rhythm and beat of the music. A band of people formed a circle around me and suddenly all eyes were on me, cheering me on and dancing along. It was a crazy night. It was the night that I fell in love with drugs.

Shane and I spent the next month driving and drinking our way around the country, doing more ecstasy whenever and wherever we could. At some stages we found ourselves living out of our car. We spent time in Crossmaglen with his family. This was a little town on the border of Northern Ireland and Ireland. We traveled to Dublin, to Galway and to other parts of that beautiful country. In the meantime, I had somehow managed to start seeing Orla; we would always stop by to visit with her on our travels and I would end up in her bed. She was a beautiful girl, so I didn't mind so much.

Shane and I, Orla and her friend spent the weekend away at the Giants Causeway. We were out one night and Shane had finally hooked up with Orla's friend; he came rushing over to me saying he needed a condom. I only had one on me so I gave it to him. Later that night, Orla and I went to bed together and had unprotected sex for the first time; we were usually very careful. The next morning, she was worried, so we went to the pharmacy so she could take the morning after pill just to be safe. We never thought anything more of it.

Next stop for Shane and I was Gothenburg in Sweden; another cousin of his had moved there for work and we went to visit for a few nights. I think it was every boy's fantasy to go to Sweden and hang out with beautiful Swedish girls, luckily the language barrier wasn't much of a problem as most Swedes could speak great English. We went out to many bars and clubs taking photos of ourselves with every girl we could find, like idiots. At one club Shane and I hooked up with two best friends and spent the evening with them. My girl was Mathilda, a beautiful brunette with piercing blue eyes, and Shane spent time with her best friend, a Norwegian girl living in Gothenburg. They were both nurses. Mathilda and I exchanged details and promised to stay in touch with each other. I told her I would go back and visit her at some stage.

About one week after getting back to Australia, I received a call from Celine and Orla. I thought it was a call just to say hello, but that was not what it was. It was a call telling me that Orla was pregnant and that she needed one thousand dollars to travel to London to have an abortion, as it was still illegal to do so in Ireland. I didn't know what to do; I wasn't ready to become a father. Orla and I spoke about what *she* wanted to do; whether she wanted to keep the baby and how she felt about terminating its life. I've always been of the mindset that if I ever got a girl pregnant, no matter my age, I would be there for her and accept *her* choice. Ultimately, it's her body and her decision. If she wanted to keep the baby, I would be there for the two of them; I could never abandon her or a child that was mine. It's a part of me, a part of who I am, I created this child and I would always be its father. Celine gave me the bank details and I sent the money needed for the abortion. Orla and I spoke a lot over the next few days. We spoke about my moving to Ireland or her coming to Australia to be together if she were to choose to keep it. I sat by the phone waiting for the call that would determine the fates of so many. It was a strange feeling being so far away; not being able to be a part of the journey with her. I felt useless and disconnected, powerless to it all. Orla had ultimately decided to terminate, a decision that sat well with me at the time, and from time to time I still think about to this day.

Being back home in Queanbeyan was always tough for me; the memories and the depression would come flooding back, hitting me hard in tidal waves of grief and anxiety. I could be having a 'normal' day, as happy and as healthy as I could be, and then suddenly, out of nowhere I would be triggered, have a negative thought or feeling that would knock me straight down. It was usually associated with a smell or a sound, sometimes a touch, and that was it. I would fall into an abyss. At times, I felt like I had been hijacked; I couldn't talk, I couldn't see, or be around anyone. I was beginning to cry a lot, sometimes unprovoked and for no reason at all. I was feeling empty, alone and completely dark.

I just watched tv, spoke to absolutely no one and, if anyone asked me what was wrong, I would always say *"nothing,"* or *"you wouldn't understand, so please leave me alone."* To my family's credit, they never did leave me alone; they were always worried about me and tried to do everything possible to help me; but I wanted nothing to do with them. I was also going out more, binge drinking and doing drugs on a weekly basis all in the hopes of curing my deep depression and unexpected mood swings. Ecstasy was readily available in Canberra so I was going to Heaven night club, a gay club and Red Room and

Blue Room, two rave clubs. Sometimes I'd go with friends, other times I'd go alone. I was meeting people and becoming friendly with them, not that I cared for them or wanted to be their actual friend. I was doing it for the drugs I could get from them. I was popping pills as often as I could; spending a lot of money, buying a few at a time, taking them home, hiding them away and saving them for a rainy day.

Sometimes I'd sit in my room alone, take a pill, lie on my bed, listen to music or dance for hours. I became reliant on pills and alcohol to get me through the dark times. I needed them when I went out; otherwise, I felt like I had nothing in common with anyone anymore. I found it was getting harder to have conversations, to open up and relate to people.

Around six months after being back from my Ireland trip, Celine came back to Canberra. Conan was living in Sydney and Shane had moved to Wollongong for university. Celine and I became close, going out together, doing drugs, partying all night and having fun. Most of my friends in Canberra weren't really into it, except for my friend Rob. Rob was two years older than me and my cousin's best friend, and aside from Celine, he became the only close friend I had with whom I could do drugs. We would usually drive out at night, drink, do drugs, and then drive home with the sun coming up. We were young and stupid and living dangerously, and I didn't care at all.

Chapter 15

Work was going well; I had advanced in the Finance Section to as far as I could go. There was a position opening in the Audit Section and through all of my finance experience, I was recommended for the job. I applied, had an interview and got the position; I was now the junior auditor for the Attorney-General of Australia. *Me an auditor, what a joke!* I was earning a good deal of money, traveling the country and auditing the different Government Departments that came under the Attorney's portfolio. I had an assistant/secretary, and my own office. I travelled to every state in the country besides the Northern Territory; it was a great way to see the land. I visited Kirribilli House and The Lodge, the two residences of the Prime Minister. I audited at Parliament House, major law courts, power stations in Sydney, even airports. I got to see Tasmania, Melbourne, Perth, Adelaide, Sydney, Brisbane; all of the major Australian cities. It was a great job and I enjoyed it as I wasn't trapped behind a desk all day. I befriended Paul; he was about ten years older and worked in the section next to me. We hung out when we could; took two-hour lunches, went into the city and would do as little work as possible. He was a funny guy, a gay guy who was in a relationship with an older man living in Sydney. They loved their Golden Retrievers and they loved me just as much. They actually named one of their dogs Nathan, after me. They had a penchant for naming all of their dogs after guys that they liked. I had a great relationship with them, it wasn't sexual at all; we were all just good friends.

For the 1999/2000 New Year, Shane, Rob, Gianni, myself and a group of six friends travelled to Perth for a week. Shane's parents had moved there and they had an empty house for us to use for half of the trip; the rest of the time we stayed in a hotel.

Aside from Shane, I was the only other person who had been to Perth. I travelled on the plane with about ten ecstasy pills on me; I wrapped them up tight, hid them on my person, and got through security just fine. As soon as we landed in Perth, I called Shane to pick us up at the Arrival's Terminal. I gave him the pills and he safely hid them in his car. It was a great trip; we were all into our sports. We spent a lot of time in the ocean, jet skiing, drinking, playing tennis, went to a cricket match and to the horse races. We went to Rottnest Island for New Year's Eve, about eleven kilometers off the coast of Western Australia. We arrived there midafternoon and Shane, Rob and I took our first pill. We were flying; going from party to party on the island, dancing, kissing girls, having fun in and out of the water and acting like savage idiots. We counted down at midnight, kissed a few more girls, and continued to get high. Shane and I found a dirty old table sitting behind a toilet block; we had the genius idea of crushing up two pills and sniffing them off of the table. I made sure to lick what was left over on that dirt table, making sure we left nothing behind, and we danced the night away. We finally managed to catch the ferry home with the sun already rising in the morning sky. Everyone went to bed besides Shane, Rob and myself; we decided to shower and go to the horse races. Sometime between leaving the island and driving to the horse races, I lost my ability to talk, had a stutter and nothing was coming out. The overuse of drugs and the reckless licking of that table left me with a chemical imbalance that lasted for a day or two. I was worried, but the boys found it all very amusing.

Gabriela was in Perth at the same time; she went to celebrate the New Year with other friends. I left the boys for a night and drove with Gabriela to Monkey Mia. We got up early in the morning, went to the beach and watched as the dolphins swam into shore. We went on a catamaran cruise and, while lying on the net that sits just above the water, we spotted a huge Tiger Shark as it swam beneath us. We quickly jumped off that net and hopped back onto the boat, reeling from the amazing experience. Perth is definitely a beautiful city, with the most incredible weather and beaches, it is also the most isolated city in the world.

Besides work, I was spending a lot of time in the gym. I was lifting weights most days, but always did cardio and fitness training in between. This included a spin class, a boxing session or going for a run. I was becoming as fit and as strong as I could; eating healthily and working out with plenty of the male members. There was a community feeling in the gym and I enjoyed my time there. I told myself that the fitter I got, the more I could drink, the more drugs I could do, party and recover without a hangover. One night while I was depressed, I went out with Celine. We took ecstasy, drank, and stayed up until the early hours of the morning. I didn't want to go home; I wanted to spend the night with her, but she said *"no."* She was right; we had a great friendship, we never kissed or broke a boundary, perhaps out of respect for Orla and Shane, but I was very much attracted to her. She told me it was time for me to go home and, driving back to Queanbeyan I found myself on the backroads that lead to Fyshwick. Her rejection of me precipitated a self-destructive fever; I began hating the world and hating the *'amazing'* life that everyone thought I had. I couldn't stop myself and I ended up in the cruise lounge. It would sometimes stay open to all hours of the night. I drove my car around the corner and snuck in, no matter what time of day it was I made sure no one would see me. I was depressed and under the influence of drugs and alcohol, and I was in desperate *need* of this place. I needed to be abused and hurt, as this was all I could relate to deeply. My self-loathing had turned into a fierce addiction, and my addiction brought me right back here, every time, even if only sporadically.

Once inside, I kept my head down, kept to myself and found the right guy; a young guy, strong looking. He came over to me; I don't know if I was even able to stand straight. We went into a private room; he kept trying to kiss me and I kept pushing him off. I never kissed any of them. He was very persistent; maybe I liked it that way so I could retaliate with aggression toward him. I pushed him hard and he hit the wall in shock. I just stood there waiting for him to hit me back; maybe he thought it was a game because he came back trying to kiss me again. I pushed him off even harder this time and he got aggressive and pushed me back; I showed no emotion and asked him to rape me. I'm sure he thought it was a game or a fetish of mine. He grabbed me, turned me over and did what he did to me. I felt nothing emotionally and mentally; I was dead to the whole thing and pretty much lay there a broken man. I pushed him off half way through; I was done and I needed to get out of there. I didn't give a fuck about him and his needs. I got dressed and left the room, leaving him there to finish himself off. I walked to my car, got inside and started driving home. I felt like a zombie, numb to it all. I had left my body and was a shadow of my former self. I had so many emotions pulsing through me. I started to pick up speed, driving faster and somewhat out of control. A few hundred meters down the road on a corner sat a large gum tree, and I was heading straight for it. My time had come; I was over my life; over the person I'd become and I didn't want to burden anyone anymore. I didn't think anyone would have really cared or missed me anyway and I was ready to die.

"I spoke to your parents and they told me that you are a miserable little boy and they don't like you anymore...You have to continue living with them but they don't want you to speak to them..."

Over and over, I heard the Man's prophetic words taunting me, reverberating in my memory.

*"I love you and I am going to take care of you and make you happy...
Now remember, I will kill you and your family if you ever say
anything... This is our special little secret because this only happens
to special little boys."*

I kept my foot on the accelerator, unbuckled my seat belt and, for the
first time in a very long time, I felt alive and free. It was my time. But
for some unknown reason, the world wasn't ready to let me go, for
fifty meters from the tree towards which I was heading, jumped out a
kangaroo, followed by a second. I slammed my foot on the break so as
to miss them. I did. The car spun around in a one-hundred-and-eighty-
degree circle, landing me head first facing potential oncoming traffic.
Luckily, no cars were on the road at that morning hour.

I felt as if my heart had literally ripped itself out of my chest and was
running away from me down the road, even though it was already dead.
I couldn't believe what had just happened and what I just tried to do. I
sat there for what seemed like an eternity, my hands gripping the
steering wheel, I started pushing back and forth aggressively against
it, crying. I was screaming at the Man for hurting me, for leaving me.
I was replaying old traumas in my head, angry and confused. I
violently punched the roof above me until the strength and anger
drained out from inside of me. I could fight no more.

Quietly, and with an attitude of defeat, I composed myself, turned the
car around and slowly and carefully drove home. Canberra Avenue
always had dead kangaroos and wombats on the side of the road from
people hitting them. Luckily, none of them had to die because of me. I
made it home, jumped in the shower to sober up, and got into bed. I
was up for most of the night thinking about what had occurred. I
believe things happen for a reason, and I saw the kangaroos that
jumped out in front of me as a sign. Perhaps it was a message from a
higher power telling me it wasn't my time; assuring me that I was

meant to be here, to go on this journey and to share this story with you. Or maybe it was just luck.

<u>Chapter 16</u>

I was turning into a bit of a lady's man and I was getting cocky about it. It was becoming increasingly easy for me to meet and pick up women and I was becoming pretty good at doing it, going from girl to girl, having sex with many of them to fill a void and chase the emptiness. I was becoming the envy of most of my friends who were living vicariously through me. However, it all felt very empty. Yes, I was sleeping with beautiful girls, but I was finding it harder and harder to do so. There was no enjoyment in it; as soon as I would cum, I had to get out of there. I was finding it harder to show these girls any form of affection; finding it harder to hold them, to be close to them or to kiss and cuddle them after sex. I was becoming increasingly closed off, putting up a wall with everyone I was meeting or already knew, pushing them all away and needing to isolate at home. My communication skills had all but disappeared and I was starting to revert back to the eight-year-old boy who had to suddenly grow up into an adult to survive. I was saying and doing childlike things.

It never stopped me from trying to be with women and, if anything, I tried even harder to make up for my wanting to be alone. Over the years I had become close with one of my sister's friends. She was often at our house and, for a while, she and Janice were inseparable. Janice had since moved to Malta and other countries within Europe to teach English with her boyfriend, Simon. She also wanted to be closer to our grandparents as they were getting older, so I pursued this woman and we started a relationship. We dated for about six months; I was infatuated with her; she was a voluptuous girl, very sexy. We told

Janice we were dating; I don't think she was happy with the news, but she was on the other side of the world and wasn't too surprised.

It was easy for us, she already knew, and had relationships with, my close friends. We all went out together; she was against the drugs so I would sneak them in when I could, behind her back or when I was alone. I had a yearning to join Janice in Malta and to travel through Europe; I wanted to be there for the European Summer and continue to stay on for as long as I could. Toward the end of our relationship, I did it again; she fell pregnant. This time I was there for her and told her that, as much as it was both our decision, it was ultimately hers; it was her body and I would support whatever she wanted. She decided to terminate the pregnancy. I dropped her off and picked her up once the procedure was done; I bought her flowers knowing that it probably didn't make much of a difference to how she was feeling. It was a very quiet drive home and night at her house. I felt so much love and sympathy for her; I could see the deep pain she was in physically, emotionally and mentally.

I turned inward and thought about my role in all of this. I thought about the outcome if she had chosen to not go through with the termination. Perhaps it would have solved all of my problems and got me on the straight and narrow. Back then it all seemed so perfect; we would have stayed together and given it a real go. However, eventually the trauma, secrets, lies and shady life choices would have caught up with me and surfaced, and I probably would have destroyed the relationship. We went our separate ways not long after this. I'd be lying if I didn't say that part of me still wishes she kept the baby; another moment in life that I'll always remember.

It was time for me to get out of Canberra, again. I was twenty-two years old, my life there was killing me and I needed a fresh start. Off to Europe I went. I was running away from my problems, though I didn't know it at the time. I was living a lie, pretending that my life was amazing. My ego was getting bigger and becoming a large part of the problem. The drugs, the drinking and the sex with random women was growing all-consuming. Hence, I planned an elaborate escape from the inner darkness.

First stop was Copenhagen in Denmark; Shane was there with two of our other friends and we all met up. We travelled through Denmark, hanging in Christiania for a day, smoking marijuana and taking drugs. We then went on a ferry to Norway, where Shane reconnected with a Norwegian girl that he'd met back in Australia. (They are still together to this day and have two beautiful boys.) Oslo was a great city, very clean; and the people were beautiful and friendly. I had stayed in touch with Mathilda from Sweden, whom I met a few years earlier when I travelled there with Shane. We would call each other when we could, using phone cards and public phone boxes. Our relationship grew via telephone and we sent letters and photos to each other. It was exciting to receive a letter in the mail every month or two. I told her I was heading back to Europe and she told me to visit and stay with her. Mathilda lived in Gothenburg, on the west coast, a beautiful port city with winding canals and picturesque boulevards. I arrived towards the end of summer; we went on many walks through the beautiful Botanical Gardens near where she lived. Some of Mathilda's friends had a boat that we would sail up the coastline around the little islands surrounding the city. The water was cold but pristine, and swimming became a wonderful part of our days.

In this part of the world, the sun would stay out for what seemed like a full day. It would get dark around ten at night and it would rise again at four in the morning, which preempted any attempts of my sleeping in. Mathilda and I had a strong relationship at first, even though her tiny apartment created unexpected moments of tension. I had difficulty finding a job, even a cash job that would pay under the table. I inquired at an Aussie bar, 'The Dancing Dingo,' but without a working visa, the opportunities were very limited. Unemployed, I tried my best to stay out of her way as much as I could; but my inability to speak the language, coupled with not knowing anyone else in the country, made the situation ever more tiring. As the weather grew colder, the days grew darker and there wasn't much I could do besides walk in the parks and explore the city, cook dinner for Mathilda and keep the house clean. I was gradually growing depressed as the winter weather began to welcome the rain and snow, and the low temperatures were unlike anything I'd experienced before.

I found a gym close by and that is where I began to spend most of my days, but I was burning through money quickly. It felt like Mathilda and I were getting on each other's nerves, and the resentment began to set in. The love was there but she ached for her independence and space, and I was in search of my own life. I was relying on her for everything, which placed too much pressure on the relationship. A hard-working nurse, Mathilda was happy to sit home and watch Swedish television after a long day at the hospital. The easiest thing for me to do was to go to Malta, where Janice was living. I had family and accommodation waiting for me there, and I could easily find work with my Maltese passport. I knew it was the right time to go. Mathilda and Sweden were a beautiful part of my journey, and I will never regret that chapter of my life. The long days of unending sunlight, juxtaposed with cold nights of rain and loneliness, taught me a lot about the paradox of my life, namely, that I was in search of connection but afraid of the closeness both at the same time.

Chapter 17

Life in Malta, however, was an entirely different story. It was easy, it was fun and it was crazy. I was living between our beach house in St. Paul's Bay with my grandparents and Auntie Lina, and in Attard, at my mum and dad's old place with Janice. The house in Attard was where mum and dad lived when they were first married and living in Malta. It was also where Janice spent the first few years of her life before moving to Australia. I arrived in Malta just as summer started.

Malta is one of the best places to be in Europe during the summer months. The warm European sun would mix with the North African heat and winds, causing cloudless skies and unrelenting heat to hang tirelessly over the crystal-blue Mediterranean Sea. My day consisted of getting up at six in the morning because of the heat; I would go for a run followed by an ocean swim or a peaceful walk through the quiet suburban streets. Depending on which house I was at, breakfast came next before joining friends and swimming until lunch time; then off to another beach with friends and cousins to swim some more. We would go home late afternoon to shower, before heading out to dinner, finishing with drinks and dancing all night.

Several days after arriving in Malta I met Fred, a Maltese/Australian just like me. He had met Janice a week or two earlier. They were at a bar in Bugibba, a resort town of Malta; Fred asked someone for the time, he didn't know how to speak Maltese. Janice heard the Aussie accent, offered him the time, and a friendship began. Fred is two years older than myself, a short guy, solid and well built; he was a scrappy bastard and he loved a good fight. He left school when he was in Year

Nine to make money and help out his family. What he lacked in book smarts he made up for in street smarts. He couldn't read or write well and this held him back a little in life. We became inseparable. It was an amazing summer; we had a great group of friends, we were out every night, meeting amazing people and having the time of our lives.

Shane came to visit for a week. We literally stayed out every night until six in the morning, drove home drunk and, on the way, stopped at St Paul's Bay, near my family's house, stripped to our underwear, jumped into the ocean and swam out to a beautiful speed boat or yacht that was tied up. Though we had no idea whose boat it was, we would climb aboard anyway, sit for a good while and soak in the morning sun, fall asleep and enjoy the peace that was the Mediterranean Sea before the exciting chaos of the day began. We would stay aboard the boat until we were spotted by someone sailing past who would call out to us, or we would be suddenly awakened by the sound of a boat horn or the rocking of the sea.

Shane and I spent a lot of time with my cousin Karen; she was our unofficial tour guide and took us around Malta, introducing us to clubs and bars at night, and beaches, day clubs and private swimming pools during the day. Karen knew everyone on the island; and she could get us in everywhere without having to pay or stand in any lines. One afternoon I will never forget, Karen was driving Shane and I to a private swimming club. I was in the front passenger seat and Shane was in the back. They were talking about the fun we had the night before; I wasn't paying much attention to them. I was staring out the window with my arm waving in the wind, side to side, up and down. The song 'Have a Nice Day' by the Stereophonics started playing on the radio. I turned the volume up and stared out of the passenger side window as we drove along the coast with the turquoise Mediterranean Sea in full view, when it all hit me. For the first time in my life, and still the only time to this day, I felt absolute peace and joy emerge from within and wash all through me. I had never felt such a feeling of not having a worry in the world; it was different to the drugs. I cared for nothing and was truly in the moment, fully present, relaxed, and even more than that, *I was at peace.* My troubles and my past just melted away, something I had never been able to make happen or feel until this day. It was a feeling I will never forget and one that I hope to feel again someday. I started crying as I'd never felt anything like it. I made sure they couldn't see my face and, for that brief moment in time, I knew what it was to be free, to feel pure joy and peace.

Janice and I spent a lot of time with our grandparents. She had a special bond with them being the first and only grandchild born in Malta and, as the golden child, she surrendered some of her social life to spend more time with them; she was never a party girl or big drinker. I think my grandparents would look at me and ask, *"Where did he come from?... He's not one of us!"* In reality, they didn't have to look too far, because every male in the family loved their alcohol. Beer and whisky were the drinks of choice. Dad and grandfather would have a Cisk Lager and J&B Scotch or two daily. Every time I visited Malta, I made certain to buy my grandfather a bottle from Duty Free and drink half of it with him.

My life in Malta was the complete opposite of my life in Australia. I committed no violence toward men in the way I did back home; I was only dating women, and drugs weren't a high priority. We were mostly just high on life. Malta was the most amazing place to be in the summer and we were living it up. I met plenty of girls and had a lot of fun with many of them; I was going to the gym, swimming, running and keeping myself fit, which made me happiest of all. I was in a great place.

It was September 11, 2001, Janice, myself and our friend Aldo had gone out in his speedboat and jet ski cruising between the islands, when Janice received a call from Simon to get in front of a television immediately. Two planes had hit the Twin Towers in New York; none of us could believe what we were seeing. A few weeks before that, I had planned on going with Fred to Libya, on the North African coast, to lay fiber-optic cables in the ground and get paid a lot of money for it. Fred's cousin had a company in Malta and was contracted by the Libyan government to do this work. The United States was about to declare war on Afghanistan and, since Libya was a Muslim country, it was best I stayed away from that part of the world.

Janice moved to Belgium soon after to be with Simon; he was working in Antwerp at the height of the IT boom and was doing very well for himself. Janice found a job there teaching English to the locals. I stayed in Malta and got a job at a new restaurant in Paceville, the bar and nightclub district of Malta. It was called Mongolian BBQ, a buffet style eatery where customers would pick the meats, seafood and side dishes they wanted, bring them to a grill station where I would barbeque their food for them. Not long after we opened, we were held up at gunpoint; two men came in with shot guns and held us up as we were closing. The public had all left and it was only staff remaining. I was forced into one of the bathrooms with one of the female staff; she was hysterical, crying and frightened for her life. Half way through the robbery they grabbed us from the bathroom and put us with the other staff members in the middle of the restaurant as they robbed the place. I remember it clearly, standing there with a gun held up to my head and not feeling anything at all. I even laughed at them when they spoke to me; I was numb, disaffected by the situation and not afraid for my life, while everyone else feared for theirs.

"I will kill you and kill your family if you ever say anything to anyone. I will see you again soon."

I flashed back to the day when I was assaulted by the Man in the pool as a child. I heard his voice; his warning and his threat resounding in my head. And suddenly I realized that in order to survive those memories, I had become numb and unmoved by fear.

Aside from the hold-up, the restaurant was a great place to work. The staff were all young and we got along well, always getting together after work to socialize. I mainly hung out with a set of cousins, Jane and Mary, and our other friend, Brigette, who was a lesbian. Most nights after work, the girls and I would drive back to Jane's house, stay up drinking and smoking weed. Brigette and I would sometimes wrestle and, on occasion, make out. It all became a bit incestuous; I would have sex with Jane at her house, with the girls in the other room, then drive Mary back to her house and have sex with her in the car. The girls both knew what was going on but didn't seem to care, so neither did I.

One night at work, a bachelorette party came in to celebrate over dinner. They were a quiet group of girls; not really drinking or making much noise. I was working behind the bar that evening, so I asked the girls if I could bring some shots or other drinks to their table, trying to start their party. They shut me down with a firm *"no."* Soon after, the female staff asked the party the same question; they were rejected once again. However, one of the staff members thought up the idea of having me strip for them and asked the party if they wanted to see that. They all said *"yes!"* The bride-to-be had no idea of what was going on and neither did I. The staff came back and told me that's what they wanted and I flat out refused; there was no way I was going to strip for them, but they went back and told the party that I had agreed to do it. Everyone was happy and on the same page, except for me.

The girls talked me into it and I thought *fuck it, why not? I'll have some fun and maybe I can sleep with one of them.* We asked the owner if it was ok and he agreed, thinking it would be good for business. I went down into the cellar, grabbed two empty beer kegs and started doing bicep curls, jumped to the floor and did some push-ups to pump up my

141

muscles as best I could. I returned upstairs, took a few tequila shots and was ready.

The girls cleared the table in front of the bride, who still had no idea what was going on; the lights were turned off except for the blue halogen spots that lined the perimeter of the restaurant. The song 'You Can Leave Your Hat On' by Joe Cocker was turned all the way up on the stereo. I jumped onto the table, not really knowing what I was doing, took off my shirt and started dancing in front of the unsuspecting bride. I got the bride up on the table with me and danced all over her. I finally took my pants off, fortunately I had a nice pair of undies on that night! This was a Saturday night, the restaurant was full, everyone was cheering, the girls at the party were having a great time and so was the bride. Confetti cans were spraying silly-string all over us, and regular confetti was flying over us as well. We were a joyous mess. I didn't get naked; the bride was super happy and I made about fifty pounds in tips. To me, that was a successful night. Once the party ended and I was back behind the bar, a girl who was sitting at another table asked me if I would strip for her friend's 21st birthday party a few weeks away. I ran through the logic; *I need the money, I am going to meet a bunch of girls, I'm young and I'm single. I'd be stupid not to.* I was all for it. My stripping career lasted for three evenings; it was great fun and something I could tick off of my bucket list. I never wanted to get naked, but on one occasion, the girls successfully ripped my undies off. It was all part of the job, I guess.

For the next few months, I was returning home at all hours of the night; sometimes drunk, sometimes sober. I could only imagine what my family was thinking; watching or hearing me come home in a reckless state, making a mess of myself. Being religious people, they must have been horrified by what they were seeing. I know they were ashamed and embarrassed by my actions, and they would tell me so on more than one occasion. Sadly, I didn't care.

Chapter 18

Heading into winter, things declined even more for me. I couldn't fake the 'amazing time' everyone else thought I was having. I was simply too exhausted to keep up appearances. I was crying myself to sleep; depression was heavyset, flashbacks and unwelcomed desires came clawing their way out from deep within me. I was missing, craving, the drugs and the violence, wanting to feel it all again. I didn't want to be in Malta any longer; the November air was turning cold and the world was quieting down. My family needed a break from me and I them; so, I went to Belgium to spend some time with Janice and Simon.

I flew into Brussels in anticipation of a new adventure and an attempt to suppress all the feelings that were surfacing in Malta. In other words, I kept on running from my problems and continued to put on a new face. I lived a new lie and pretended, yet again, that my life was great. I caught the train down to Antwerp; Janice met me at Central Station and we walked home, a few hundred meters down the road. It was a cold and snowy night; I was excited to be there. Janice and Simon lived in a great building that was a mix of Belgian citizens and other foreigners, Australians, English, South African, Dutch, Italians, and French, and we all got along very well.

Every Friday evening, once everyone had finished work, we would all gather downstairs on the ground floor at a makeshift bar and we would drink until the early hours of the morning. For the first few weeks, I explored the city either on my own, with Janice and Simon or with a friend I had met in the apartment block. We visited the many museums, market places, Antwerp's main square, and the diamond district. We explored many of the Belgian pubs and cafes, drank classic Belgian beer or hot chocolate and ate waffles and world-famous Belgian chocolate.

One cold and dark afternoon, my next big adventure began. I was in the elevator on my way up to Janice's apartment. I arrived at our floor, doors opened, and a beautiful girl stood before me, patiently waiting to get in. She took my breath away. I was supposed to exit as she entered, but I stayed in there so I could speak to her. As we rode the elevator down to the ground floor, I introduced myself and she said she knew who I was. Apparently, Janice had earlier told her that I was coming to Antwerp to visit. Her name was Olivia. We walked out of the elevator together and I escorted her to the building entrance, asking if she would like to go out sometime. She told me she would love to but that she was very busy with work and not sure if it was a good idea. I asked her if she attended the Friday night drinks in the building with everyone and she said that she rarely did but would try to make it so we could have a drink together. She left me breathless, standing at the entrance, and as I watched her walk to her car, I thought to myself, *I need to know this girl.* She told me a few weeks later that when she got into her car that day, she called her best friend, telling her that she just met the man that she was going to marry.

Friday night couldn't come fast enough. I was downstairs in the building with the other residents. It was a large empty space with ground floor apartments to one side, a large indoor garden and seating area to the other. There was an old bar that was brought in for our entertainment. There were about twenty of us. Alan, an older South African gentleman who had been living in England for the past few years before moving to Antwerp, was the main instigator who brought everyone together. He was an alcoholic who would drink himself to sleep every night; a funny man with many stories. He liked Olivia himself, and had asked her out many times, so when I told him that she might join us for a drink, he was sure she wouldn't show. Everyone there that night was sure that she wouldn't show. They said she was a mysterious one, no one really knew anything about her, what she did for a job or had going on in her life. It was always a friendly hello and only a brief conversation when they saw her.

It was the night of the European MTV music awards, the year Kylie Minogue released 'Can't Get You Out Of My Head' and won most of the awards. I remember it being on TV as we drank and went between apartments and the bar area where music was playing and most people were hanging. We had been drinking for an hour or two when Olivia turned up; I think everyone was surprised but me. She came over, said hello to everyone there, gave me a kiss and a cuddle and said she had just finished work and was going to her apartment to freshen up and would be right back. Alan could not believe what he was watching; saying *"I have never seen her like this!... What did you do to her?"* It was all said in fun and I gave it back to him just as hard. Not long after, she returned with two drinks in hand; one for her and the other for me. We had a great deal of fun with everyone, before she invited me up to her apartment for a few more drinks.

Her apartment had a cozy, loft-style layout; the kitchen, living area and bathroom all downstairs, and a bedroom upstairs. We got comfortable on the couch and she opened a bottle of red wine and put on 'Depeche Mode'. This is where my love for English 80s rock bands started. She also got me into 'The Cure'; two of her favorite bands. We rolled a joint and began talking about life, who I was and who she was. Looking back now I realize how clever we were as we each left out huge chunks of who we truly were. I was into her and I could tell that she felt the same way about me. We stayed up for most of that night talking, getting to know each other. We kissed, we got naked and we spent the night together. There was something very special, but equally mysterious and secretive about this girl and I hungered to know more.

145

I hadn't really spoken to my parents in a long time; I didn't speak to them much when I was in Malta and now, in Belgium, I had no need or want to reach out to them. Janice could tell them that I was doing well, I thought, and if there was ever any emergency, they knew how to find me.

On the outside I was living my best life; traveling all through Europe, out every night, enjoying lots of alcohol, drugs, women and sex. However, on the inside I wrestled with a deep, dark emptiness that was growing by the day. I needed more than this. What everyone didn't see was the other side of it; all of the secrets I kept hidden deep down; the lying, cheating, self-loathing and overwhelming shame. I was hurting myself more every day and I still didn't know it. I was searching for more, trying to find my place in the world, trying to find where I belonged, but I couldn't. I wasn't ready. It's funny how people truly think that they know the ones they love, but often have no idea who that person really is.

Olivia and I got together when we could, which actually was most nights of the week. I think Janice and Simon appreciated the time I was away from them; it gave them time alone, as I was sleeping on their floor and taking up whatever little space was available in their apartment. We were going out to bars and clubs; she seemed to know all the right people, security, bartenders; we were well taken care of and wanted for nothing. She introduced me to her best friend Mark and his girlfriend Sara. We went to their house and, luckily for me, they spoke English reasonably well. The bottles of wine were flowing and Mark pulled out what seemed like an endless supply of cocaine. This became the start of my strong and dangerous love affair with amphetamines. We proceeded to do cocaine all night and have our own little dance party. Mark loved the DJs Laurent Garnier and Felix da Housecat, so we were going between both for most of the night. They told me that most of their friends were either in jail or dead from drugs and violence. They talked of how they would stay up for days at a time, not sleeping until they had so much gunk collecting in their eyes that they physically couldn't keep them open. Mark invited me out with him and one of his best mates; I needed a boy's night out and was looking forward to it.

Olivia and I had been seeing each other for a few weeks and I still didn't know what she did for work. I would ask but she said she wasn't comfortable telling me; that it would change my opinion of her and that I wouldn't want to see her anymore. Little did she know that I had my secrets too. I had tried to find a job whilst in Antwerp, but like Sweden, without a working visa, it was hard and no one was willing to pay under the table. Again, I had plenty of time on my hands and I would go to the gym during the day, which was not too far from where we lived. No matter where I was in the world, I always tried to keep up with my fitness. I would try to meet Olivia after work but she regularly refused me, saying she would just meet me at home. One evening, however, she did allow me to meet her after work.

It was a bitter cold night; icy rain was coming down as I made my way to our meeting place. She had asked me to walk her home and, it was here that she was ready to tell me what she did for work. I reassured her that it didn't matter to me what she did; that I wasn't going anywhere. She started crying, telling me that she really liked me and was terrified that I was going to run away. I grabbed her, held her tight and told her it was all going to be OK. She finally summoned the courage and told me that she was a sex worker. Hearing this had no impact on me at all. I didn't care. I didn't think any differently of her, nor did I judge her or look down on her. We were both going through our own big challenges at that time; doing whatever we needed to survive. Who was I to judge her? I had my secrets. I wasn't innocent, far from it. She said that when she told most guys they would leave her or try to have all of their friends fuck her. I simply replied *"I'm not*

147

going to leave you, I don't have any friends anyway, so you're safe with me." This broke the tension and we had a laugh. We walked the rest of the way home in silence, had a quiet night and never spoke of it again.

A night or two later, I was able to show my romantic side for the first time. I created a picnic for the two of us in her apartment. While she was at work in the afternoon, I went shopping; bought a few different cheeses, salami and prosciutto, crackers, fruit and nuts, and a few bottles of wine. I placed blankets on the floor, candles throughout the apartment, and laid the food and wine out in classily catered style. She was so surprised as she walked through the door that night. She told me it was the nicest thing anyone had ever done for her. It felt great to see her happy, especially after revealing her truth to me.

My night out with Mark had arrived. He picked me up with his friend, Lucas, a big guy, a bodyguard and doorman at a few establishments around town. I felt a genuine connection and friendship with Mark; he was a straight shooter, a loose cannon, and a little crazy, but I could tell he had my best interest at heart. He was my height, but more solid; a genuine killing machine. He had been in and out of jail for drugs and violence. Mark and Lucas were not the most popular guys in Antwerp; they had a lot of enemies and were always on their toes, prepared to move fast in any situation. Lucas wore a bulletproof vest under his shirt the night we went out. They told me sternly *"...if trouble goes down, just get out of here fast, don't worry about us, the last thing we want is for you to get caught up in our mess..."* We went to a bar where the two were friendly with the staff. The first thing they always did when entering a venue was to see who was in there, locate the exits and check the best place to sit or stand where they did not have their backs to anyone. We hit the drinks and cocaine hard and soon found ourselves at a rave. The guys loved a good dance party and always knew where the good ones were at.

148

As soon as we entered the venue Mark handed me an ecstasy pill and proceeded to give me another seven more throughout the night and well into the morning. Literally every hour he fed me another pill and I took them all. We didn't sleep for about three days, staying up, drinking, dancing, non-stop drugs, at times philosophizing about life and other times talking shit that felt really deep, but wasn't. This was fast becoming my new life and I was liking it more and more, yet sinking deeper. Mark was always secretive about what he did for work. I later found out that amongst other things, he was a hit man; he would get paid a lot of money to make people disappear. He told me that he would travel through Europe and do what he did, then return to his 'other life' like nothing ever happened.

An apartment soon became available in our building and Mark moved in; we were one big happy family. I would spend most days with Mark in the apartment when Olivia was working. We would always listen to his favorite DJ's and music all day. He introduced me to liquid ecstasy, which also goes by the name of 'GHB' or 'GBH', 'Fantasy' or 'Liquid E'. It gave me the feeling of being uninhibited; a sensual and sexual mix of freedom and rapture where I escaped everything I was, everything I had been and everything I was feeling when I took it. It allowed me to be free; to feel nothing, be nothing and escape all reality. Ketamine, also known as 'K' or 'Special K' is another drug that he introduced to me. It is often used as an anesthetic on animals, and sometimes referred to as a horse tranquilizer. It's a hallucinogenic and makes one lose all sense of reality; a big club and sex drug. The first time I tried it I literally couldn't stand or walk. I had to lean up against the wall, I was completely out of this world. I felt like I was walking on clouds with no head, literally holding my own head in my hands. I was in a state of euphoria, ecstasy and pure happiness and I wanted to stay in that state forever. I never wanted to get out of it, I wanted more of it and wanted it every day. On another occasion when I took 'K', I fell into a 'K hole', a state of complete detachment from consciousness and reality which normally lasts about thirty minutes depending on how much you take. It could be described as a temporary state between intoxication and a coma, normally brought on from taking too much. Not a great feeling at all.

Chapter 19

I was spending more time with Mark and Olivia and less time with
Janice and Simon. Janice was never able to get in contact with me; I
hardly ever answered her calls, and when I did, I would be short with
her. She noticed that something was wrong because whenever I would
return to her apartment, I would sleep all day, not say much and walk
around in a stupor. Janice wasn't dumb; she was getting more
suspicious and soon, had an idea of what I was doing because of my
overall appearance and demeanor. She threatened to send me back to
Malta, or even Australia, if I didn't clean up my act. The drugs were
becoming more of a dependency and deepening my addictions. Janice,
Simon and I were going to Malta for a few days for Christmas to be
with the family. I needed it more than anything. I needed to sober up
for a while, to get away from Antwerp. However, the longer I was
away, the more I wanted to get back there. I needed to escape this life;
to escape who I was. We were in Malta for about one week. We had a
lovely time with our grandparents. They would absolutely crucify me
if they knew what I was up to. I spent most of my time with Uncle Naz
in his room. I would sit and tell him everything that I was doing, but
in a joking way, so I think he never believed me even when I assured
him that it was all true.

Sitting with Uncle Naz was like going to confession at church; I was
spilling out my sins and wrong doings, only he gave me no penance.
He just sat there and listened. Uncle Naz was a large man, on the heavy
side. He was missing two or three fingers and, when I was a kid, I
would always play with the parts of his hands where his fingers should
have been. He was a gentle giant. I don't know why we had such a

strong connection; we were complete opposites; however, they do say opposites attract and he was literally the only person with whom I could truly be myself. He smelled of cigars, tobacco pipes and urine. He was perfect in my eyes. I wouldn't want him any other way. He was my soul mate.

For New Years, we were back in Antwerp and I planned a trip to Amsterdam with Olivia, Mark and Sara. The drive took a little over two hours and we were there for three sleepless nights. On the drive there, we passed a massive car accident that always sticks in my head; one car was completely mangled and in flames. We later learned that two passengers died in that accident. Sometimes I look back on that moment as another warning sign for where my life was heading and the reckless choices that I was making.

Amsterdam was a wild time, I had been there before with Janice, but this was a completely different experience; the four of us stayed in the same hotel suite with separate bedrooms. The three of them were very comfortable with each other; always walking around naked, the girls bathing together. Mark had slept with Olivia years before and I'm sure Olivia and Sara had slept with each other as well.

We explored the city, frequented many parties and clubs, took a ridiculous number of drugs and, for New Year's, attended a rave in an abandoned warehouse. Mark was so fucked up that night that he threw up quite regularly on the dance floor, and then took more drugs as soon as he could to quickly replace whatever he threw up. As fucked up as I was and lost within myself, I was wondering;

What is he running away from so hard to go to that level of desperation and escapism?... He really needs to take a break... when is enough enough?... Was this a reflection of myself here?

Toy Cars   Nathan Spiteri

It's a wonder we all survived those days.

One of the tenants in the building where we lived had vacated for a
month and let me stay in his apartment whilst he was gone. It was
convenient for everyone, I got my own space, which I severely needed.
Janice and Simon got their apartment back and Olivia had some much-
needed time to herself. Mark had disappeared for a few weeks and we
weren't sure where he went or when he was coming back. Olivia was
working most nights; so, I found myself wandering the streets alone,
lost in my head and my loneliness. I always had cocaine on me and a
little K or liquid E; Mark was sure that I was well taken care of before
he left. I checked out different bars and clubs and, depending on how
fucked up I was, I would wander into a gay bar to get my fix. I was
still getting violent towards these poor men; the last thing they ever
expected was to receive a beating after having a sexual encounter. The
drugs were a temporary fix; a few hours of escapism, helping me to
forget about life until they descended into depressants. And they
always descended. As high as the highs were, the lows were always
much lower.

I would lock myself in my temporary apartment and speak to no one
for days, unless it was Janice. When I spoke with her I was fake and
positive, reassuring her that everything was great. Sometimes I would
shower and clean myself up and go to Olivia's apartment; she had
given me a key to come and go as I pleased. We had an understanding,
an unspoken and unhealthy agreement (also known as a 'Coward's
Bargain'); I would never ask her to stop what she was doing, and she
would act as if she knew nothing about the things I was doing. We
were living in a codependent relationship; we both needed and relied
unhealthily on the other for mental, emotional and physical support.
We were enabling each other's addictions and vices so that we could
do what we needed to *survive*. Then we would return to one another,
act as if all was normal and as if we were in a healthy, loving

partnership. Here, we would get approval from each other on how amazing, beautiful and in love we both were.

Olivia had her issues, granted, but deep inside of her existed a genuinely beautiful and caring person with a lot of love to give. She was extremely street-smart and intelligent. She told me that, one day, she would love to use these dark experiences and turn them into something positive and healing. She dreamed of becoming a counselor or therapist for troubled youth. I believe that she would have been amazing at it. She told me never to ask why she was doing it, and I never did. Her reasons, as sad as they may have been, were none of my business and, at the time, I didn't care. We had a contract; she dealt with her demons her way, and I dealt with my monsters my way. She did mention that she had a much better relationship with her mother than with her father, that he wasn't kind to her mother, and that she resented him immensely for that. Her older brother had left home when she was still young and he had little to do with her.

Olivia loved to party. She loved her drugs, especially marijuana, and her free and open sex life. She had slept with many men outside of what she did for a living. She had mentioned me to her parents and wanted me to meet them; they lived an hour out of Antwerp and were coming to the city to treat her to dinner. She asked for me to join and I agreed. Before we left her apartment, we did a few lines of cocaine and had a few drinks to help us feel calm and relaxed. Once in the restaurant, I found myself sitting opposite her father at the table; Olivia sat facing her mother. Her father was an educated man who held a high-profile job working for the Council of the European Union. Her mother seemed to be very sweet and lovely; I don't remember what she did for a living. We ordered wine; the conversation was cordial. They asked the standard questions, about Australia, what I did for work, for how long I would be traveling and if I planned to stay in Belgium. I answered them to the best of my ability and, I think, sufficiently, although I was probably mumbling utter nonsense to them.

Everything was going well, they seemed like lovely people. But before we ordered our food, Olivia thought it would be a great idea to put her hand on my leg. It seemed innocent enough at first. She then proceeded to move her hand up and place it on my penis. Soon she was stroking my penis from outside of my pants. At this point I wasn't sure what was happening, but I didn't push her hand away. I grabbed the menu, which was a large book with many pages from which to order. I held it up at the edge of the table, right in front of me, trying to conceal what was happening. Thinking that I wasn't uncomfortable enough as yet, Olivia proceeded to undo the button on my jeans, put her hand inside my underwear and masturbated me. I have no idea how her parents didn't notice the motion of her arm moving up and down in front of them, or my sudden gyrations and facial expressions. Panicked that her parents or the waiter would see what was happening, I struggled hard to have a normal, decent conversation. Olivia wouldn't stop. She was on a mission and I surrendered to the forbidden pleasure of it all. I came. I then excused myself to the toilet to clean up, returned to the guests at the table, and enjoyed the remainder of the evening without anyone finding out. A very satisfying meal for me!

Dinner was done and I thought we were going to go out or back to her place to enjoy the rest of the evening, but instead she told me she had to go into work. She said that she was requested by one of the high rollers who was in town for a short time. I knew I wouldn't see her for a few days and for the first time I found myself upset about it. I still don't know if it was jealousy or anger. I've never been a jealous person so this was all new to me, and I didn't like the feeling. She dropped me off at the apartment building and was off. I went inside, no one was around, I checked in to see what Janice and Simon were doing but they were out so I went back to my apartment. The incessant self-loathing and depression were back, taunting me, forcing me to stew in my thoughts;

*Why the fuck is she going?... Where the fuck is she going?... Why the
fuck is she still doing this?... How the fuck could she do this to me?...
Doesn't she love me?... What am I doing?*

I snorted some cocaine, took a hit of K and stumbled out of the building, unable to walk in a straight line. I went for a cruise through the red-light district, checking out the ladies in the windows, thinking that I may have seen Olivia. Instead, I bumped into a couple who invited me to a sex party and, with the state of mind I was in, I was up for it. This party was more high end than the dirty swinger's parties I had been to. It was in a big, beautiful house in the suburbs with access to only a handful of rooms. Very 'Eyes Wide Shut'.

One room was cleared out with a DJ booth toward the corner playing cool, deep house music. There were two or three rooms filled with beds, mattresses and bean bags. There was a huge formal dining room with a stunning old wooden table, medieval style, drawing attention to the middle of the room. On one end of the table was a bar with more alcohol than anyone could ever drink; and at the other end was a veritable confection of illegal drugs; A drug addict's paradise. There was a large bowl of cocaine, with lines made up for whomever wanted a hit; and a bowl filled with pills of varying colors and sizes. If I remember correctly, the party cost about 100 Euro to enter and there were at least a hundred people entering and leaving throughout the night and into the next day. I was only able to enter because of the couple I met who frequent these events quite often, (you normally needed to have a partner with you.)
It was literally a 'free for all'. People would have a dance, do drugs, have sex, and then start all over again. There were orgies going on everywhere, people fucking where they wanted and with whomever

they wanted. I had never seen anything like this before; the swinger parties I frequented in Canberra were nothing like this. I felt as if I was in a porn video. I cannot tell you the number of people I had sex with that night, or whether I even used protection. At one point I passed out and woke up to someone giving me oral sex. The debauchery lasted all weekend. I left in daylight, many hours after I entered. I felt ill, dirty and I just wanted to run away and bury myself in a deep hole. I wasn't happy; I wasn't sad or angry, I felt nothing. I walked away from this event as I usually do, in slow motion, empty and depressed. I was a completely hollow vessel with nothing left inside of me. I was done. I made it home and stood under the shower for what felt like an eternity, water streaming down as hot as I could handle. The bathroom was drowned in steam. I couldn't see a foot in front of me. I was invisible in the mirror and just wanted to remain that way forever. It was still winter and the weather was freezing cold and it felt like it stayed dark twenty-four hours of the day. I finally wandered over to Olivia's apartment, no questions were asked by either of us. I acted happy and high on life. It was exhausting.

After some time, there was a knock at the door. It was Janice and she was not at all happy. She didn't say hello, just ordered me outside into the hallway. I stumbled out, closing the door behind me. I must have looked like death because I certainly felt like it.

"I have been trying to contact you for days, you did not reply to any of my messages and have not called me back... You need to leave, I do not want you in Belgium anymore.
I don't want you here with me anymore... I know about the drugs; I know about the partying and the sex... I don't want you dying here on my watch."

She was short and straight to the point, then she stormed off back to her apartment. I could feel her anger, disgust and disappointment, beyond all of that I could feel her heartbreak all through me. For the first time, I actually felt her pain and it hit me hard. I stood out there for a while and really thought about what I must have put her through over the past few months. Janice is unlike any other, she's an angel. She never touched drugs and drank only very rarely. She has a heart like no other and would do anything for anyone, no matter if she knew them or not; she wouldn't, couldn't, hurt a fly and doesn't have a bad bone in her body. She is the kind of sister I always wished for, and I had completely taken her for granted and destroyed our relationship.

Within a few days I left Belgium and went back to Malta. I was back living with my grandparents and back working in Paceville, this time at a little late-night Mexican cafe and bar, up the road from the Mongolian BBQ. We only served quesadillas, burritos and beer, tequila and mezcal, which is tequila's huskier and smokier cousin with the worm in the bottle. I drank many a mezcal and sucked down many a worm for added taste. It was a fun and easy place to work; I began to know many of the returning customers and we would bet on who would eat the worm. It wasn't a hallucinogenic; it was a Maguey worm which feeds off of the agave plant. It was added to the bottle, some say, for the taste and others say for marketing reasons.

Olivia came to visit me a few weeks after being back in Malta. I got us a hotel room in Paceville where we stayed for five days. The weather was a little cool, nothing like it was in Belgium, as winters in Malta are quite mild. We drank a lot and dined out on great food. I introduced her to the sights; showed her as much of Malta as I could. One night we were at Axis, the biggest club in Malta at the time. I knew one of the bartenders who worked there, so she took good care of us. We were quite drunk and we stumbled our way back to the hotel. We were having sex, she needed to urinate, stood above me and, in a circular motion, urinated all over my body. She then jumped back onto me, wet and bewildered, and continued having sex. That pretty much sums up our relationship. The day she left Malta we spoke about always being in each other's lives, but knew it was best that we stopped seeing each other. Between the codependency, the drugs, and the complicit contracts going on between us, we were never going to be good for one another and we both knew it.

I stayed in Malta for a few more months. My mother told me that I was needed back in Australia as my job at the Attorney-General's Department was going to be made redundant and I needed to be there otherwise I wouldn't get paid out. It got me home where I needed to be.

Chapter 20

On the way back to Australia, I stopped off in Dubai for a few weeks and stayed with a girl I met in Malta; she was working for Emirates Airlines as a flight attendant. It was before the country had become so westernised. I was staying on the 30th floor of a high rise building in an apartment with three girls. It was situated in the middle of the desert and, every day, I would sweep away a layer of sand that had amassed on our balcony, only to return and do the same thing the next afternoon. There was an amazing amount of wealth in Dubai, even back then; wealth beyond anything I had seen before. I didn't have the greatest time, it was somewhat uneventful; however, it was a welcome change from everything I had been through in Europe. It was a good time to detox from the drugs, and to prepare myself for what was awaiting me back in Canberra.

During the entire time I was away, I hadn't dealt with any of my demons. I was still running from myself, from my past, from the depression and jumping from relationship to relationship. I did care for the women, the friends I met and the family I stayed with, but I was unable to invest anything emotionally with any of them. It was the 'Jekyll and Hyde' thing all over again, I genuinely cared for them, but on the other side, I didn't care for anything or anyone. I was detached and didn't give a fuck. There was a constant pull between these two internal forces.

I was being true to myself because I always did what I wanted irrespective of its impact. My higher self was nowhere to be found. My communication skills were nonexistent, I couldn't trust myself or anyone else, I couldn't access love. It was out of reach. I continued to put up walls and push away anyone who got too close. Rather, I spent my time using people for whatever I could get out of them.

I was back home in Canberra and it was actually quite nice to see familiar faces. I was exhausted and needed a good few week to acclimate back to familiar surroundings. I went back to work as an auditor; however, the audit department was being outsourced and privatized, so I was transferred to a different position in the Department. I was given the new role of Assistant Property Manager, on a six-month contract. The job was fine; I took control of both current and future maintenance work being performed at the Department, organized tenders and meetings for a new security system being put in place and implemented a new energy rating system for the Department. There was only a small group of us working together. I did the work with ease, but I was developing a strong awareness that public service life wasn't for me. It was never for me. I realized that if I stayed working there much longer, I would have woken up in thirty years, severely depressed, after having a breakdown thinking ... *what have I done with my life?... I resent and hate myself and everyone around me.* How ironic though, everything that I didn't want to have happen in thirty years' time was actually happening live, right now in my life. I was just too messed up to see any of it.

Fred was back from Europe; he was living in Sydney and in love with Janice. I would visit him on weekends. He had a wild group of friends who were also into the party scene. It was different from Europe though; there, I was free, whereas, here, I had responsibilities. After weekends in Sydney, and not sleeping for nights on end, I was given a handful of Rohypnol (the date rape drug) to help me sleep. I would take one after a huge weekend of partying when I knew I had to work the next day. I never once used Rohypnol on anyone else, nor did I share them with others; I used them purely for sleep after a big weekend. It became so bad that one time, in a Monday morning meeting with a gentleman regarding a building issue, I fell asleep. I apologized and told him I had been up all night due to food poisoning and that I wasn't feeling well. He completely understood, was sympathetic to my illness, and we rescheduled.

Paul was still working in the Department; still sitting next to me, and we were still up to our old tricks, taking two-hour lunches, escaping into the city or going back to his place to chill. We did anything not to be at work. He was on an independent contract, reporting only to the head of the department and on his own schedule, so I put myself on his schedule when I could.

I went to visit my drug dealer in Canberra one evening. I was there to buy drugs and get high with him. He was smoking crack cocaine and I had a hit; I had never done it before. Crack is the crystal form of cocaine, it is the strongest and most potent form of cocaine, rendering it the most dangerous. It is usually between seventy-five to one hundred percent pure, making it far more potent over regular cocaine. Smoking crack reaches the brain much quicker, bringing on an immediate and far more intense high which normally lasts around fifteen to thirty minutes depending on the hit. It is also much cheaper than cocaine in the powder form, making it much more marketable, but it is also much dirtier. I bought some from him; he had a new pipe, which he gave to me, so I was set. The thought of going into work, doing something that I had no interest in, was getting to me, so I would sometimes take my pipe to work and leave it under my car seat. I was still working with my mum, as well as my auntie and cousin, so we would all car pool together. We would share the driving load, one driver per week, which meant I would only take the crack with me one week per month. I kept it in a little leather pouch and, on those fateful weeks, I would take a hit or two during lunch. I would sit in my car, make sure no one was around, and do my business. It was an immediate escape from reality; from the mundane existence which I was living. When not at work, I would smoke when I was down, depressed or in a bad place emotionally. It wasn't an everyday thing.

I was getting along well with mum and dad, Peter and Karl, working in the public service and making money. That's what was most important to my parents; money and job security. I had bought an apartment as an investment property in Canberra with Peter; he was also working in the public service. However, unlike me, Peter enjoyed his post. I envied people who could work a 'nine to five' job, sit behind a desk, not necessarily enjoying it, but do what is necessary to pay the bills. I knew that would never be me. Peter was quite opposite to me; he was playing representative rugby union and league. He drank, but in moderation, and he never did drugs. Janice broke up with Simon and moved to Japan to teach English; we were speaking over the phone and were in a better place in our relationship. No matter what I did or said to that girl, she always forgave me. Karl was in primary school; a cute little boy. I would sometimes play soccer or football with him at home. He was turning into a great sportsman, just like Peter. The gym was still a very big part of my life. I found myself going every day after work and on weekends, getting very fit but not too big. I never cared for big muscles, it was always more about fitness, being lean and in good shape.

Surprisingly, as mentally and emotionally disconnected as I was, I was able to talk to women very well and it was becoming even easier to sleep with them. Maybe it was from years of hanging with the girls at the chemist when I was younger and my experience in Europe. I knew what to say and what they wanted to hear, but as soon as they asked anything about me, I would lie or run away. I was hanging with new friends, getting into a lot of mischief, doing a lot of drugs. Ecstasy and cocaine were still my drugs of choice, but I was also experimenting with speed, although I was never a big fan of it. It was the only drug that would get me physically ill; it tasted disgusting and it would bring me to the worst comedowns. My friends liked it though; so, I took it because I literally couldn't say *"no."* We would get ridiculously messed up, march into parties like we owned the place, trip over ourselves, collapse to the floor, unable to talk, unable to stand straight, and we would make absolute fools of ourselves.

We got tickets to an AC/DC concert through a lady I was dating; she was the General Manager at the hotel where the band was staying. She gave me six tickets to take a bunch of friends. Three of us decided to drop acid, a hallucinogenic drug, and we went wild in the mosh pit for the duration of the concert. It was a reckless and wild time. The grandmother of one of the boys I gave a ticket to lived across the road, so we all decided to meet there once the concert was over as we knew we would have separated throughout the night. Drenched in sweat, a friend and I were the first to arrive at her house, and she invited us in while we waited for the others. I was well into the middle of my acid trip and was swaying from side to side. I took a seat on her couch and asked for a glass of water; I wasn't looking straight, sitting straight and everything in the room was moving and rocking. The furniture came alive, dancing around me and talking to me, spraying splashes of color out of make-believe mouths all over me. The fan on the ceiling was spinning and I thought it was getting closer and closer to my head with every rotation, effortlessly ready to chop my head from my shoulders.

The rest of the boys were starting to show up; everyone was feeling fine and not in the horrid state I was in. I needed to get out of the room, I asked where the bathroom was, and, holding onto the walls for dear life that I could have sworn were caving in on me, I made it to the bathroom. It was only down the hallway, a few meters away, but it took what felt like five minutes to walk there. I was tripping hard; sweating, hot and feeling as if I was going to pass out. I looked at my reflection in the bathroom mirror. My eyes were crossed and popping out of my head; my jaw was chomping down involuntarily and I thought I looked like some kind of alien. I came up with the genius idea to jump into the shower fully clothed to cool off. I walked back into the living room saturated. The poor grandmother must have been thinking, *"who is this boy and what the hell is going on?"* Before I knew it, I was quickly ushered outside to dry off and to try to compose myself. We made it into the city, continued to party, took more acid later that night, and the rest was a blur.

Chapter 21

My time working at the Attorney General's Department and in the public service was nearing an end. My six-month contract was up, and I was offered a new role in a different section of the Department for less money, or I could take a redundancy package. I chose the latter. It was my chance to get out of a career that was slowly suffocating me. I decided to take a personal training course through the Australian Institute of Fitness and got a job at Odd Bods in Queanbeyan, the gym I was already training at. Working there was easy and pleasant; I knew most of the members through my many years of training there, and I was already familiar with how the gym worked. I was in my element, getting myself super fit, training hard and teaching up to ten classes in a week. These included abdominal, boxing, spin classes, Les Mills Body Pump and Body Combat. I was earning less money but I was finally doing something that I was good at and made me happy.

Soon after starting at the gym, I was celebrating a friend's birthday and I saw one of my first crushes; her name was Lea. She was seven years older than me and I first saw her at the gym when I started going as a teenager. I was now twenty-three years old and she was thirty. She was huge into her fitness and competed in physique competitions. The party was in a mutual friend's backyard. I mustered the courage to approach her, told her about my crush on her and asked her out. To my surprise she said *"yes,"* and she introduced me right back into the Canberra club scene. I started hanging with people her age, some married, others single. I found myself back in the culture of taking ridiculous amounts of ecstasy and cocaine and living a fake life; loving everyone, talking nonsense and acting as if these people were my best friends, staying out until the club would close at six in the morning. I would then kick on at someone's house, take more drugs throughout the day or go back to Lea's place and have sex until I passed out. I would hardly speak to any of these people outside of the club scene; when I would see them at the next party or club, we would behave as if we were all best friends, and do it all over again. It was a seductive and vicious cycle.

I stumbled upon a big drug culture in Canberra all those years ago, and I'm sure there still is now. Canberra is a small city; it had a population of around three hundred and fifty thousand in 2003 and a lot of us solely lived for the weekend. We all worked hard during the week and partied even harder on the weekends. For all of us into this scene, we would end up at one club, Lot 33, in Kingston, a suburb of Canberra. It was a small and intimate place, big enough to dance but small enough that you were never far from anyone or anything. It felt like everyone I knew was at this club. I made many connections at Lot 33; some good and some definitely not so good. Lea and I were at different stages in our lives; she was looking for someone to start a family with, and I wasn't in that mindset at all. We dated for a few months, she was my summer love, and then we went our separate ways.

My work schedule was always alternating, sometimes I worked early morning, other times the night shift and every other weekend. I enjoyed this schedule and it made me get out of the scene for a while. Soon, training, health and fitness became my drugs of choice. I treated my body as if it were my temple; I was eating healthy, getting fit and staying away from all of the seductive addictions that I *thought* I needed and wanted.

I was able to take breaks from it all; as much as I was reliant on the drugs, alcohol, sex and partying, I was always able to get away from it for weeks or months at a time. This made me become more of a homebody, I stopped going out, stopped seeing my friends and also stopped seeing everyone who *enabled* me. I stopped all of it and fell back into the familiar setting from when I was a kid, sitting at home alone watching a lot of TV and movies.

I was back in my safe place.

I began to model in local Canberra magazines, brochures, fashion shows and television ads. I was introduced to the National Acting School and started attending classes. I enjoyed being around actors and other artists, acting in small scenes, memorizing monologues and performing them in class. I guess all those years as a kid, sitting alone in front of the television for hours did something to me. My love for film and TV was always there, but I never really expressed it, just as I never really expressed anything that I liked or wanted. The very first movie I was in was a little independent film, shot in Canberra. I played a hiker with my girlfriend and we were kidnapped. We managed to escape, but were then caught and murdered. I had a fight scene and was stabbed to death. I loved being on set surrounded by like-minded people. I loved rehearsing the scenes, shooting the many takes, the make-up, and the *"Action"*, the awe and the energy. Mostly I enjoyed finally being a part of something meaningful and constructive and I felt important on shooting days. I kept it all a secret and hardly told anyone because I felt ashamed, a fraud and unworthy. I felt like a failure; unable to express or show anyone that I was happy. I didn't deserve this; I didn't deserve any success. I kept it as a thing I would do on the side; no one would know the joy that I had finally discovered through theatre and film.

I soon found myself in another codependent relationship with Veronica, whom I met through a friend. She had been in a physically abusive relationship before she met me. She had a sweet little three-year-old son. She was a heavy drinker, but she was against drugs and wouldn't touch them. It was the first time I was in a relationship with a woman who had a child. I spent a lot of time with the little man playing 'Thomas the Tank Engine' and building train tracks with him. Veronica and I would drink a lot together; sometimes when she drank, we'd have a great time, other times she'd take to hitting me, yelling abusive words and waiting for me to cheat and hit her. Her ex-boyfriend beat her up a few times and cheated on her with her best friend. She was not very stable; she was unsure of who she was and what she wanted in life, telling me that she wanted more kids but only with her ex. We battled and fought a lot on that issue until I eventually gave up. I cared for Veronica and at the time I really tried to make it work. She was living with her parents for support, although she didn't really get on very well with them.

Veronica won a cruise around the Great Barrier Reef in a raffle; she had never been on a trip before and was very excited. She took me with her. I was really looking forward to it as I had never been up to the reef. We spent two nights in Port Douglas and three nights cruising the Whitsundays on a little ship with close to one hundred people aboard. It was an amazing time cruising the Barrier Reef and some of the surrounding islands, snorkeling and diving. It was unlike anything I had ever seen; the size of the reef, the colors, the fish and sea life was out of this world. We swam with rays, giant turtles and reef sharks. For lunch we would get dropped off at different islands for seafood feasts, BBQ's and free time to relax and explore the island.

It was hard dating someone with a child because I fell in love with, and cared for, the child more than I did my partner. He was an innocent, sweet little boy; he didn't know what his mummy had gone through and, because of the horrors I went through, I would subconsciously look out for him and make sure he was always safe. Veronica was always in contact with her ex about their son, as they would share custody doing week on/week off. She told me that, although she hated him, she still wanted that second child. I slowly noticed her drifting away and, one night out, I saw them together and I knew that we were over. She eventually fell pregnant with their second child; it was what she always wanted. For the first time being in a relationship with a woman, I was upset that I had been dumped and it hit me hard.

I kept pushing my shit further down inside of myself, burying it, not wanting to face all that was boiling beneath my façade. I had the gym, my friends, the occasional acting class, however, the place I felt most comfortable was the same hideaway I went to since I was eight years old; home alone, lost in my own world, watching movies and listening to music. I listened to old school U2, Depeche Mode, The Cure as well as a lot of techno and dance music. I loved epic movies like Braveheart, Gladiator, and Saving Private Ryan. I would get lost in these movies, pretending I was one of the characters. Other movies I enjoyed were The Untouchables, Reservoir Dogs, Casino, Goodfellas, and many foreign films. I loved watching all types of documentaries, especially about animals and war. My favorite place in the world to visit is the War Memorial in Canberra, the most powerful, beautiful and sacred building I have ever been in. I would take myself there, and just walk through it alone for hours, studying all the wars (especially the First and Second World Wars) and check out all the artifacts. Reading about the soldiers, the evil that was Hitler and the Nazis, the POW camps, the Holocaust and the battles, inspired me more than anything else to better my life because of what the soldiers and the victims went through. It was their bravery and courage, knowing that they might die while running into gun fire, that kept drawing me in. To me, they were the bravest men and women in the world and I wished that I had an ounce of their strength and courage, to face my past, but more than even that; to face my life.

One movie I was fascinated with was 'Requiem for a Dream.' I felt as though I was Jared Leto's character. I was living in that world, maybe

170

not as extreme, but I was heading down that path. I understood his character well. Like him, I struggled to find a way out, I surrendered to the seductive cravings that pulled me back in, and *in I went*, ever more deeply.

The next few years my desperation grew, my deep need for validation was out of control and I continued the downward spiral into sex and drug addiction. I am not writing about it to glorify this lifestyle. Rather I am writing about it to describe my continuous fall into darkness. I did these things to survive; to somehow feel validated. I hurt people through my vain attempts at self-understanding and my ever-failing search for love. I did what I wanted, when I wanted, I was a nasty person, a real arsehole and I hurt those who got in my way. Looking back, I can see that I did these things because I was grieving my lost childhood and was feeling fucked off that I had my life taken away from me.

Odd Bods was full of middle aged, married, divorced and single women. I was flirting with all of them and most of them were taking my classes; some also doing personal training with me. I was good at what I did and I took advantage of that. I started having affairs with two of the women, separately. I'm sure they didn't know I was sleeping with the other. I would visit one woman at her house during the day while the other would visit me at home. Their husbands were never around. I would take ecstasy with one and have sex, then I'd go into work, teach a class and do personal training. I thought I would have so much energy, but it had a counter effect, it wiped all the energy from me and I literally couldn't do anything. Half-way through teaching a class I would have to make up a story that I hurt my back and needed to rest; I would sit on stage, instructing, unable to move. I was reckless; the drugs and alcohol were my life force, and I relied on them to make it through some of the days and weeks.

I was out at a pub in Queanbeyan with some friends and my two lady friends were out together at the same pub. They were drunk, flirting, and kissing one another in front of everyone. They were trying to get me to dance with them, but I wanted nothing to do with it. The whole pub was watching them and the last thing I needed was to be involved with what was going on. They persisted, but I continually said *"no."* I told them I was leaving, that my car was parked around the corner and for them to come meet me in fifteen minutes if they wanted to. Fifteen minutes later they jumped into my back seat and I started driving out to Canberra where one of them was to meet up with her husband. They were making out and going down on each other in my back seat as I was driving. I pulled the car into the car park of a retirement village, pushed the front seats as far forward as they would go and joined them. When we were through, we composed ourselves, finished our drive to Canberra where the husband and a few of his friends were. We all proceeded to have drinks with them like nothing had happened.

Her husband left early and asked if I could drop his wife at home later that night. I said *"yes"* and we stayed out to drink a little more. It was late, close to four in the morning, when I drove them home, drunk as usual. However, before we arrived at one of their houses, we stopped around the corner, jumped into the back seat and went at it again. I dropped them both off, made it back to my house where I cried myself to sleep because I hated who I was and what I was doing to people. I was without the strength and mental capacity to change who I was. I saw the two women at work the following week and they were cool; no one at the gym suspected anything. I left the gym soon after, I was getting myself into too much trouble.

Chapter 22

I started working at Deakin Health Spa, a premier gym in Canberra. It had a fifty-meter Olympic size swimming pool that was converted into an aerobics room. I was told it was the biggest aerobics room in Australia - we would sometimes get close to one hundred people in a class. I always felt a rush teaching to that many people.

Janice had returned from Japan and was living in Kingston, not too far from Deakin. It was good to have her back in Canberra and close by; she and I were in a good place and were hanging out with each other and our mutual friends. I continued with my personal training and teaching at the new job. I was teaching classes at a few other gyms around town, getting well known in the area for my work, and was contracted to teach a class or two at many different venues as well. I was still very close with Fred; he would either come down to Canberra for a weekend or I would go to Sydney. He was still in love with Janice and, when she moved back to Canberra, he decided to move down to be closer to her. We found an apartment in Kingston together, about a ten-minute walk from where Janice lived. It was convenient for work, a great location and we had a pool, tennis court and gym in the complex, so we were set.

Fred grew up around drugs and had been growing weed since he was a teenager, so we thought it would be a great idea to start dealing in Canberra. We would drive to Sydney together (a little over a three-hour drive), pick up close to five hundred ecstasy pills, an ounce of cocaine and get as high as humanly possible, without crashing on the drive back home. Once home, we'd divide the cocaine, put them into smaller bags, hide them behind walls and light switches and in the air conditioning ducts of our house. Our apartment became quite popular when the word spread. Fred and I thought we were the coolest kids in town, everyone's friends, but for all the wrong reasons. We were foolishly acting like we were living the high life; kings of the kids. There was a problem with what we were doing; we loved the drugs more than anyone else did, so we did a lot of them ourselves, especially cocaine. Most nights at home we would pull some out and do it. I'm sure we were probably some of the worst drug dealers around as we never made any money; I actually lost money. We never had enough money to repay our suppliers on occasion so I was always pulling money to cover our end. Moral of the story... don't be a drug addict and try to sell drugs!

I loved living with Fred, as much as I was self-destructing. He was a great cook, so we would always prepare meals together, have BBQ's, but that always came with some sort of alcohol or drug. One of Fred's best friends from Sydney, Anthony, an amazing singer, came down and lived with us for a few months, sleeping on the couch. He was a large Fijian guy. I trained him every day. We became very close, spending a lot of time together. I would take him to the gym with me to do my classes, we would box together and go to the oval across the road, where I would take him through many different workouts until he threw up or collapsed on me. I worked him hard and, as much as he hated doing the exercises, he appreciated it and saw the changes he was making to his health and life, losing over thirty kilos. I loved the time I spent with him and the deep bond we formed, which is strong to this day.

Depression was always close, in and out of my life. I was mentally, emotionally and physically exhausted; always being 'on' for people, trying to please everyone. It was impossible for me to say the word *"no."* I was over-committing myself to people, breaking promises and brushing friends off to sit at home alone or to go see a girl. I wasn't a good friend to many and definitely let a lot of people down. I was taking up to, and well over, ten ecstasy pills over the span of a weekend, as well as large amounts of cocaine. To my friends, I was the nicest guy; I deferred to their every whim, whether it was the restaurant they wanted to go to, or the bar or the club they wanted to drink and party at. I would just go with the flow, do whatever was needed to make the other person happy. I never fought them on anything.

But when I was in my self-destruct mode, when I hated myself, I was the biggest arsehole to these very same people. I wanted nothing to do with anyone and again, didn't care who I hurt or what I did to them. I was once at a pub, drinking alone, when my friend Ruby invited me to have a drink with her. Her best friend and the best friend's boyfriend were also at the table. I sat opposite the boyfriend and the two girls sat opposite each other. I was immediately attracted to Ruby's best friend and we kept looking at each other. The best friend said she was going to the toilet and I decided to go up to the bar to buy us another round of drinks. We immediately went into the bathroom together where we proceeded to have sex. As soon as we were done, I went back to the bar, bought the round of drinks and went back to the table like nothing happened. These are the things I did. I was getting more desperate, reckless, cared less about my impact on others and was becoming more daring.

On occasion, I would get so fucked up that I would somehow stagger my way into a bathroom somewhere, knowing I was going to be sick, and instead of lifting the toilet seat to throw up, I would sit on the seat and throw up all over myself and the floor around me. I was physically incapable of doing the simple task of lifting up the toilet seat and throwing up into the bowl. Many times, after being kicked out of a bar and unable to walk and think straight, I would pass out in the gutter or an alleyway, being awakened in the morning by a stranger, or by the sun hitting my face, covered in my own vomit. It was a true 'walk of shame' home. I couldn't get much lower. I was incapable of getting any help and I didn't want it either.

I became so hungry for drugs that I would do them anywhere I could. I was out with a friend; we went into the woman's toilets to do some cocaine. We were so desperate and out of our minds that we lifted the toilet seat and decided to use the wet, ceramic bowl from which to snort our coke. She wiped the bowl with toilet paper, thinking it would dry, divided the cocaine into two massive lines, rolled up a note and we did our lines, leaving half the cocaine there because of the dampness on the bowl. I ran my finger over what was left and put it in my mouth, and tasted the dirtiest cocaine I have ever had. I remember sliding down the wall, sitting on the floor, unable to get a hold of my senses. I was getting tonsillitis or a fever often, getting sick regularly as my body was so run down, my immune system was shot and couldn't handle what I was putting into it.

One afternoon as I was leaving the gym, I walked past a girl whose eyes I could not escape. I thought I knew most faces in the gym but hers was one I had never seen before. I quickly turned back around and chased after her to introduce myself. She was sexy as hell and resembled Olivia from Belgium. She had red hair, freckles and walked to the beat of her own drum. She didn't seem to care about what anyone thought of her. Her name was Claire and her mother and brother were business partners and owned the gym, but Claire rarely went there to work out. We exchanged numbers and got together soon after, hit it off and started dating. I soon met her mother and brother and became friendly with them. We would hang out a lot at her place; she lived in Deakin with some friends, close to the gym. I would often stay with her and go straight into work when I had an early class or client the next morning. She introduced me to R&B, rap and bands such as Portishead and Radiohead. She owned her sexiness; she had so much confidence about her and was without ego. She was the coolest, and the most chill girl I had ever met. She loved drinking cider, watching cricket, hanging at home, having BBQ's and watching movies. I had never met anyone like her.

Christmas had passed. I spent it with my family. It was nice to be with them all but it was rather uneventful. Fred was up in Sydney with his family and we had planned a big New Year's Eve party at our place. Janice and Fred were hanging out a lot; but she wasn't interested in him in a romantic way. Lots of family and friends attended. We had a projector playing from our balcony, shining movies onto the building wall in front of us. There was a DJ, Anthony sang a few songs too. Fred talked Janice into doing ecstasy for the first time and didn't that turn out to be a bad idea. She took half a pill and as soon as it started to kick in, she became paranoid and spent the rest of the night in the bedroom scared she was going to die. Fred spent the night taking care of her. Throughout the night we must have had close to one hundred people come through the door.

Our lease was up, so we found a two-story house in Deakin with a huge yard; a five-minute walk from the gym and local shops. There was a spare bedroom and a friend from the gym named Denae was looking for a room to rent, so she moved in with us. She had no idea of what Fred and I were doing and was not a part of the drug and party scene. She offered exactly what I needed; stability and structure. Fred and I were still dealing drugs; we all lived upstairs and used the downstairs rooms and the inner walls to hide the drugs. Denae and I got on extremely well; we would hang at home together when I wasn't with Claire, watching movies and talking all night. She didn't like Fred at all and they would argue sometimes (I think he may have been very sleazy towards her one night and tried to pick her up). The only good thing I had in my life at this time was Claire, she was everything to me, although I had no idea how to express that to her. I was incapable. As much as I was spending time with her, I was still spending more time alone and away from everyone.

It was my twenty sixth birthday, and I had a joint party with one of Janice's best friends named Melanie. It was at a bar in Civic, and I didn't want to be there, I didn't want to see anyone. A few hours before the party I sat on the roof of my house, hiding from the world, wanting to jump and end it all. Severe depression, my one true and constant companion through time, was back, yet again, rearing its ugly head. I eventually stumbled my way into the party, already heavily intoxicated. The place was packed with my family, gym friends, my best friends, and Melanie's family and friends. I shot into the party like a cannonball; I was all over the place and I spent half the night alone in the corner, crying, unable to talk to anyone. I continued to drink and to do more drugs as that was my solution for everything. Everyone sang happy birthday to us, then it was speech time; Melanie got up and made a beautiful speech and I followed with mine. Janice recently reminded me that I actually started my speech by saying *"I tried to kill myself today."* The rest of the speech was obviously a blur and people weren't really sure how to take what I had just said. Everyone knew I was fucked up, and some may have thought I was joking or looking for attention. I don't remember anything else from that night.

Chapter 23

About six months after moving in, Denae moved out. She found it too difficult living with Fred; they weren't getting along at all and she couldn't live in an environment like that. Soon after, I fell into the biggest hole I'd **ever** been in. I quit everything and moved back home with mum and dad. I had to get away from everyone in my life at that time, as well as the drugs, alcohol, sex and violence. I had hit rock bottom, was in a severe depression and was thinking often of suicide. I could not stop crying, sat home all day, unable to talk to anyone. My family, whom I was now starting to realize actually did care for, and love me, was scared and concerned. Mum and Janice continually asked if I was ok, what was wrong and what they could do for me. Peter was worried too, and as tough as he was on the football field, he was very sensitive, with a really big heart. Dad showed love in other ways, putting his hand on my shoulder, or sitting next to me in silence. No matter what anyone did or asked, I would just answer with *"Everything is fine,"* or *"You wouldn't understand."* I would otherwise say *"I don't know what is wrong", "Leave me alone"* and *"Don't worry about me."*

In all this time sitting at home, the Man never came into my mind. I had buried him deep inside my psyche; *he is a part of my past,* I told myself; I convinced myself that I had forgotten him. I was losing weight, always in bed sleeping or watching movies. The only person I really spoke to and saw outside of my family during this time was Claire, she was a constant and important part of my life.

When I finally did leave the house, it was to visit my cousin Marissa. Having just returned from her honeymoon, she and her husband had

179

moved into their new home and invited us all over to celebrate. I didn't want to go, but mum said it would be good for me to get out for a bit; that it would be relaxing to be with the family. It took me forever to get ready. I was thinking of every excuse not to go, but there was no way I could have gotten out of it. Mum, dad and Karl left early, leaving Peter and me at home waiting for Janice to pick us up. On the car ride there, I sat in the front passenger seat and Peter was in the back. I couldn't look at them, and stared straight out the side window as I could not stop crying. I didn't know what I was crying about, I just couldn't stop. I think Janice and Peter were hoping I would open up to them a little more without mum and dad around. They asked me *"what is wrong, has something happened to you? Are you ok?"* All I could reply back to them was, *"Don't worry, you wouldn't understand."* These few words seemed to be my answer for every question that came my way. We finally arrived at Marissa's house and I managed to compose myself enough to look like everything was fine. I walked in and was greeted by Marissa, who was in the kitchen preparing some food with her mother. Literally everyone was there, my grandparents, aunties, uncles and all my cousins; there were over twenty people, and I discovered that this was exactly what I did not need.

The first thing Marissa asked me was; *"are you ok?"* As soon as she asked, I started crying again, told her *"everything is fine,"* and went to the bathroom to clean myself up. I sat in the house for a few minutes to relax. Marissa said,*" if you need to, you can speak to my husband as he suffers from depression from time to time."* I finally went out back, said *"hello"* to everyone, kissed my grandparents and sat to the side, away from the happy crowd sitting around the garden table. Everyone did say *"hello,"* but they were a little hesitant to ask any questions and acted like everything was fine. I could feel everyone's eyes staring at me, silently judging, questioning and watching me as I sat there searching for privacy. I couldn't stand it any longer so I got up and played with Karl and my little cousins; they were all between ten and fourteen years old. We kicked a soccer ball around for a bit but as soon as I stopped or thought about things, I would become emotional again.

Lunch was served; an indulgent feast ranging from BBQ to lasagna to an array of sumptuous salads. I continued to sit to the side, away from everyone and ate alone. I could feel everyone's eyes on me once again, so I retreated to the house and sat in front of the TV. Mum came in and asked *"Do you need anything?"* I told her *"I just want to sit inside,"* and she let me be. Shortly thereafter, Janice came in and sat with me and, as soon as she did, I welled up with tears again. I didn't know how to stop them; I had gotten to the point where I simply had no control. The family let me be; they didn't know how to handle me or what more to say. I come from a close, but sheltered, family where my mum, her sister and her brother still live under the rule of my grandfather. Anything he says, goes; no matter how old his children are. Depression never *happens* in my family; toxic masculinity and mental illness are things we don't talk about, even though we've had cases of mental illness and suicide in our extended family.

Janice did some research and found a therapist for me to talk to. I couldn't live like this anymore, I needed something to change in my life. I walked into her office, not really knowing what to expect. After seeing many movies and shows where therapy took place, I expected to see a long leather couch with a therapist sitting opposite me; and that was exactly what I got. There was a box of tissues sitting on a coffee table between us. I had been crying all week and promised myself that I wouldn't cry in there, but as soon as she asked me the first question, I burst into tears. I literally cried through the entire session. However, I still couldn't open up; I still didn't know how, I wasn't ready for it. I couldn't answer her questions, I couldn't really talk to her, I told her the bare minimum and what I thought she wanted to hear. I didn't know what was wrong with me, I couldn't explain it or wrap my head around any of it. I definitely wasn't ready to talk about anything from my past. I did open up to her about the drinking and drugs, but not about the sex with men or the violence towards them. I didn't trust her enough. I didn't trust anyone and definitely didn't know how to communicate with true emotion. For a large part of the time, we just sat there in silence. I did recognize the room as a safe space and this lady as a safe person. I had three therapy sessions with her and don't really remember anything that was said, what I discovered or what I took away from the experience. I did, however, walk away thinking that I was *all better* and ready to move on with my life.

I knew I needed a break from personal training and took a few weeks off from teaching classes. I needed to work, to get out of the house, to get my mind off my dark state of being. Dad got me a job working with one of his best mates, David, a very successful Concreter and dad was the best man at his wedding. I spent close to a year working with David and his band of merry men, and I feel that it saved my life at that time. David had a team of four men, including himself. Mike was a wise older guy, a successful concreter in his own right, however, he also had some big life lessons and was now working for David. Justin, a man in his mid-thirties, liked to stir trouble amongst the group for fun. Stuart, who had been concreting for years and started working with us after I'd been there for about six months; he was my age, a skinny guy who was living just up the road from me. Working as a concreter got me into a healthy routine, into bed by ten or eleven o'clock at the latest, and up at five the next morning. I would drive to David's house, then together we drove to the job site in his truck, ready to pour concrete by six thirty. I started working with the boys during winter, so it was definitely cold outside in the early mornings. One good thing about Canberra though is that through the winter months, as cold as it is in the morning, by mid-morning the sun is usually out without a cloud in the sky. As much as I hated those early mornings, I also loved them because my day was usually done by three PM. I was in charge of doing all the shit jobs they didn't want to do, like washing and cleaning tools, shoveling concrete and dirt, digging trenches and getting the footings and mesh ready for the next day's pour. Mainly, I was just taking orders from the boys.

I loved my new job; it was hard work, which I enjoyed and it got me fit and strong in a different way than the gym. It took me away from the old life, away from who I was and what I was becoming. What I loved most was hanging, interacting and talking with the boys. They were real and easy; no ego about them whatsoever. I was fortunately gifted with the nickname *"Hollywood"*. The boys would buy their girlie magazines and we would flick through them, not for the centerfolds, but for the home girls on the back pages. I was spending most of my time on site with Mike; he saw that I was a fit boy and the first thing he told me was *"your muscles mean nothing here boy and are no good on this work site, it's what's on the inside that matters."* He put me straight, gave me tough love, told me about his life and how he used to be married with a son who, at that time, would have been in his late teens. He told me how he had his own successful concreting company, lost it all and some big life lessons came out of that. He had since found his way and now lives a very simple, real, connected and uncomplicated life which was now all about quality over quantity. He didn't care for bullshit, the ego and noise. He chose to live in a simple house on a beautiful property in Bungendore, a little country town twenty-minutes from Queanbeyan.

We would talk on the job site for hours almost every day and he would tell me about the evils of ego and about the illusions of life; how people live in a bubble. He schooled me in ways that I'd never been educated before; spoke to me like I'd never been spoken to before. We also talked about love and what was real and what was fake. I would hang with him outside of work, too; go to his property and help him cut firewood or clear his land. I loved the manual labor; the hard work and working up a sweat. It kept me out of trouble, out of my head and on the 'straight and narrow'. He was dating a woman, Mary, and she was on the same spiritual path as he was. She lived by the same values that he did and she reminded me that love was indeed a possibility in my life.

Mike followed a lot of the Native American traditions and introduced me to the world of Sweat Lodges and Smoking Ceremonies. Sweat lodges took place in a dome shaped hut, mostly made by natural materials and covered with blankets. It was called a *'purification ceremony'* or a *'sweat.'* A sweat is intended as a spiritual ceremony, it is for prayer and healing, to purify the mind, body and soul and to promote healthy connected living. It can only be authentically led by people who have been taught and initiated into the prayer, ritual, language, songs and traditions in the right ways. Mike had been practicing this ritual for years and was thus a leader in the community. There were usually ten to twenty people participating in the sweat and, once inside, Mike would lead us in chanting, prayer, drumming and silence. In the middle of the hut sat basalt stones that had been sitting in fire for hours becoming super-heated. Once taken out of the fire and put into the hut, the stones were doused or splashed with water and medicinal herbs, the steam from the stones would enter our bodies and drive out the waters holding trapped emotions within, as well as the memories that inflicted pain. The hut would get close to 50 degrees Celsius, or 120 degrees Fahrenheit and, as the title suggested, we literally sweat buckets. The 'sweat' could last anywhere up to an hour and I would sit in there for the duration, with rounds taking up to ten minutes with a few minutes break in between, where the tent door would open for some fresh air and sometimes a sip of (prayer) water.

It is strongly encouraged to sit upright to be able to meet your prayers with integrity and honour, but one can also lie down if it becomes too intense. As much as the heat was getting to me, it was more my own self-doubt, my thoughts and heaviness weighing on me that posed a greater challenge. I would question what I was doing there and what I was doing with my life. However, coming out of it created a lightness, a cleansing of sorts, and layers of doubt washed away with the sweat. After my first sweat, I told Mike that it was the most intense thing I have ever done.

Mike would offer community cleansing smoke (smudging) ceremonies every Friday in a yoga studio in Canberra, another purging and awakening of the mind, body and soul. This was also intended for removal of impurities, and it connected us back to the earth. He would get a great group in attendance, sometimes upwards of thirty souls all sitting in a circle. He would burn tobacco, cedar, sage and sweet grass in a shell with a smudge stick and wave the smoke around the room. Then we would follow in suit, start from the head and move around the body in a circular motion down to the feet. We would do this using an eagle's feather to clear away evil spirits and impurities that might be in, or attached to, the body and room. This was combined with singing, chanting and prayers. The ceremony would go on for an hour and once this was done, some of us would go to the Chinese Restaurant next door for a great feed and to talk about what we just experienced.

Mike was a charismatic and handsome man with a deep, sexy voice who was always full of jokes and old Italian songs, and he would entertain us on the work site as well. I was happy going to work back then. I looked forward to seeing the boys, spending time with them, talking nonsense, having a laugh, watching them argue about literally every single thing. It did me a world of good and I was starting to feel much better. Though I wasn't ready to return to therapy, I was indeed benefiting from this therapeutic environment. I have to say, at the time, all of this saved my life. But as much as it pulled me out of my darkness, I still wasn't in any way prepared to face the abuse from my past head on; nor was I ready to appreciate the depth to which the abuse was ruling my current life. At this stage, I still didn't want to know anything about it.

Chapter 24

I had hurt many people along the way and I needed to make amends. I called about seven or eight women whom I had cheated on, lied to, or with whom I acted poorly. I took complete ownership of my wrongdoings and my past, told them how sorry I was for what I did to them and asked for forgiveness. I told them that I hoped we could one day be friends again and, if not, I completely understood and would never hold it against them. One of them said *"go fuck yourself and never reach out again."* I totally understood where she was coming from and accepted her decision; while all of the others said that it took a lot of courage to call, and they each accepted my apology. Some said they forgave me, others said that they needed time or couldn't forgive. I remained friends with a few of them, the rest I have never spoken to again. I needed to do this for myself. I needed to be vulnerable and honest in order to move forward in my recovery. My intentions, and remorse were real and heartfelt. I also needed to do this for the women, to give each of them an explanation and to offer each of them closure. I just hoped that I would be able to keep on living in this new way, committed to evolving with greater awareness for myself and those around me.

A few months into working as a concreter I was asked to go back to teaching my fitness classes. I wasn't missing the teaching so much as it was the actual fitness that I longed for. I went back to the gym and was starting to see more of Claire. I would take a change of clothing and go straight from concreting, normally covered in dust and mud, shower at her house and stay with her for the night. Her brother owned a few video and DVD stores, and she would bring home a different movie every night. I was trying to spend as much time with Claire as I could. However, just as I did in every other relationship with a woman, I began to build that wall, brick by brick, and push her away. I still found myself unable to commit, unable to let someone in. I knew I was going to hurt her, even though I had discovered a lot about myself and had cleaned my act up a bit. The more I liked someone, the harder and faster I pushed them away. I couldn't stop myself.

In some ways Claire was much smarter than me; my unrelenting pattern of withholding communication was something she saw through pretty early on, and she called me out on my bullshit. Not wanting to put up with it, she pushed me away and broke up with me before I did her. I decided it was (again) time for me to get out of Canberra; I had done enough damage to people that I loved there. I had a craving to live in Sydney ever since I was a kid and went on that trip with my grandfather. The time was right; as much as concreting saved me, I knew it wasn't something I would do forever. I will forever be grateful to David for taking me on, and to Mike for showing me the way to live a healthier and more spiritual life. To this day, he is still a mentor and someone that I hold dear to my heart. I was trying to implement everything he taught me, but I still wasn't ready to put those lessons into action. I had a few friends in Sydney, friends that had moved up there from Canberra, so I figured I'd begin my sojourn with them.

Before moving, I went up for a few days to find a place to live. I stayed on Alan's couch. Alan was now the ex-boyfriend of Paul from the Attorney-General's Department. Alan was an older gentleman, paralyzed from the waist down from a car accident he and Paul had been in years earlier. He had a full-time caretaker, someone who helped him get in and out of bed, dressed him and prepared him for the day ahead. The caretaker was moving out in two weeks and Alan asked if I'd like to move in and help him out. I said *"yes."* Alan lived on Victoria Street in Potts Point, one street over from Kings Cross; in the middle tower of three brown buildings half way down the street. He lived on the ground floor, and had converted two small apartments into one bigger one that was wheelchair accessible. It was a beautiful space with a balcony that overlooked Sydney Harbour and the Bridge, the botanical gardens and the city skyline. I was going to continue personal training, so whilst there I went to Bayswater Gym in Kings Cross and asked for a job. It was a boutique gym with a predominantly gay member base; about five minutes' walk from Alan's house. I went there, flirted with the management and staff and asked for a job. They said *"yes"* and to let them know when I'd be back. I drove back to Canberra, collected my belongings, said my goodbyes, and was off to Sydney.

It was a necessary change; Canberra was a bad place for me at the time. It was too easy to get what I wanted and needed (drugs and sex). I knew too many dangerous people, hurt too many loved ones and burned too many bridges. Sydney presented me with a new start. I had become a little closer to my family and best friends; but, for the sake of our relationships, I felt I needed separation from them. As much as they all knew me, they didn't really know me at all, and it was exhausting trying to be someone that I wasn't. They were truly amazing and supportive; I just didn't see it at the time, and I didn't know how to handle their love.

I moved to Sydney about a month before Christmas. The weather was beautiful and I was settling into life in the big city. Living with Alan was great; he and I got on well and I was happy to support him where needed. I was up early most mornings, around six, to help him up and into the shower. He had a nurse that came three times per week to change his bandages and clean his wounds and dressings. He was unable to move from the waist down and, since he lived in his wheelchair and bed, he was prone to bed sores and infections. His muscles were atrophied from the waist down. Once he was dressed and back in his wheelchair, he was good to go for the rest of the day, until bedtime. Some nights he would have the strength to get into bed on his own; other nights I would help him. I would put the pads down first in case he wet himself, sit him on the bed, take his clothes off and settle him in. He didn't have control over his bladder, but would go to the toilet at the same time every day, like clockwork, so there was rarely a problem. He would wear his 'old man nappies', as I would call them, and he was generally fine. We worked around each other's schedule.

I started work at Bayswater Gym about one week after moving up to Sydney, and quickly immersed myself back into the gym culture. I picked up clients quickly, taught two boxing classes per week, and relieved some of the other trainers who had an overload of clients. Most of the trainers at the gym were straight, good looking, and fit. We all knew what to say and how to flirt, and we all did well. I quickly started dating a female trainer that was working there, a few years older than I was, from New Zealand. That didn't last very long, which was probably for the best, after everything I had been through in Canberra, it was probably a good idea that I stayed single and focused on myself for a while.

2006 was upon us and, for New Year's, Alan had a party in the apartment overlooking the city and the harbour. I invited a few friends from the gym and we watched the celebrations and fireworks from the balcony. It was a funny feeling, the firework display was amazing, as was the atmosphere, but inside I still felt so alone and empty. I had new friends, was living in a dynamic city and doing what I enjoyed, but the feelings I always had deep inside **never** escaped me. I still wanted to be alone and away from everyone. Thus, I immersed myself more into my work. I was busy every day, getting up before sunrise working with clients most mornings and evenings. My first session began at six either at the gym, or I would drive to Bondi Beach or Coogee Beach to train private clients. These sessions were my favorite;

it was great training outside early in the morning, then going for a morning swim before the rest of the day began. Sometimes I would work out two to three hours a day, lifting weights, doing cardio or teaching a class. Since I was Les Mills qualified, I started teaching classes at Fitness First Gyms around the city and leading outdoor sessions with groups of twenty people.

My other favorite outdoor session was at Observatory Hill Park, right near the entrance onto the Sydney Harbour Bridge. We would train in the park and sometimes run across the bridge. Sydney really is one the most beautiful cities with a spectacular Harbour. Once my morning sessions were done, I would normally go home, have a second breakfast or snack, and make sure Alan was fine. I'd then take 'Nathan', the dog, named after me, for a walk. We would normally walk to the end of our street, down to Embarkation Park, which also had amazing views of the city and harbour. I'd let him off his leash and he'd run around. It was always a little embarrassing when I would meet someone in the park who would stop to pet him, introduce themselves and ask my name and the dog's name. I would introduce myself as Nathan, and I would tell them the dog's name is Nathan as well. They would always give a look of confusion and concern. I would then explain that I moved in with someone who already named their dog Nathan, and that it was a mere coincidence. I would never tell them that they named the dog after me years ago when we first met.

Some days I would finish work in the afternoon at around five o'clock, and other nights I would work through to about eight o'clock. I loved going home in the evening, sliding open the retractable glass doors leading onto the balcony overlooking the city, cooking dinner, breathing in the beautiful Sydney air, listening to the sounds of the thousands of fruit bats from the Botanical Gardens flying overhead. I was socializing with the other trainers and some of the members that worked out at Bayswater; it had a real family and community feeling.

We would drink like fish and the drugs would always appear at some point in the night. My problem was that if someone put alcohol, or a drug, in front of me, I couldn't say no. This invariably led to more alcohol, drugs, sex, violence, and mood swings in my personality, and more bouts of depression.

Sometimes, after I would put Alan to bed, I would go for a walk to the park, sit on a bench and look out onto the harbour and the city, contemplating life and what it was all about. I always had the same conversation with myself;

> *What the fuck am I doing with my life?...Where do I want to be*
> *physically and mentally?... What is going to make me happy?... Am I*
> *ever going to meet someone right for me?*

I would go for walks through Kings Cross, which wasn't a good idea because I would sometimes wander into one of the many strip clubs on the avenue. I became friendly with one or two of the strippers and would go backstage and hang with them, do cocaine and on the odd occasion, have sex with one of them who I became friendly with. On my walk to and from home, there was always a junkie sitting on a side street or in an alleyway shooting up heroin. I always wondered what that felt like, but I promised myself I would never do it.

One thing I tried to do every day (as it helped me to get out of my depressive slumps) was to run down to the Andrew (Boy) Charlton pool. This is probably my favorite pool to swim in anywhere in the world, along with the pool at Bondi Icebergs. It was about a ten-minute run from my place, through Woolloomooloo and the Royal Botanic Gardens. There I would find the beautiful, outdoor, fifty-meter salt water swimming pool on the shore of Woolloomooloo Bay in The Domain of the Royal Botanic Gardens. It's where I learnt to swim well. Usually twice per week, I would drive to Coogee Beach, run around the headlands to the South Coogee Stairs, a steep set of two hundred and ten stairs. I would run them four times, never missing a step; then follow it up by missing every second step, and repeat. Once I was done, I would run to my car, take off my shoes, grab a towel and run two laps on the beach and finish the workout with a jump in the crystal-clear blue ocean. These were the things that were starting to bring me so much life, energy and happiness.

I loved running in the middle of the day; the hotter it was, the better it was. It felt like a punishment but it also felt like a reward; working out in the scorching Australian sun wasn't easy. One afternoon, after I finished my stairs and beach session, I was having a shower at the outdoor showers on the beach and a gentleman was looking at me, a fit guy, a few years older than me. He came over to the shower and was waiting for me to get out; I just thought he was wanting to use the shower. When done, he came over to me telling me I had a very fit body. He asked if I was gay and I told him that I wasn't. He then offered me three hundred dollars to go back to his house, stand in front of him so that he can masturbate and get off; he told me he didn't want to touch me, he just wanted to look at me. I did think about it for a few seconds; I needed the money, believed there would be no touching and with where my head was at, I decided to go with him. I followed him back to his apartment, parked under his building and we rode the elevator up to his place together. I didn't know a thing about this man, he could have killed me for all I knew. Looking back on moments like these, I was living and moving with whatever was presented in the moment. I didn't even care.

He lived on Bourke Street in Surry Hills, in a beautiful apartment high up with gorgeous views of the city and the harbour. Once in the apartment, I just stood to the side, like the eight-year-old boy who was trained to wait for his orders. He was actually a nice guy and quite respectful. I asked him how we were doing this; he told me to take off

193

my clothes, gave me a pair of his speedos to wear, and asked that I lean over the couch with my arse in his face. He went into his bedroom and got out a bottle of poppers, the chemical term being 'Amyl Nitrate'. Poppers are in liquid form; sold in a small bottle that you inhale by placing it up to your nostril and taking a deep breath in. Poppers give you a relaxation effect, mostly affecting the throat, anus and vagina, and are used to increase blood flow and relax the sphincter muscles. It is widely used in the gay community during sex and in the rave scene. When you inhale the drug, it typically gives you a high and a rush that lasts for a minute or two. He got naked and began to masturbate, looking at me from behind and, on occasion, would ask me to turn around so he could see the front of me. After he came, he cleaned himself up, asked me if I'd like to have a shower and was very respectful of my needs. As I was leaving, he asked if I'd like to do it again the following week. I thought to myself, *he's a nice guy with needs, and I could help him meet those needs and make money at the same time.* It was between he and I; no one was ever going to know. We exchanged numbers and I left. This went on for the whole time that I was in Sydney, once per week, sometimes twice.

Over time we got to know each other quite well; he told me about his life, that he had a partner who was away for work a lot. I told him a little about myself; we did what we did, which evolved a little from the first time we met. He would offer me lunch or a snack, sometimes have a meal together, or make us both a protein shake; he was also into his fitness. We never met out in public for a drink, it was always just at his house. He was a good guy, there were never any feelings or intimacy involved. To me it was just a transaction; he got what he needed and I got what I needed, which was money and a dirty sexual encounter, which was a feeling I craved back when I was a kid. It was a feeling I wasn't sure would ever go away.

Chapter 25

Alan had a mean streak to him; he was sometimes angry and bitter with the world, and he lost his temper quite easily on poor, unsuspecting strangers. It was understandable considering his situation; he was watching himself slowly deteriorate, becoming ever more aware of his mortality. He would periodically get gangrene on his ankles and feet. This brought on very bad infections, so having to change his bandages and clean his wounds would make me dry retch. The emanating puss, a green-like liquid, would drip off of his skin and fill the air with the scent of rotting flesh. He would spend months at a time in hospital, having operations, and on heavy medication to clear the infections and the gangrene. The doctors recommended amputation of the legs from the knees down, but he told me that this would make him feel like he had lost the battle and his injuries won out. On occasion, I would take Nathan to the hospital to comfort him. He would meet us outside when he was allowed out of bed. Eventually, after I moved out, he did get his legs amputated; it was either that or his life.

When not helping Alan, and not at the gym, I spent most of my time in Sydney alone. Days were filled by going to the beach, working out, and falling in and out of my depression. I had put an end to any romance or friendships that came my way for the most part. I was at a low point one night and I went out with a few of the trainers and a group of the gym members. I remember being pretty fucked up, having taken cocaine and ecstasy, dancing on my own. We were at one of the many gay clubs around the Oxford Street/Darlinghurst area of the city. One of the members from the gym came up and started dancing with me; we started making out. This was the first time I ever kissed another man. I remember feeling the stubble from his beard on his face and that freaked me out. I pushed him off of me, not wanting anything to do with him. I was turned on by the kiss, but also angered by it. He came back at me and kissed me again and this time I didn't push him off. As soon as the kiss was over, I looked around to make certain that no one saw us.

The good thing about living in Potts Point was that it was always a short walk home from the bars and clubs. The guy I kissed lived just around the corner, a two-minute walk away on Darlinghurst Road in Kings Cross in a beautiful pre-war building. He had gutted and refurbished his apartment; it was a beautiful space. We walked home together with one or two others who lived in the area, parted ways and, thirty seconds later he called me asking if I wanted to come over for a drink. I knew the situation and what he wanted and, as much as I didn't want to go, I needed to. It had been a long time since I last had sex with a man. I went over, had that drink, and had sex. I must have passed out straight after, because I woke up a few hours later not knowing where I was and who I was with. Once I got my bearings, I dressed and snuck out of there as soon as I could. I was at peace with what had happened; I kissed and had sex with a guy and, for the first time, I didn't want to hit him, I didn't hate him and there was no self-loathing. I walked out of there and didn't really feel anything. Maybe I wanted to have sex with this guy to see if I actually liked it; to see if that was me, who I really was and what I preferred. It didn't make me happy, nor did it clear up any feelings I was having that maybe I was gay. It didn't make me think, *Oh, this is what I want or who I am.* I felt the same, nothing had changed or shifted within me, it wasn't a light bulb moment. I got home, showered, and made myself something to eat.

Later in the day, the self-loathing, hatred and sabotage kicked in. I was angry, confused, and now I wanted to be violent; to do something stupid, find one of the junkies on the street shooting up and take a hit.

I went for a long walk to calm myself, reached out to a woman I was seeing, asked if she wanted to come over for dinner and to stay the night. She did; we had a bottle of wine; cooked some seafood on the BBQ and retreated to the bedroom. This time, however, it felt different. I wanted to see her, but I also wanted to prove to myself that women were what I wanted and who I liked. I felt bad because I knew I was using her; she was an object for me to ascertain how I really felt about women. I knew right from wrong, and I cared for her a lot, but my mind was confused and my self-loathing ruled my actions. I learned that sex with women was just as empty as sex with men. However, I realised that I had sex with women because I *wanted* to, not because I *needed* to, like with guys. I was creating a pattern of searching for love through sex. I did see the guy again at the gym and we acted as if nothing had ever happened. He had had a boyfriend who was out of town so the last thing he wanted was for his boyfriend to find out. My search would continue.

Denae introduced me to one of her best friends, Kelly, who moved up to Sydney for work from Canberra and was a senior editor for a magazine. We befriended one another and became close; she was one of the boys and we enjoyed each other's company. She got me a job teaching a spin, boxing and 'Les Mills Body Pump' classes at the boutique gym in her building. The gym catered to all staff that came under the publishing house umbrella; they printed a few different magazines. It was a great place to work, there was a beautiful indoor pool in the building and I would swim laps after every class, followed by a dip in the ice pool. I'd try to stay in there as long as I could, then would sit in the hot tub for a while to relax. Kelly was invited up to the Gold Coast by a new phone carrier to attend a surf competition; they were the major sponsor for the competition and they wanted Kelly to write a piece about them in the magazine. She had a spare ticket and invited me. I hadn't been to the Gold Coast for almost twenty years; the last time I went was for the World Expo in 1988 with my family.

We went, had a great time, everything was paid for and we got to go to a cool surfing competition while hanging out on the Gold Coast for a weekend. She wanted to sleep with me but I kept on pulling away in the nicest way possible as I was on holiday with her and wasn't really interested in her in that way. We did end up sleeping together, which made things a little uncomfortable on my part, but eventually had the talk and agreed that we should just be friends. I was trying to grow up and be responsible. Normally I would sleep with a woman and worry about the consequences later. The whole time she totally felt the same as me, that we should just be friends.

One of the members at Bayswater gym was an actor who was previously on 'Home and Away' for a few years. I told him I had done a little acting in Canberra and wanted to pursue more. He introduced me to his old acting coach, Anne; a beautiful, little old lady from Newtown, a suburb of Sydney. She was about five foot and the most honest person I'd ever met; she had a mouth like a drunken sailor, used every swear word known to man, and told you straight to your face how she felt about you or the situation. She definitely made me laugh, but also scared the hell out of me. I started meeting with her twice weekly; she was as much a second mother and therapist as she was an acting coach. She seemed to know instinctively about my past and what I had gone through. She never directly said it, but she was amazingly intuitive and knew how I was feeling before I even did. We would talk about life; my family and my plans for the future. Anne gave me specific books to read. She was big on Shakespeare's sonnets, requiring me to read three per week, write about them in my own words and draw a picture that best represented the sonnet in my eyes. We worked on monologues and scenes, we also went to the cinema and theatre together. I enjoyed doing these things with her, she was becoming a very influential person in my overall development and an important part of my life.

Over the months my relationship with Anne flourished. I wasn't as afraid of her anymore and looked up to her as someone I could deeply trust and rely on for advice and direction. Sometimes after a lesson we would walk her dog through the beautiful, old cemetery across the road. I was taken by the ornate beauty of the old gravestones, but was even more amazed at the rows of Moreton Bay Fig Trees that lined the cemetery paths. I marveled at their imposing and elaborate root systems forcing their way into the sacred grounds. We would do laps of the cemetery with her dog and it was here that she told me I should go to the USA to pursue acting. I had already been playing with this idea in my head for a few months before she mentioned it to me. Anne told me about HB Studio in New York as she had sent a few of her other students there.

"I believe you have the talent to make a go of this and really do this as a career, but I feel that you have a few obstacles in your way that you need to clear first."

She really did know me better than I knew myself.

I thought about it for a few days and was in agreement with the idea. I always had a fascination with New York, having heard stories about it being the biggest city and the center of the world, as well as having seen it in so many iconic movies and TV shows. I loved Sydney, but I wasn't settled, I felt lost there. I always had a voice in my head telling me that there was something bigger out there for me and, since I had nothing keeping me in Sydney or Australia, I decided to take this chance. I returned to Canberra for a weekend to tell the family of my plan. They were a little worried about my moving to the States on my own after everything I had recently been through. They also knew that they couldn't stop me and told me that as long as I was happy, they were happy for me.

Alan was feeling better, out of hospital and back home. I told him my intention to move to New York. He completely lost his cool, screaming and yelling, before kicking me out. He accused me of owing him thousands of dollars in rent and for the use of his car. I didn't know if he saw me as taking advantage of him, or was bitter that I was moving onto the next chapter of my life, leaving him behind and, in his eyes, abandoning him. He even had a lawyer draft a letter with an itemized account of what I owed him. I was worried that this would hinder my ability to leave Australia. He said that he was going to sue me and take me to court if I didn't give him the money. I spoke to my family, they told me to give him the money, they didn't want me to get into trouble and lose my opportunity to go to the US. I already had my visa and only had a certain amount of time to enter the US before my visa expired. I contacted a lawyer (to learn about my options) and decided to call his bluff. I packed my things, loaded the car and drove away.

I needed to be in Sydney for at least another week as I had work commitments, so I stayed with Kelly for two nights and spent the next five days living out of my car. I showered at the gym, parked my car in a safe place to sleep, bought and stole food and drink when I needed it. Depression and self-loathing, my unbidden companions through time, reared their ugly heads, and for the first time in years, I bought some crack and smoked it. It helped me to relax, to forget all about my problems, put me in a state of euphoria and helped me to sleep. I was having conflicting thoughts about going overseas, leaving everything I had in Australia (not that I really had much). At the same time, I was excited for a new life where absolutely no one knew me. I could start over and be me, not that I had any idea of who 'me' even was. It was the same thing I was chasing when I moved from Canberra to Sydney.

I drove back to Canberra; my car filled with everything I owned. There wasn't much, just some clothes, boxing gloves and pads, a medicine ball, plus a case of expensive wine that I stole from Alan as a parting gift. I spent two weeks in Canberra preparing for my move to New York. It was nice to be home to see family and friends; I didn't have the same resentments, anger or trust issues towards them that I had growing up. I was, however, still rather closed off from them, not sharing too much, only the necessary details about Sydney and what happened with Alan. Anne contacted one of her former students and asked if I could stay on their couch for a week until I found somewhere to live. They said yes, as they were in the same position as me at one point in time. I spent a little more time with Claire before leaving, my feelings for her hadn't changed, even after moving away to Sydney. I just couldn't open up and give her what she needed and deserved. I knew that I had already hurt her, was continuing to do so and would have done so again in the future. She didn't deserve that; she deserved the world. None of the women from my past deserved to be treated the way I had treated them.

As I got closer to my departure date, I had many mixed emotions in my head. I was excited to start this new chapter, a new adventure in my life, but I was nervous as well. I smashed my crack pipe in Sydney before leaving, thinking I was going to New York to be clean, healthy, drug-free and away from the loveless, dirty sex. I said my final goodbyes to Janice, Peter and Karl. I'm sure Janice and Peter were thinking, *"What the fuck is he doing?... Why is he moving away now?... He is not happy or in a good place in his life"* Karl and I had become closer, even with the eleven-year age gap; he was very much a 'mini me' and would come hang with me in Sydney whenever he could. He loved a good party, drinking and was starting to experiment with recreational drugs. He had turned eighteen earlier in the year so he was finally 'legal' to go out. On several occasions I had told him not to be like me; that I was a mess and definitely not a good role model for him. He was excited for me to be moving and was even more excited to come and visit.

Chapter 26

Sunday, August 26th, 2007, a day and date that I will never forget; the day I left Australia. I was all over the place that day, mentally and emotionally. Mum and Dad dropped me off at the airport; it wasn't an emotional goodbye for me, though quite a difficult goodbye for them. I knew I was going to miss them; I did love them and wanted them to be proud of me, but the separation was what I needed. I flew from Canberra to Sydney early that morning where I had a two-hour stop. I remember sitting at the gate waiting for my connecting flight, looking out the window at the planes, the runways and the Sydney skyline in the distance. I started to cry, I was both very excited and very scared, then… 'Jekyll and Hyde' kicked in;

What the fuck are you doing with your life?... Are you even doing the right thing?... You are such a loser... You fucking hate yourself... You can't do this!

Then the flip would come;

*Yes, you can!... You are going to be a success and do something special in this world... There is a reason why you are here on this earth and not dead after everything that's happened... You **are** going to prove everyone wrong with your success.*

I continued to soothe myself with the belief that moving to New York would bring me closer to finding out the answers to all of my questions.

I boarded the plane for Los Angeles in that emotional and mental state; I took my seat and prepared myself for take-off. Once in the air, I was fine. I watched movie after movie after movie, tried unsuccessfully to get some much-needed sleep, and thought about the whole of my past throughout that fifteen-hour flight. I landed in L.A. close to six o'clock Sunday morning, the same day as I left Sydney but five hours behind my Australian departure time. I finally made it to New York at four-thirty that same afternoon, thinking to myself; *Now what? Where do I go?*

I got on a bus heading to Grand Central Station, stared out the window like a big kid, and thought to myself, *holy fuck! I'm in New York, the greatest city in the world, the center of it all!* As the bus made its way past Cypress Hill Cemetery, I marveled at the length and breadth of its sacred ground. It seemed to extend on forever; it was huge and beautiful. The New York City skyline came into view and immediately brought tears to my eyes, its imposing towers and steeples calling out to me. My eyes located the Empire State Building, the Chrysler Building, as well as many other iconic monuments that I'd only ever seen in movies from my youth. We finally arrived at the Grand Central Terminal and, with a breath of pride and wonder, I told myself, *I am finally here, I made it to Manhattan.* I got off the bus, inhaled the New York City air, the hustle, the heat and the grittiness of it all. I loved it; it was the end of summer and the weather was inviting and beautiful.

My destination was One Hundred and Fifty-Fifth Street in Washington Heights on the Upper West Side. I walked into the Grand Hyatt Hotel right next to Grand Central Station and asked the concierge for directions. He told me that I could either take the subway or I could jump in a cab. I had my suitcase and another big bag in tow, and, since I had absolutely no idea how the subway worked, I hailed my first New York City cab. I was on my way. Driving through the streets, I was mesmerized by all of the people, the traffic, the staggering buildings, the ordinary yet stimulating life going on around me. I had to pinch myself to make sure that I wasn't dreaming. After a good forty-five-minute cab ride I finally got to One-Fifty-Fifth Street, found my building, rang the buzzer for the apartment and was welcomed inside by an Irish lad who was also living there. The contact that Anne had put me in touch with was out for the night. Soon after letting me in, the Irish lad also left. I was finally able to sit, take a deep breath and relax; I was exhausted. I got comfortable on the couch, my bed for the next week, and watched some television.

I woke up early the next day; the combination of jet lag and excitement preempted my ability to sleep-in late. I went for an early morning walk around the neighborhood, which was populated predominantly with African American and Hispanic people. It was all very surreal and exciting, New York all around me. I went back to the apartment and met Anne's former student and his girlfriend, both Australians now living in New York. It felt comforting to be with a few Aussies; they explained how the subways worked, which stops to get off for HB Studio, the classes to register for, and the general rules about the city.

I did as was directed and I jumped on the subway, sat there cautiously, making sure I didn't miss my stop. I managed to make it down to the West Village on the 'A' train, got off at Fourteenth Street and Eighth Avenue, found my way to Bank Street and the Studio. HB is named after Herbert Berghof, a Viennese actor/director who started the acting Studio in 1945. It is one of the original New York acting studios. In 1948, Uta Hagen, an iconic American actress joined the Studio as Herbert's artistic partner and authored the bestselling acting text, 'The Respect for Acting,' which is the same text I used as a student of the Studio. Some past students of the Studio include Robert DeNiro, Gene Wilder, Faye Dunaway, Jack Lemmon, Harvey Keitel, Jeff Bridges, Whoopi Goldberg, Geraldine Page, Matthew Broderick and Stockard Channing.

As I climbed the long flight of stairs that led me to the main office, I could feel the presence of the thousands of well-trained actors who ascended these steps years before me. I filled out my forms and registered for classes such as; Acting Technique, Scene Study, Script Analysis, Movement, Alexander Technique, Voice and Speech. I posted on the notice board that I was looking for a room to rent. I had my first meal at the Bus Stop Cafe (a quaint little diner around the corner from the Studio) and wandered through the streets of the West Village to get familiar with the area. I set up a bank account, got myself a US phone number and began to feel like I could make this place my home. From the first moment I got off of that bus at Grand Central I felt at peace with my decision. I felt like I belonged. I felt an ease and was already in my groove. It wasn't too busy for me or too crazy and I already had a real love for the place.

While walking over to the Studio the following day, I met an older gentleman and his best female friend (both actors), who introduced themselves to me. I told them I had just arrived from Australia; was doing a two-year full-time course and the friend told me that she, too, was interested in taking classes at the Studio. They asked if I'd been up to Times Square or if I'd seen any of the sights of New York, to which I responded that I hadn't. They offered to spend the afternoon with me and we walked around the village and then up to the Flatiron Building and the Empire State Building. We had a bite to eat and waited for the sun to go down before walking over to Times Square. I was in awe. I had never seen anything like it; the action, the billboards, the people, the craziness. The streets down there were ablaze with light and life, and I was starting to understand why New York is called 'the city that never sleeps.' We walked around Times Square long enough for us to feel annoyed at the myriad tourists with their heads tilted up, oblivious to where they were going, sometimes stopping abruptly without concern for the others behind them, just so they could take a photo. My new friends invited me to see the Broadway Musical 'Hair' in Central Park with them and another friend in a few weeks. I was pumped!

The following day, I received an email from Carol, a teacher from the Studio (whose Acting Technique and Scene Study Class I had enrolled in), stating that she had a room for me to rent at her house. That weekend I went to Carol's house to look at the room. It was in Weehawken, New Jersey, just through the Lincoln Tunnel, on the other side of the Hudson River. I took the subway to Forty-Second Street/Port Authority and from there caught a bus and got off at the first stop. The house was a two-minute walk away. On my walk, I met Sam, a Canadian girl who would later change my life forever. Her mother was an acting teacher in Canada and friends with Carol. Sam was staying with Carol for a month until she found a place of her own. She had actually enrolled in the same full-time acting courses as me. She was on her way into the city but directed me to the charming little two-story house around the corner.

As charming as Carol's house was from the outside, the inside was even more so. Carol was a beautiful, generous lady who had been teaching at HB Studio since 1968 and had taught all over the world. She was an integral part of countless theatre productions and wrote the book 'Acting and Living in Discovery: A Workbook for the Actor.' She showed me the room, which was actually an entire floor of the house. She lived upstairs; I'd be downstairs, and we would share the kitchen. My room and bathroom had the character and feel of a little old lady, it was the room where Carol's mother lived before passing away; but it was good enough for me. The rent was cheaper than rent in Manhattan, it was quiet and it seemed like it could keep me out of trouble. Carol and I agreed upon a month-to-month lease, allowing for either or both of us to change our plans if needed. Perhaps the best part of the arrangement was that every Thursday through to Monday, Carol would be away at her country house where her painter husband worked and lived, so on weekends I'd have the entire place to myself. I moved in the following week.

One of my first memories of New York was one of the first times I went to a gym in the city. I hadn't worked out for a while and was feeling somewhat sluggish. As the Studio was in the West Village, I went to 'Equinox' on Greenwich Avenue. I would always try to sneak in because it cost a fortune, and I was normally successful. I had a good workout, showered and was dressing in the locker room. I looked up and saw someone with huge breasts walk past me. I panicked, thinking I was in the women's change room by mistake. I took a second look and realized they were transgender with a towel around their breasts and their penis exposed. We smiled at each other and I was thinking, *only in New York.* It was one of the coolest and craziest things I had ever seen; people in this city were able to express themselves freely; to be who they really wanted to be without bias and discrimination.

School started the following week. I was a little nervous as I hadn't been in a classroom for over ten years. There was a good mix of people in class; international students and Americans all representing a wide range of ages. I knew two people already; my new friend Sam and one of Anne's students from Australia. The international students were from Argentina, Peru, England, Canada, Brazil, Israel, Italy, China, and, of course, Australia. Carol's Acting Technique class started with easy exercises that gradually progressed into more complicated ones. In Scene Study class, we were all assigned a partner with whom we met outside of class to rehearse. Speech class was my favorite to begin with as it was filled primarily with international students who were learning to speak with an American accent. This always provided me with a good laugh.

It was time to see 'Hair' in Central Park. I met my new friends early afternoon and waited in line with them for several hours until the seats were all assigned. I met Neil (a friend of theirs who was also invited), a very successful gentleman, who owned one the biggest PR Firms in the country, and later became a manager for several 'A-list' celebrities. Neil and I clicked straight away and spent the hours in line huddled in great conversation. We forged a very strong friendship; he became a mentor to me and we spoke on a weekly basis. He was a genuine, caring man who had my best interest at heart and wanted to see me succeed. We managed to get into the theatre and had great seats in front of the stage. It was a beautiful, quintessential New York night; I was watching a free Broadway Show in Central Park with this amazing city surrounding me and feeling good about life. Afterwards, Neil took us to the iconic restaurant, 'The Russian Tea Room' for dinner.

One of my personal training clients (back in Australia) introduced me to some friends living in New York, so I reached out and met up with one of them. She was an Aussie girl, the same age as me and worked as a manager at the W Hotel in Union Square. I met with her and a group of her friends, some from New York and a few very wealthy people who were in town from Scottsdale, Arizona. We were a mix of Aussies and Americans and we had a great night out for dinner and drinks. They invited me up to Toronto a few days later to go to the Toronto Film Festival. One thing I was realizing was that I could use my charm and looks to my advantage, and one of the guys from Scottsdale offered to pay for me. I was good at flirting, even better at making them feel special and touching them in the right way. I took full advantage of it at the time, not truly caring who I hurt in the process.

I was flown up to Toronto on the following Friday and I stayed through to Monday. I met up with a group of ten people who had already been there for several days. Toronto was a cool city, definitely a lot of fun during the film festival. I saw a few films, went to many parties, great restaurants and bars, and visited the beautiful wineries and tasted many glasses of amazing wine. It was a great time; I met some amazing people on that trip and was grateful to my new friends for inviting me. Living with Carol in Weehawken was going well; on days I was in her class, we would travel into the city together. On the way home we would go grocery shopping together; she was thoughtful that way and we had a respectful and understanding relationship. She liked her alone time at night, so this became a time for me to explore the neighborhoods nearby. One bus stop away from me was Hoboken; a great little town full of bars and restaurants. On nice afternoons I would run there and workout in a local gym. On most nights, I would hear the sounds of heavy bass and the beat of music, only to discover that our backyard was adjacent to the back of a strip club. The owners were nice to me and always welcomed me into the club and took care of me, as they knew I lived behind the place. I tried to get a job behind the bar there, but once they discovered I was only on a student visa, they refused me. One morning as I was leaving for school, I came upon a stripper passed out in our front yard. I leaned down and shook her to make sure she was breathing and, after waking in an angry stupor, she asked if I could drive her home. Then, as if she didn't remember what she was saying, she walked off and headed back in the direction of the club.

It was time for me to get a job. I definitely didn't have enough money to sustain me for the duration of my two-year program. Anne had suggested that I get in contact with one of her old students, Harry, who had been in NY for years and given up on his acting dream to open two Australian restaurants, 'The Sunburnt Cow' in the East Village and 'Bondi Road' on the Lower East Side. I rang Harry and he pretty much offered me a job on the spot because of his love and respect for Anne. As I only had a student visa, he agreed to pay me cash under the table. My first shift was a Saturday brunch, one of the two busiest shifts of the week. In New York restaurants, it is customary to do four training shifts to learn the ins and outs of the restaurant. I, however, was thrown into the deep end; the best way to learn. I walked into the Sunburnt Cow, on Avenue C and Ninth Street, and besides being a busy Saturday Brunch shift, it was also the semifinal of the 2007 Rugby World Cup between Australia and England. The place was crazy. The TV behind the bar was playing the game and there were two projectors to the side of the bar and another in the back room of the restaurant. That was the day I met what was to become my new dysfunctional New York family for the next few years.

Our group consisted of Kristen, Tom, Zane, Chris, Kate and our fearless leader Amy. Everyone working there was either Aussie or from New Zealand. We all got along well, looked out for one another, loved to party and took full advantage of our time together in this weird and wonderful city. I was working as a server and learned the menu on the run. The Cow had one of the busiest and booziest brunches in New York, fifteen dollars for your meal and all you can drink. Drink choices were Mimosas, Bloody Mary's, Screwdrivers, Greyhounds or Beer. Patrons would get absolutely hammered and we would have to get the tables up as soon as they finished their meal to allow the next group in. It was a chaotic atmosphere and we had too much fun, but we made it work. I flirted my way through many mistakes during those early days at work, and I got away with all of them. We weren't paid an hourly wage; we worked solely for tips, so we all learned to flirt with customers quite well. We pooled our tips together and divided them up equally amongst the group. As Aussies in New York, we could literally say and do almost anything we wanted and get away with it; Americans thought we all were care-free, fun and sexy. The restaurant was always filled with young guys and girls in their twenties looking to hook up with an Aussie. They loved us, thought we had the sexiest accent and were exotic because we came from so far away. I tried to tell them how wrong they were, but to no avail.

I was working out at the gym one day when a man came over and offered me a job as a dancer at Splash Bar on Seventeenth Street in Chelsea. It was a gay bar where guys would dance on the bar or on stage in just a pair of tiny shorts or speedos and have the patrons tip in cash. As this was happening in the front room, all kinds of debauchery went on in the back rooms or any dark corner. I spoke to one of the dancers there, asking what it was like, he warned;

"You can make great money, but guys will put their hands all over you when they are tipping... Be prepared to be propositioned by a lot of the men all throughout the night... I have been offered up to one thousand dollars to receive oral sex from a customer."

I stayed and watched what went on for an hour before deciding that I would give it a go. I wanted to make money and thought I would be able to handle having guys put their hands all over me. I went back a few days later for a trial run since management needed to check if I was a 'good fit'. I was nervous when I got up on the stage, danced for about thirty minutes, and was offered the job. I promised myself that I'd do it for one night then make an actual decision, but after my first shift I quit. I was being triggered as memories came flooding back from my time at the Cruise Lounge in Fyshwick. Guys were aggressively grabbing at me when they tipped, shoving their money into my pants and groping me without any consent. Men offered me money for oral and for sex. Thoughts of violence and self-sabotage were starting to re-enter my mind and I was ready to hit someone. I knew that this job would only lead to darker days, filled with relapse and trouble. Half-way through the shift I went out back to get changed; I saw one of the other dancers receiving oral sex from a patron and I knew I needed to get out of there. I apologized to management, telling them that it wasn't for me. I left and never went back.

School was going well, I was making great friends, enjoying my classes and learning a lot; not just on the acting side of things, but also with my breath work and body. One of my favorite classes was Dance; my teacher Michael would give us a contemporary dance routine and we would learn it over the course of a few weeks and then perform it for class. I was actually pretty good at it and had great rapport with Michael; he was always pushing me to go harder and further than what my body would allow. I was doing Kundalini Yoga (which powerfully combines movement, breath and prayer) and the 'Alexander Technique' which concentrates on movement and posture. These were great classes for me to get in touch with my body, to discover where I was blocked and how to release tension, stress, trapped emotions and heaviness. I felt like a kid again in some classes, being told to *"stop talking"* on more than one occasion. I was actually separated from my friends for being a disruption at times. Sam and I had most of our classes together; we were hanging out all the time, during and outside of school. It was not sexual; we just clicked and became best mates. She was only nineteen when we met, and seemed much more mature than that, sometimes even much more mature than me. I would always sneak her into bars and clubs with me. I introduced her to drugs; she would also come to see me at work and I would fill her up with booze and cocaine.

We would normally stay at the Cow drinking to all hours, then venture over to Bondi Road, have a drink or two there, pick up the rest of the crew and go out all night. We would go to clubs like 'Rivington 151' and other dirty, grunge, dive bars in the area until all hours of the morning. I was working at the Cow only on the weekends; I would work on Friday night, do a double shift on Saturday (brunch and dinner service) and either brunch or a double shift on the Sunday as well. The journey back home to Jersey was over an hour and the last bus was at two in the morning. Sometimes I would make it back home but usually

I would stay with one of the guys I worked with or I would go home with a girl I met. It was all becoming too easy.

One night I was on my way home after work and I stopped in at 'Papaya Dog' for a hotdog on the corner of First Avenue and Fourteenth Street. It was late and I needed to rush to make sure I could make it home. As I ordered my hotdog, there was a girl standing next to me and when she heard my accent, she asked where I was from. Upon hearing that I was Australian, she offered to buy my hotdog, then straight out asked me to go home with her. I looked at her in disbelief, telling her that she didn't know me at all and we had only said two words to each other. She didn't care, she said she loved my accent, the fact that I was from Australia and wanted me to go home with her. I needed a place to stay because I was working early the next morning, so I went home with her. That's how it was for me for the first few years in New York. The vicious and seductive cycle was gaining momentum again and I was falling back into my old ways of sex, alcohol and drugs. All three were easy enough to get and I was falling in love with all of them again.

I had school Monday through to Friday and I attended every class. Being an international student, I would have been kicked out of the program and lost my visa if I missed above a certain number of classes. I was going to the theatre and to the movies quite often during the week with friends from school or with Neil every few weeks. After each show, we would talk about what we just saw and break down the characters, the writing, directing, plot, blocking and cinematography. Neil always gave me advice on the industry and how it worked; he taught me a lot. We grew closer over this time and I enjoyed the moments we spent together. There was a lot of mutual respect between us.

Chapter 27

Winter had arrived, I don't think I'd ever been so cold in my life and I wasn't prepared for it. I had to buy a big winter coat, scarf, gloves, beanie, the whole lot. It felt like no matter what I wore, the wind would rip right through me and the chill in the air would saturate my bones, wipe me out and make me miserable. I didn't want to be outside; people would always tell me that I would get used to it. I'm still waiting for that day to come.

I spent my first Christmas in New York with Sam and my friends from the Cow. We went to a house where a few of the staff were living together, had a big family lunch, ate a lot, drank a lot and did a lot of drugs. We then went out to a bar and partied late into the night. On New Year's Eve I worked at the Cow, went out afterward with Zane, met up with Sam at a house party and did ecstasy for the very last time. I haven't touched it since and haven't wanted to.

2008 had arrived and it was my thirtieth birthday. It was on the same day as the Super Bowl between the New York Giants and the New England Patriots and it was an extra special day in New York with the Giants playing. I worked brunch at the Cow, which was as wild as always and extra boozy because of the Super Bowl. I was now getting away with anything I wanted, with whomever I wanted. I also pretty much said whatever, as well. It was great for all of the right and wrong reasons. I was now an obnoxious douchebag with an ego the size of Manhattan. I made out with a few girls just because it was my birthday, drank too much, inhaled too much cocaine and partied like an idiot-rockstar. Sam and a few friends from school came to the restaurant for brunch to help me celebrate. Once brunch was over, we all hung around, people sang happy birthday to me, I cut my cake and we celebrated some more. We watched the first half of the game at the Cow and for the second half we went to the iconic local bar, 7B, on the corner Seventh Street and Avenue B. This was the same bar made famous from the first 'Crocodile Dundee' movie. The bar was full and the Super Bowl was on every TV. The Patriots were winning for most of the game until the fourth quarter, when the Giants delivered a game winning drive. Everyone went nuts and we continued to party deep into the morning.

I was auditioning for student, short and feature films, as well as for theatre, even though it wasn't really allowed whilst being at school. I auditioned for a feature film being shot in St. Petersburg, Florida. It was a low budget, independent film, written and directed by the lead actor. A gritty film about four friends dealing with the hardships of life; they plan and execute a bank robbery and later deal with the consequences. I must have done well in the first audition and the callback because after a few days I got the call saying that I had the role. I was very happy, thinking that this was my big break and the start of something huge for me. Though we weren't shooting for a few months, I was given the script to prepare for the role and I met with the cast for a 'read through' and to get to know everyone. We got along very well and were excited to be going down to Florida for a few weeks to shoot.

Before shooting the film, I went back to Australia to attend my brother's wedding. Peter was marrying Bec, a girl I really liked and thought was great for him. Peter asked me to be the best man; I was surprised and honored. I'd never been part of a bridal party before and it was the last thing I was expecting. I made it home a week before the wedding so I could attend the bachelor party, organized by his best friends. We went up to Sydney for the weekend, which was a wild and crazy time. The theme song for the weekend was 'Killing In The Name' by Rage Against The Machine. (Don't ask me how or why, but it was very fitting with what went on.) There were over ten of us and we traveled in a minibus. There was plenty of alcohol, sex and drugs. Peter had never touched drugs, for which I was really proud of him, considering most of us around him were doing them.

It was nice to be back home for a short while. Everyone was happy, excited and in a good mood with the wedding ahead. I got fitted for my suit and didn't have any other responsibilities that week, besides preparing my best man speech. During the week leading up to the wedding, I fell into a depression, although I didn't let anyone know. A deep heaviness had come over me. I looked at Peter, my sister and what they had both accomplished. They were moving forward with their lives, making major decisions and passing important milestones, and I was running around the world, masking my pain with drugs and alcohol. It didn't help being under the scrutiny of my parents constantly. They were always telling me *"...please come back home, settle down, join the public service, get a secure job, meet a girl and have a family."* There was no malice in it; they said these things out of the deepest love and concern for my well-being. They saw that I wasn't happy; they had witnessed the breakdown I had not too long ago. Mum always said to me *"I'm your mother, I know you best and you can't hide anything from me."* The last part wasn't entirely true, but she did know me best, noticing when I was going through things and calling me out on them, even though she missed the biggest thing that shaped my life forever. Peter was happy and in love, committed to his partner; Janice was finishing her master's degree in education.

*Am I ever going to experience these things?... Am I ever going to meet someone that I could commit to, not cheat on, actually feel love for and be able to let in?... Am I ever going to be **normal**?*

216

It was a joyous week for everyone but it was hard for me to feel any real emotion or connection. I loved my brother and was truly happy for him but I hated everything about the occasion and where I was in relation to him at the time. A few days before the wedding I saw Fred and got fucked up with him; which only drove me further into a dark hole. I left his place, feeling self-hate and desperation. I drove past Fyshwick for the first time in years. I needed *that* validation once again, I needed to act out. I was angry, I felt like the whole world was against me. I was numb, living at the threshold between earth and hell. I felt empty, there was nothing there, inside or out. I was lost and everything that I was doing to move forward, to survive, was pushing me further into darkness. I stood in the corner of the cruise lounge, away from everyone, disconnected from that place, from life itself. A couple of guys approached me and I aggressively pushed them both away. It had been fifteen years since I first walked into a cruise lounge and yet nothing had changed; I was still acting the very same way as I did as a lost fifteen-year-old boy. I finally let a guy go down on me and, as he did, I tucked my head into my arms with shame and disgust. The pain and anguish felt heavier than normal and it was bursting out of me. I couldn't look at him, I couldn't talk to him, there was definitely no emotion and I just wanted to get out of there as quickly as I could. I hated being there but the feeling of still needing it and wanting it was as strong as ever. Even after all of these years, I still hadn't escaped and I was back reenacting the same old vicious patterns.

There was still no attraction towards men or wanting to be with men on an emotional and sensual level; I just needed to feel the same feelings that I did as an eight-year-old and relive the depth of pain that I felt during that time. The pain is what fueled me; it fueled my actions and guided my anger, sabotage and loathing. It's what made me want to act out, to be violent towards guys and, on this occasion, I was violent again. It was becoming easier for me to punish them; this was the last thing these guys ever expected. I pushed him off and hit him with a one-two punch and ran out of there, leaving him bleeding on the floor. I was replaying myself from fifteen years ago; the tape had never changed. I jumped into my car, lost, feeling like I wanted to throw up, hating myself more than ever yet also filled with so much satisfaction at getting off sexually and being violent. I wanted to shake the steering wheel off its brace; to punch a hole in the roof as I railed against my fate. But surprisingly, I drove home in a very calm and somber mood, like nothing happened. I had to keep living in this life, being lost and heavy; crying myself to sleep knowing I was doing wrong, hurting people and hurting myself. No matter how much I grew, I seemed to keep falling backwards as if on an endless loop of self-hatred and despair.

The wedding day had arrived; it was a beautiful but hot day. The wedding was at Bec's family's church and the reception was at Regatta Point on Lake Burley Griffin, a beautiful indoor/outdoor venue, very relaxed and easy, just like Bec wanted. It was a fantastic night, full of laughter and fun. My best man speech was a hit, although it did contain a dirty joke, some curse words and an innuendo that may have made a few religious guests uneasy. I ended up in bed with Janice's friend later that night; the same one I got pregnant seven years earlier. We still had a love for, and an attraction to, one another. The tape in my head was playing on repeat; first the feelings of despair and loneliness, then the sexualizing and the violence against men, then the shame and self-loathing, and finally, the self-soothing through unsatisfying sex with a woman. It was an awkward, dangerous tape I played, and it was becoming all too familiar and unstoppable.

Chapter 28

I was back in New York and it had a comfort and security to it and it was starting to feel like home. I was back at school; classes were going well and I was enjoying my time there. I liked all of my classmates and would hang with them outside of school on occasion. Sam and I were as close as ever, going out and doing everything together. Peter and Bec actually came to the States for their honeymoon; they visited the West Coast and then the East, it was great to show them around New York and have them meet some of my friends. I looked forward to working on the weekends, it took my mind off of school and the sadness that lingered inside of me. I was meeting a lot of girls and sleeping with most of them. Drugs and alcohol were playing an ever-important part of my life; they were sometimes the first thing I did in the morning when I woke, they were constantly with me during my day, and they were starting to play the lead role in my life.

I went to visit my friends in Scottsdale, Arizona for a weekend. I hadn't travelled throughout the States yet and was looking forward to visiting the desert. It was beautiful out there and not too hot. I stayed with my friend who flew me up to Toronto; although I paid for the trip this time. It was a weekend of eating out and partying in my friend's spacious house and at the bars that he owned. We happened upon his friend's bachelorette party, so we jumped in on that with the girls and ended up at a male strip club. I ended up sleeping with one of the ladies from the bachelorette party. A few weeks later she rang to tell me that she was coming to the city for a week, would love to see me and for me to stay with her in her hotel. As the owner of a major corporation with an earning potential in the millions, I told her; *"The only way I will stay with you is if you get the penthouse suite at the Waldorf Astoria."* This was one of New York's most expensive and luxurious hotels. She rang back about thirty minutes later telling me that she booked it. It was an amazing room; austere with antique furniture, gilded wallpaper and paintings that hearkened back to a different era. We had our own private butler who cooked whatever we wanted. She spent her days shopping at high-end department and boutique stores, and came home in the evenings with thousands of dollars' worth of designer handbags, sunglasses, clothing and shoes for herself and her kids. (She was divorced with four children.) She bought me an eight-hundred-dollar cashmere scarf, which I absolutely loved. I thought it was fascinating that someone actually had that kind of money to spend.

I returned to work after that expensive weekend and made the decision to try harder to make money. I had acquired a few new personal training clients through working out at the gym, and they paid cash under the table. I also picked up a client or two from working at the Cow, some of whom I kept for quite a few years. Some clients I trained in gyms, others I would train in the parks around the city. I bought some boxing gloves and pads, dumbbells, skipping rope and a medicine ball. I would do a boxing/circuit workout with them. It was always fun training clients in the parks, weather permitting, which also made it easy to pick up new clients. I was very diligent about working out myself; I would get to the gym most days during the week, before or after class, as I knew I was working all day on the weekends. Every Tuesday night I took a spin class with an instructor I liked; I was very strict on my diet, cooked for myself and made enough healthy food to last me for days. Sometimes I tired of the meals I made, but I knew I wouldn't be eating well on the weekends being at work and drinking the nights away.

We were getting ready to finally shoot the film down in Florida. The director wanted me to shave my head for the film; I was excited for that as I'd never shaved my head before and my hair is my life. Even when I was a little boy, I always had my hair styled with gel and would never let anyone touch it. I decided to shave about two weeks before the shoot, which was scheduled for May. The staff from the Cow were having a big party and we gathered at Kristen's house, she and I had become close and we were seeing each other on occasion. I shaved my head at the party. I wanted to have some fun with it and asked for them to shave the top only, leaving the sides as they were. I wanted it to be like the George Costanza look from the show 'Seinfeld'. Kristen and one of the boys did it; I looked terrible. I had the Costanza look but with a classic comb-over. I kept it like that for the weekend before shaving it off fully. I enjoyed the shaved look; it made my life much easier as I was able to get up and go quickly and easily without spending large amounts of time trying to style it. A few days after shaving it, I learned that the film was to be delayed until after the summer. I was beginning to wonder if we were ever going to shoot.

The summer was upon us; I had completed my first year of school and many of the Northern Hemisphere, International students went home for the break. I stayed in New York, worked at the Cow and enjoyed the summer fun frequenting lots of carnivals and festivals all around the city. I was still meeting and rehearsing with the main cast for the film and getting to know them much better. Throughout all of the craziness going on, I always made exercise, healthy eating, acting, rehearsing and school a priority. I was out most nights; I wasn't a big club guy, I didn't care for the people, bottle service, the egos and attitude that came with it all. I preferred the bars, a speakeasy, or a dark, dirty, dive or grunge bar. It was easier to get away with so much more in these places, and I felt comfortable and at home with the clientele and bar staff. I was going out a lot on my own; from Weehawken I'd walk to and from Hoboken, enjoying the amazing views of the New York City skyline. As much fun as I was having with Sam and my Cow family, I always enjoyed my own company more than anyone else's. On occasion I would go to Williamsburg in Brooklyn, to party with Sam. She and I slept with each other one night and, the morning after, I told her that we should keep it a secret and not tell the others from school, which is what I thought we both wanted. That was the first fracture in our relationship. She didn't talk to me for a week or so after that. We did recover from that time, but I don't think it was ever the same. I loved her dearly and the sex hadn't changed anything for me; but it did for her.

Here I was, in the greatest city, with millions of people and hundreds of bars, yet, I was still the loneliest person in the world. I hated my life more than ever. I was taking drugs, drinking and having sex to pick me up, to make me feel better about myself, to help me forget the unwelcomed memories and thoughts swirling in my head. But as much as my vices got me up for that moment in time, they were also depressants, forcing me to crash in waves of pain and numbness; facilitating acts of violence toward guys, and making me dig an ever-deepening grave for myself. The sex was becoming a chore too and, as soon as I was done, I would feel so distant from the woman I was just with that I couldn't talk to her, I couldn't look at her, or even touch her. Sometimes a woman would notice my distance and ask me what was wrong, or she would ask to be touched and held, but I would recoil and just pat her on the back from a distance. I needed to get out of there more than anything. Internally, I was losing my mind, going crazy trying to figure out what was wrong with me. The sex was clearly an addiction and I couldn't stop it. I wanted it, I needed it and I hated it. It was a mixture of desperately chasing external validation, to prove (to myself) that I wasn't gay, combined with a need to feed my ego knowing that I could have them. I hated myself, I hated the situation, I hated cumming. I would hate myself as soon as I would orgasm, I would spiral into disconnection from myself and the other person. I didn't deserve any pleasure, I wanted to curl up into a ball in the corner and fucking disappear. I was again starting to not care who the women were or about their situation; single, married, or in a relationship. It was again getting dangerous.

After a year of living with Carol, it was time for me to leave. I was grateful for the time that I lived there and for the time we spent together; I learned a lot about life, the craft of acting and the industry itself from her. She also gave me my privacy and trusted me with her home. I never took advantage of that trust; I never took any of my recklessness home with me, but I felt I needed greater independence and privacy. I moved in with Zane from the Cow, along with three other boys; two from Australia and one from the States. I moved into a little room in their massive loft on Murray Street in Tribeca. It was a huge space with four bedrooms on the top floor of what was once a warehouse. It was the ultimate bachelor pad. At night we would go up to the roof top and hit golf balls into the city, the most amazing golf course. Looking back, it was stupid, dangerous and irresponsible. We had a lot of fun in that place, lots of parties with the Cow family; Sam would always hang with us as she was seeing one of the boys for a little while.

I was back at school for the start of my second year. I had enrolled in more advanced level classes; there were a lot of new faces and some old familiar ones. One month into the semester, it was time to shoot the film. I was flown down to Tampa, Florida with another actor in the movie. We were picked up by Eddie, the director, writer and lead actor in the film and we were driven to St. Petersburg in Clearwater, the location of the shoot. We filmed the movie in two weeks, half of the time drunk and high. On one of our 'shoot' days, I filmed a scene alone in a bar. The shoot began early in the morning and, by ten o'clock, I was already drunk. The director kept pouring me alcohol for each 'take' instead of using a non-alcoholic substitute. This movie was one of the first legitimate productions many of us were ever in, so we weren't the most professional cast and crew. (This became obvious by the way the film turned out.) Eddie was facing his own demons; he was also self-destructing, drinking and drugging, and we were encouraged to partake.

It was a reckless and provocative time; two of the best weeks I'd had in America up to that point. The weekends were work-free and the St. Pete beaches were packed with buff men and beautiful women, all drinking and having fun. We were out most nights; I smoked my first and last bucket bong, this is a bong that uses gravity and air pressure to draw the smoke into a large chamber, which then gets expelled quickly into the lungs. It gives a much larger hit, allowing you to get stoned very quickly, with a relatively small amount of weed. Needless to say, I coughed up a lung and got very stoned. Perhaps the best things to come out of it were the friendships I made with several of the actors on set, especially Jordan, Eddie's friend, an amazing woman who had been through a lot herself.

Back in New York, I resumed my studies at the Studio and I took the experience I learnt from the shoot with me, putting it into my work and studies. I wasn't letting what was going on outside of school interfere with my studies, I never missed a class; I gave them my full attention and effort, which was as cathartic and therapeutic as it was educational. I also returned to my job at the Cow. All was the same there; still a shit show; everything was escalating; more drugs, more drinking and more sex. I got to the point where I was blowing cocaine up my arse with my friends. We would use a long straw and pack one end with cocaine, bend over and stick the straw up our arse while someone blew it in from the other side of the straw, providing a more immediate and bigger high. The owner of the Cow let us all get away with a lot of reckless behavior; provided we didn't get caught or jeopardize his business. I eventually got a call from him.

"Nathan, I am so disappointed in you, you are completely taking advantage of my place. You are taking advantage of women, you are taking too many drugs, drinking too much and have slipped up one too many times. Anne would be so disappointed in you. You came to New York to act and you are fucking it all up."

I needed the job; I needed the money and I couldn't work anywhere else because I still didn't have a work visa. I promised him that I would not let him down anymore, or Anne, as she had vouched for me. He himself was an alcoholic who fell off the rails on occasion, often finding himself in a good bar fight. I felt like I was looking at myself in him.

Chapter 29

I wish I had listened and kept the promise I'd made to my boss, but I did not. Soon after making that promise, I met a couple who were about to take me on a journey that had no return. With them, I went as low as I could go, but I also reached the highest of highs; a frightening darkness catalyzed by an experience of pure enlightenment.

The couple invited me back to their house after a wild party; their drug use was, even for me, at a whole new level, and their filthy apartment reflected that. It was just the three of us. The guy took out a pipe and suggested we all smoke some Crack. I felt at ease and comfortable with this situation. He retreated to his bedroom for a minute and returned holding a little tin box and sat down on the couch next to his girlfriend. He pulled out a syringe, a large rubber band, a spoon and heroin. I had never seen anyone do heroin before so I just sat there, quiet and lost in my thoughts. I couldn't move. He tied the rubber band around his girlfriend's arm and she clenched her fist a few times. He placed the heroin on the spoon, cooked it with a lighter; it was a dirty brown color as it pooled on the instrument. I should have realized it was a bad idea just by the color alone. The heroin was then sucked up into the syringe and transported into her hungry vein. I remember staring at the process, mesmerized and unable to speak. Once in the syringe the heroin had changed colour into a rich golden honey. Upon injection, his girlfriend let out an ecstatic, long moan, like she just had the best sex of her life. He released the band; she gave him a kiss and she sunk into the couch partially awake but completely gone, and very content with where she was. He looked over to me with a big smile like he was proud of what he had just accomplished. I sat motionless.

He said two words to me that shook me to the core and I suddenly wanted to disappear into the couch;

"You're up."

My heart skipped a beat then immediately began to race and I started to sweat; this was something I never thought I would do. He threw the rubber band at me; I wrapped it around my left arm and tied it as tight as I could, being left-handed, the veins in this arm were always more protruding than in my right. I didn't speak. I couldn't. I didn't know what I would say even if I had opened my mouth. I made sure he used a new needle; he put less heroin in the syringe than what he had served his girlfriend, knowing it was my first time. He walked over to me. I couldn't take my eyes off the syringe as I pumped my fist in slow motion. It felt like everything was moving in slow motion.

He placed the syringe close to my arm;

"You ready?"

I suddenly flashed back to the day I was confronted by the Man in the change room at the pool. I remembered how he picked me up and turned me around, shoved me against the wall, making sure I wouldn't fight back. I remembered how he pulled my shorts down to around my ankles and he brutally raped me.

Back in the present moment, I looked this stranger straight in the eyes;

"Don't kill me."

He smiled at me, I smiled back, I guess for that second, I was at peace with my decision, and he stuck the needle into my vein. I watched as the heroin was injected into me and I could feel it coursing through my body. I sat there for a few seconds, feeling my eyes fully erupt with life and roll back all at once as I took in a deep breath. I thought it was going to be the last I ever took.

I sat back into the couch, staring up at the ceiling, feeling a warmth come over me. It was like I was headless; I felt my body float and I was in an enlightened state of euphoric ecstasy, as if I had just had the best sex of my life, one hundred times over, in what one can only deem as the ultimate orgasm. I saw and I felt the ocean, I could hear the waves crashing onto the shore. I was finally free, pain free, all kinds of free, and I finally closed my eyes to sleep.

If only I could remember my dreams. The effects lasted a few hours. I woke up in a disorientated state, not really sure where I was, and very lethargic. Once I got myself together, I got out of the apartment as quickly as I could. The other two were passed out in bed. The journey home was a long and arduous one. The subway was a calming experience but also felt like it went on forever. I'm sure I was still feeling the effects of the drug as I was constipated, irritable and depressed for a few days afterwards. However, I was completely seduced by the experience; in all honesty, it felt amazing, I wanted to feel that feeling again and I knew I would.

A new living situation had become available to me. My friend Tom was moving in with his girlfriend, whom I met a few times. Her name was Dani and she was from South Africa, Tom was a New Jersey boy and they were moving to Brooklyn Heights/Dumbo, just off the Manhattan Bridge in Brooklyn. There was a spare bedroom if I wanted it. It was a brand-new apartment, the top level of a renovated three-story building. Tom and I went to check it out, I liked what I saw and we moved in soon after. We had the apartment to ourselves for the first two months as Dani still had two months left on her old lease. It was a nice place and convenient for getting in and out of the city. We were off the High Street stop, the first stop on the A/C Subway line into Brooklyn, and a short walk to supermarkets, restaurants, bars and shops.

Tom and I had an instant connection; he was like a brother to me, we got on amazingly well and we could have almost passed for siblings. He was more gregarious than me; he loved to party, loved to dance and to be the center of attention. He was a bartender and that was his stage. He relished the attention he received whilst behind that bar and, when Dani moved in, we truly were one happy little family. They were in love and perfect for each other. Dani also loved a good party; she, too, loved to dance and to be the center of attention, and whenever the three of us went out, Tom and Dani were the ones getting the party started. She and I were just as close as Tom and I were; we had a connection and understood what it was like to live life outside of America. The three of us would cook together, go grocery shopping together, literally do everything together; what was mine was theirs and vice versa. We had access to the rooftop and we took full advantage of it. In the summer we bought a decent-sized inflatable pool and played around in it on those hot summer days. I would work out up there, skipping rope and lifting weights.

Tom and Dani were always trying to set me up with their single friends; they had no idea of who I really was, they only saw a happy guy on the outside. I had hoped living with them would help me to clean up; they weren't big drinkers and definitely didn't do drugs. I was going out more than ever and digging my own grave even more so than before. I was dating an Aussie stripper, doing cocaine until my nose wouldn't stop bleeding, staying up for three days partying, running nude down the street in the middle of the day for a dare. I can't believe I was never arrested. I was unravelling, all the while believing I had everything under control. At the end of my long nights out, I would end up with a strange girl or at a gay club. I was about to explode, I needed to get off

229

and let loose on a poor unsuspecting stranger. It was always the same pattern; I would hide away, I didn't want to be there, but I couldn't be anywhere else. I always waited for him to come up to me, then I would walk into the bathroom and have him follow me. There was still never any intimacy; no kissing. We did what we did and I would hide from the world with the pain pouring out of me. I needed it, not only for the feeling it gave me, but also because it validated how worthless I felt both inside and out. I was a *nothing* and I deserved failure and everything bad that had happened in my life. I deserved to feel the pain over and over again.

I began to notice that I wasn't getting so turned on anymore; half of the time I wouldn't even get an erection or cum. I would just be there motionless, mentally and physically. I would leave my body, as I did when I was a kid; there wasn't any enjoyment in this type of sexual act anymore, but somehow, I was still addicted to it. Once the guy was done, I would attack. I didn't want to kill him or knock him out; I just needed to hit him a few times, I needed to get my rage out. I was like a wild animal and I had to set the beast free. There were mornings when Tom would wake to discover that I wasn't home, only to find me outside, at the front door, passed out on the floor with a key in hand. My biggest problem was that cocaine was so cheap and readily available, there was no getting away from it, not that I wanted to. Some nights it got to the point that I would have a line or two to calm my thoughts and help me sleep. I could always sleep on it. I recently discovered that it is a sign of ADHD to be able to take cocaine and fall asleep straight away. I don't believe I have ADHD, but I do lose concentration and zone out, with a million things running through my head when I try to listen to others, concentrate or when I'm in the middle of a conversation with someone.

At times during my early years in New York, my bank account was overdrawn and I didn't know where my next meal was going to come from. I never asked my parents for any money, I never wanted them to know where I was financially, emotionally or mentally. My parents usually called me once per week to see how I was; I always told them, and my siblings, that I was doing great, all was well and that I was happy. I was starting to struggle a little in school, falling asleep in class and not applying myself as much as I should have. I was really letting myself down, as well as my fellow students, scene partners and teachers. I also let Anne down in Australia as she pushed me to come to the States and truly believed in me.

My two years at school were coming to an end and it was time to move forward with my life and my career. I was given an Optional Practical Training Visa, (OPT Visa) and a Social Security number that allowed me to work only in the field in which I trained. I was finally able to work legally; even as a bartender, waiter or other job that could support my New York life. School was my security blanket, and for those two years I didn't worry about the real world, so it was a bit of a culture shock to many of us graduates as we weren't prepared for it. We had no ceremony, received no certificate, degree or diploma; only a congratulations, a handshake and a *"Go out and get 'em."*

A week or two after school was done, Sam and I, along with two other classmates, drove up to her family's lake house on Big Rideau Lake, close to Ottawa, Canada. It was a beautiful old house right on the water. We stayed there for a week not doing much at all. We swam, sat around the fire, relaxed, read books and talked about our next career moves. We thought we knew everything about the acting industry and were ready to take on the world. It was also a good way for Sam and I to reconnect. We never lost our friendship, but she had noticed a change in me and was slowly drifting away; she could see me starting to spiral out of control. It was actually really nice to get out of New York, I needed it, as much as I loved the city, it was a tough city especially when I didn't have the money to live there. It weeds out the weak, it can suffocate and eat you up, throwing you out the other end. It was essential for me to get out and recharge my batteries once in a while. New York is the center of the world and as Sinatra sang it best,

"...if I can make it there, I'll make it anywhere."

I saw myself through Sam's worried eyes and I realized that life in New York can sometimes be an illusion; a bubble and culture like none other, filled with fake people, but on the flip side; real, strong and some of the most amazing people I have ever met. People try to live a certain lifestyle, live out of their means, in a way it almost felt like it wasn't real life.

For the next year I stayed working at the Cow, auditioning for everything I could, mostly student and short films, and I got quite a few of them. I was a fucking mess but I always applied myself one hundred percent when it came to auditioning, preparing for a role, and filming. I got a commercial agent and auditioned for a lot of commercials and Australian voice-over roles. A friend put me in touch with the creative director for an ad agency that was shooting an IT commercial; put in a good word for me, and I got the job. I was on set all day, holding a new mobile phone and pretending to have the time of my life. I got paid seven thousand dollars. I was getting into a better financial place and this commercial facilitated my acceptance into the SAG/AFTRA Actors Union.

Six months after getting back from the lake, I was walking through the West Village with Steph, an Australian actress, and another one of Anne's students. Anne put us in touch with each other and we became very close friends. It was always nice to have that Australian connection. I checked my phone, there was an email from USAFIS, the organization I used to apply for my Green Card a few years earlier. There was an attached document stating that I was a winner of the

232

lottery and could apply to move forward with the application phase. The document said that out of the 13.2 million people who had applied that year, I was 1 out of 100,000 that could move on to the next phase. 55,000 of us would eventually receive the Green Card. The reason for this was that there were many interviews to be had, forms that needed to be filled, medicals, security checks and the process was very expensive. This eliminated thousands of people from qualifying and moving forward with the Green Card process. I picked my head up from the email with tears in my eyes; I was not accustomed to winning or receiving good news. Those who were less lucky had to resort to other ways to attain a Green Card, like finding another way into the country or getting married. I had friends who paid US Citizens to marry them for their Green Card, and I was asked by three international friends if they could marry me so that they could get theirs. I didn't think it was worth it as I was still in the process of applying for my Green Card and didn't want to do anything to jeopardize my chances of winning it.

The year 2010 was the biggest of my life in so many ways. I got fired from the Cow. I was out of control and causing too many problems for the business. I was told the reason I got fired was because I was sleeping with too many patrons, taking too many drugs and drinking too much. Looking back, getting fired was one of the best things to ever happen to me; I don't know where I would be today if I had continued working there.
I had seen my heroin injecting friends about five times over the course of the year; the feelings I got from injecting heroin were always better than the time before. I guess I was a lot more relaxed going into it each time, I knew what to expect, I could be totally free and let myself go on the journey and completely immerse myself into the experience. They invited me to a party with a group of their friends; I went to the address provided in Tribeca, and made sure my friends were already there before I arrived. The address read Penthouse Apartment, so I

wasn't sure I was going to the right place. I was buzzed up and found myself in a luxurious home with views looking out onto the city. The place belonged to a Wall Street financier who liked the finer things in life, (but also the not so finer things.) He was with a friend of his, and two beautiful women by their sides. The men were older, your typical Wall Street douche bags, loud, obnoxious and very pretentious, and I was told the women were hired escorts. The women barely spoke to them and they definitely showed them no affection. Alcohol and cocaine were being passed around. I stood to the side, staying pretty silent through the night. There was a lot of talk about their love for drugs, and it appeared as if they were all experienced in taking them.

Quickly I learned that this was a party for everyone to shoot up; the host's friend was first to give it a go, followed by his lady. The host and his date were next, followed by my friend's girlfriend. It was interesting watching everyone's reactions; they all had those few heightened seconds of ecstasy, before falling into a zone that took them under. I only trusted my friend to inject me, I never did it myself. I should have run out of there and never looked back, but the need for it, the desire for the pain to go away, was so much stronger than my will. As it entered my veins, that familiar warmth came over me, the ecstasy and euphoria grew larger than the time before. The experience was more vivid; stranger and crazier. I had never experienced a better feeling at letting go of absolutely everything and finally being free. Everything I was going through in life was gone; the trauma and thoughts, the anguish, the hatred, the triggers and the sadness. For those few seconds in time, I wasn't on earth; I was somewhere else, in a completely suspended state and not of this miserable world. The effects normally lasted up to five hours.

I woke to a slap in the face, I didn't know where I was or how much time had passed. The host was out of control, losing his mind; he was having a bad come down, screaming at and punching me in the face.

234

He was accusing me of stealing money and drugs from him. I was in a post-haze stupor, but I knew that I had to get out of the apartment as fast as I could, assuring him that I had not taken anything, emptying my pockets for him. I escaped out of there and never saw any of them again.

Chapter 30

My birthday was upon me; I was turning thirty-three. I had a joint party with Tom's oldest friend at a French/Brazilian restaurant called 'Felix' in Soho. Again, it was the night of the Super Bowl so it was an even bigger party than expected. I hadn't been spending much time with Sam over the past few months. She definitely noticed the changes in me and made herself scarce. I invited her to my party, along with some old friends from the Cow, but I wasn't certain any of them would show. I was fucked up and in my own world so I really didn't notice or care who came to be honest. Two or three of the friends I had worked with at the Cow came past and stayed for about five minutes; Sam came with a few of the girls we both knew from school. They stayed for about an hour, we sang happy birthday and they left. Before leaving, Sam came over to me;

> *"...I am done with you. I can't be your friend anymore as you are no good for me, for my development and growth as a person and an artist... You have changed and I don't recognize nor do I like the person you have become... I'm moving back to Toronto, I'm done with New York and I need to be close to my family."*

She was cold, to the point and she left. It hit me for a few moments, but I pushed it away and carried on like nothing had happened. Tom and Dani left shortly thereafter, and I found myself alone on my own birthday, as I had on many nights before, to no fault of anyone but me. Self-hatred flooded in; I left and walked the streets alone, thinking to myself how much I had lost and how much of a loser I actually was. I really wanted to let the pain, anger and pity flood over and consume me so that I could justify my next move. I was again close to hitting my lowest point, my rock bottom. However, there was always a newer, lower point, and there was only one thing that could get me through it.

I wandered into a familiar gay club. As usual, I followed my pattern; I kept to myself, stood in the corner so I couldn't be recognized, or even seen. A young, short guy came over to me, trying to engage me in conversation; I ignored him. I decided to go to the bar to get a drink. I knew the bartender; it was a guy I met in acting school; a lovely guy. He asked me what I was doing there. I told him I was there looking for a friend. I went back to my corner and the same, short guy came up to me again. I finally spoke to him, giving him very simple and curt answers. He asked if I wanted to fool around; I didn't answer and walked off. He followed me. I wandered downstairs, which was empty; everyone was upstairs and outside at the rooftop bar. I went into the toilet, he followed me in and locked the door behind him. He tried to kiss me and I moved my face away. As always, it was not real intimacy that I was after. He pulled down my jeans and gave me oral; I tucked my head into my arms but, after some time, I had the courage to pick my head up and look into the mirror. Looking at myself, I was unrecognizable. I saw hatred in the reflected face in the mirror. I saw deep pain in my eyes. I came. I pushed him off of me and quickly pulled my pants up.

As the guy attempted to get up, I lost control. I grabbed him by the neck and shoved him up against a wall and said to him;

"Who the fuck do you think you are?"

He said nothing. Scared and trying to break free. I then said;

"Does anyone know you're here?"

237

These two sentences were the exact words that the Man would say to me as a child.

I remember seeing this poor guy slightly wet his pants with a look that I knew all too well. It was a face that only a victim of trauma, abuse and violence could identify; a face filled with the dread and the horror that I used to feel. I let him go and he punched me trying to get away. I wanted blood; I was out to kill and I didn't care what happened to me or to my victim.

This was it; I was done with my life; I had officially given up. I kicked him in the stomach and punched him. The poor guy fell to the floor and curled up into a ball. This image, that split-second flashback, hit me harder than anything I had seen or done in the past twenty-five years of my life. I saw myself. I saw myself in him; my eight-year-old self on the floor, curled up in the shower the very first time the Man raped me. I went white; feeling I had seen a ghost. I was going to faint. I looked at myself in the mirror; but it wasn't me. I saw the Man; I had now become the very monster who had hurt me, killed me, all those years ago. I was turning into him. However, I never once in my life had a thought of hurting another child. The violence, the lies, the manipulation toward others, this was the Man living in and through me and it was now who I was becoming.

I stepped back, hit the door behind me and started crying. I slid down the door to the floor and was at the same level as this poor guy curled up on the floor. The rage and anger, the hatred and the self-loathing had all disappeared. Guilt, sorrow and empathy took over; engulfed me. I looked at my hands; they were shaking. I sat there, looking at this guy cowering for his life right next to me and thinking;

What have I done?

I kept saying;

"Sorry. I'm so sorry. Sorry. Sorry. I'm so sorry. Sorry."

These words breathed new life into me. I knew I had to change. I was done. The vicious cycle was ending. This was the beginning of the end. The dismantling of the 'Jekyll and Hyde' inside of me.

I kept repeating these words. It was the first time I had **ever** thought about and expressed them. The guy tried to stand up, but I quickly got up before he could. He recoiled and protected himself again, thinking I was going to attack once more.

I pleaded;

"Please forgive me, I don't want to hurt you anymore. I'm so sorry, please forgive me. I'm so sorry... please."

I repeated these words again and again.

I unlocked the bathroom door, and walked out of there. As I left, I made sure that no one was waiting outside the bathroom or had heard what had gone on. There were a few people around but they were doing their own thing and were oblivious. I headed for the exit and walked out of the club as fast as I could. As soon as I was outside, I ran for my life. I ran from the club, I ran from my past, I ran from the Man who had taken root and was growing inside of me. I ran two blocks over to the subway, waited for what felt like a lifetime for the train to arrive, entered it, and sat down. I couldn't get this guy and what I had done out of my head. It was different this time. This time I knew I had done wrong, I felt it. I had to change my ways. I looked down at my hands; they were shaking, red and bruised. I put them into my pockets and held my face down. I remember just staring at the floor, not looking at

239

anyone and not wanting anyone to look at me. I reached my stop, exited the subway, and took the long walk home.
I had finally done it; I couldn't go any lower. I dug my grave and I was now ready to lie in it. *"Take me away and never bring me back,"* I pleaded. I made it home, ascended the steps to the apartment and decided to climb the fire ladder. I opened the hatch and went out onto the roof. The partial, but impressive, view of the New York City skyline mocked me as its bright lights lit the cold night air. I sat up there for hours contemplating my life. I went to the edge of the roof, thought about jumping; I wanted to do it so much. I'm not sure if I was suicidal or not but I didn't want to live anymore, I was in an unstoppable loop of violence, drugs, sex and depression, and I couldn't get out. Life and karma had finally caught up with me. I stood there, swaying from side to side, trying to stand still. The weather was freezing, my body was cold, I was empty, I had no more breath in me, no more life to give.

I can't do this anymore... It's the easiest thing for everyone... They won't have to worry about me anymore and I won't be a burden to my family and friends...Would anyone actually miss me?... Would anyone even be sad?... Or would they be happy and relieved that it is finally over and I am out of their lives for good?

I heard the Man's prophetic words in my ears, his distorted promises of love and his never-ending threats of murder. I looked over the edge from where I was standing, and pictured the jump. Over and over, I saw myself fall. But I couldn't do it. I didn't have the courage to go through with it. I think it was the only thing I didn't ever have the courage to do. I sat down, looking out onto the city and up at the empty, starless sky. I needed to change. I needed to do something different. I needed help, otherwise I was dead. It was now or never. I went back inside, had a shower and fell into bed. I wanted to stay there forever. I didn't want to wake up. I pleaded;

"It's something I've never told anyone before in my life, not my parents, my family, anyone. I was raped when I was a little boy and I need help."

I really don't think she knew what to do or say, but she held my hand;

"I am here for you and I will do everything I can to help you."

I wasn't ready, I wasn't able to tell her about the sex and violence with men because I was ashamed. I thought to myself;

"Just go one step at a time."

I don't exactly know how the words came out because I was a slobbering mess. I told her about the drugs, about my deep and unrelenting depression and about wanting to kill myself.

The conversation seemed to go on forever. As soon as I told her, I felt the weight of the entire world lifting off me. I let out an enormous breath. It was an instant awakening; my first real relief for as long as I could remember.

She continued to hold my hand;

"I am so sorry, I love you. Everything is going to be OK."

I must have been talking quite loudly because all of the tables around us had stopped their conversations; their eyes were transfixed on us. It really was a moment; a space in time that was devoid of all movement, just she and I, no one else was there, everything around us was frozen still. This is a moment I will never, ever forget. I couldn't move from that table; I was absolutely exhausted and could have passed out right then and there. I already felt different; my life had changed forever in an instant.

What the fuck just happened?... Does she believe me?... What does she think of me now?... What does any of it mean?... Did any of this even happen?... I feel so lost, I feel like I have no one... Will Sam even be there?... Does she mean it when she says that she loves me?... How could she even love me?... What now?... What next?

But I had no idea of what was to come. Sam said she was going to help me find someone to talk to. I left the cafe and, even though I had finally started the healing process, that subway ride and walk home felt like the loneliest of my life. I didn't know where to go and who to be. I felt like killing myself again, like jumping in front of the subway or a car. I was tired with life and I was sure that life was tired with me. I didn't want to face it, any of it. I wanted it all to go away and I wanted to go away with it.

A few days later I heard from Kristen, Sam mentioned to me that she might reach out to her, knowing how close she and I were. We spoke on the phone for a bit; she couldn't believe what happened to me and was very sorry. I went down to the Cow to see her; it was the first time I'd been there since I was fired. I didn't spend too much time there for obvious reasons. She gave me a big hug and said;

"I am so sorry for all that you have gone through, I had no idea, why didn't you say anything?"

It was then I realized that I actually still had people on my side who really cared and were looking out for me;

"I couldn't say anything, I didn't know how and you don't need to apologise. I am the one who is sorry. I'm sorry for the way I treated

244

*you, the way I treated everyone at work, for my behavior. I've hurt a
lot of people."*

I knew that I was going to be giving out a lot of apologies for a long
time to come. Kristen next said;

*"I have made some phone calls, I've spoken to a few therapists and I
have some recommendations. I have narrowed it down to two
therapists who I like and they specialise in child sexual abuse, They
are expecting your call."*

I cried when she told me this.

I had finally spoken to someone about what happened to me but was I
actually ready to go to therapy? Did I want to speak to a professional
about all of this? She gave me their numbers, I sat on it for a while. I
didn't call them right away, even though I had Sam and Kristen in my
ear asking every day.

Finally, I did leave a message with both; one was male and the other,
a female. I received a return call from the male saying that he couldn't
fit any more clients into his schedule and would call me if something
opened up. I remember feeling disheartened by this and again, wanted
to give up. Then I heard back from Robyn. She invited me in for a free
first session to see if we were a good match. I remember having to wait
five days for that session to finally come around; five interminable
days. Everything seemed to be moving in slow motion. I think I only
left the house to go to the gym; I would sometimes go with Tom,
sometimes on my own.
With everything going on, the gym was the only solace I had. I made
sure to go every day and, when I was there with Tom for that hour,
taking a spin class or a boxing session, I was able to forget about my
troubles. But when I went to the gym alone, and just lifted weights, my

head was polluted with many dangerous and lonely thoughts. I really couldn't get away from it.

I needed to find another job, I needed to start making money again. Luckily Tom had been in the hospitality industry for some years and knew a lot of people. He had an Aussie friend who was running the bar at Locanda Verde, a beautiful restaurant attached to The Greenwich Hotel in Tribeca and he got me a job bartending there. I enjoyed working at this place; I partook in absolutely no drinking or drugs. The Greenwich Hotel was owned by Robert DeNiro, so he would occasionally have a drink at the VIP bar when I was working. I much preferred working at this bar; it was easier and more relaxed than the restaurant bar and the bartenders divided their time evenly between both. I kept my head down and out of trouble there; I did the work that was asked of me. I was still able to charm the guests when needed; it was easy for me to chat, smile and flirt. I needed to be back at work; I needed to keep my mind busy and away from all the noise in my head.

I finally sat down with Tom and Dani and told them what was going on; they deserved to know, they were the closest people I had to family in New York and I needed all the help and support I could find. I told them about being raped, but I still couldn't talk about the violence and sex with men yet. I asked them if I ever seemed happy. They told me that they saw the change in me and that I was not the same, happy-go-lucky guy they first met. They were very supportive and there for me, we really were one happy little family and got on amazingly well. I cared a lot for them as they did me.

I remember my first therapy session like it was yesterday. I caught the subway to Union Square and walked the few blocks to Robyn's office. I sat in the waiting room while she finished her session with another client. There were a bunch of magazines that I flicked through; I was nervous, fidgety and couldn't sit still. I wanted to run out of there before it was too late. Suddenly a door opened and her client walked out. I tried not to look, but I couldn't help myself and the client looked back, as well. We shared a smile; I wondered if they had gone through a similar thing to me. Robyn kept me waiting a little longer, telling me that she'll be with me in one minute. This was my chance to run away and never come back. But as frightened as I was, I was also strangely excited to be there. She came to her door and met me. I was intrigued to see what she looked like. I was about to leave my life in her hands for guidance and direction.

Who is this person that I am going to spill my guts to?... Does she have my best interest at heart?... I can't be here... I need to get out of here... What the fuck am I doing?

She invited me into her office. To the left of the door was her desk with framed certificates above. Next to her desk was a bookcase full of books. I sat on one couch and opposite to me was another long couch, both had quite a few little pillows, and a blanket sitting atop them. There was a coffee table in the middle and, to the side of the coffee table, placed in front of a window, was a one-seater couch. Next to the couch was a mini fridge full of little water bottles. There was nothing sitting on the coffee table besides a box of tissues. I hated that fucking box of tissues! Robyn pulled her chair out from behind her desk and sat down (holding her pad and pen).

"Thank you for being here, I know this is hard for you. I have spoken with Kristen briefly, she told me a little of your story. Would you be willing to share with me why you are here?"

I couldn't find the words to start. The first word came out, and then I just blurted out all that I could. I got a few sentences in before the tears began to fall. I couldn't stop crying for a good few minutes. I told Robyn everything; we spoke about my childhood in Australia, my family and that dynamic. I told her about being raped for the first time and the subsequent years thereafter with the Man, and my relationship with him. We didn't get into too much detail of my time in New York during the first few sessions, we didn't have enough time and it was going to take many sessions of therapy to get through everything.

I was very hesitant to talk about the violence and sex with men. I wasn't sure if it was because of the shame and guilt I felt, or because I was scared that I was going to get reported and then be in trouble with the police. She was very calming, supportive and reassuring so I finally let it all out; I told her as much as I could. She didn't say much in that first session; she took notes, asked questions, sat back and listened. The hour went by quickly; I couldn't stop talking. She had to remind me that my time was up. She asked me how I felt; I told her I was exhausted, I could have curled up amongst all the pillows, covered myself with the blanket and gone to sleep. I was dead and didn't want to move. She said *"I find you fascinating and I would love to work with you."*

I'd been called a lot of things but never fascinating. I knew I wanted to work with her, I liked her. I felt a strong connection, a comfort in being around her, and I felt safe talking to her. We agreed to work together but there was no way I could afford two hundred and fifty dollars per hour. She really wanted to work with me and, knowing my financial situation, she agreed to charge me one hundred dollars. We had a deal and agreed on every Wednesday at three o'clock. I had my therapist. I walked out of there feeling a little optimistic, thinking that everything might be ok and that I had a chance at survival in this fucked up world. I fell asleep on the subway on the way home and missed my stop. I had to wait for a train going back the other way; the session really did wipe me out.

Chapter 31

I still spoke to my family back home in Australia usually once per week. My parents would always call to see how I was doing; I continued to tell them that I was doing well, all was fine, acting jobs were happening and there was a lot on the horizon for me to look forward to. In other words, I continued to lie to them. However, I did stop drinking, drugging, sex, going out; literally everything. Besides going to work, the gym and therapy, I led a very simple life. I met up with Sam a few times, she was concerned for me and wanted to make sure I was in a good place. We were also on better terms and mending our friendship. I saw Kirsten a few times, as well. Those two girls saved my life.

I was seeing Robyn every week and it was tough, a real struggle; and, at times I wanted to quit. It was hard to open up and talk to her about my past; to remember things, the good and the bad, though there wasn't much good to remember. There were sessions when I would just sit there in silence for up to twenty minutes, not say a word; it was just a safe space for me, a place of trust. At times I would bury myself in the pillows, or lie under the blanket. I had never cried so much in my life and I had never been so mentally and emotionally exhausted. In one of our silences, I fell asleep and she needed to wake me up at the end of the session. For those first few months with her, I was completely wiped out when I left her office; I had nothing left inside of me. I had poured out every ounce of me in that little room. In saying it all, I didn't want to be anywhere else; I grew to love being there, to love Robyn, my time with her, and to love therapy. Another life saver. I looked forward to every Wednesday afternoon, to opening up, to speaking my truth, growing and feeling the weight fall off of me with every session. At the same time, there was also weight piling up on me with every session, as I was in a brutal discovery of all my actions. I was admitting to what I actually did, learning about the root of my behaviors, my thoughts about myself and others, as well as the impact of it all. Robyn warned me that it was going to get a lot darker and heavier before it was going to get any better. I was learning new things about myself; about the meaning of 'Stockholm Syndrome' and how I was a victim of it. Stockholm Syndrome is a psychological disorder that describes how a victim of abuse forms a 'traumatic bond' with, and attaches unconsciously, even lovingly, to their abuser. I discovered that I had many of these symptoms as a child during the abuse stage, as well as throughout my life.

As the sessions wore on, Robyn and I talked extensively about my violence and the sex with men and why I 'acted out'. I came to the realization that it was my grand 'fuck you' to the world, my way of attempting to get my power back. I was learning that I needed to feel those feelings again; it was the only thing that made me feel alive, made me feel real. It was all that I knew and all that I wanted because it validated my sense of self; my inner core, which was flooded with erroneous feelings of self-hate. At the very same time it was the most disgusting thing in the world and I loathed it. I was learning to forgive myself; growing ever more aware that, when in these aggressive sexual situations, there was minimal interaction with the men. I wanted nothing to do with any of them, and I wanted them to have nothing to do with me. There was no intimacy; no kissing, no cuddling, no holding hands or holding of each other. No love. It was only ever about the act, about recapturing the primitive and complex feelings trapped in my body from my childhood. Yes, I got a hard-on. Yes, I came. Yes, I 'got off' during these sexual encounters.

Robyn asked me on more than one occasion;

"Are you gay?"

This is a question I have asked and debated with myself many times and it is a topic we spoke about at length. My answer, or the conclusion I always came to, was;

"Maybe I'm bi-sexual. Maybe I'm straight. I don't call myself gay because I never was, or have been, romantically or physically attracted to men. I never looked at men thinking, I want to take you home to hold, kiss and make love to you. It was the closest thing that was wired deeply inside of me, that I believed to be love. As much as it killed me, it gave me life, it was all control, power and dominance."

As people, we become addicted to the emotions that we feel on a regular basis. Emotions are chemicals that get released into our bodies and we become addicted to feeling them, especially the heightened ones. The rage literally became a specific chemical cocktail that I needed to experience to feel normal, to feel myself; this is where and how the addiction cycle was created. It's literally the same process as drug, food and alcohol addictions. The emotions I would feel after the act would match the blueprint of all the complex emotions that I needed to feel, that were imprinted onto me from when I was a child; the confusion, the anger, the rage, the self-loathing, the hatred, all of them. I was recreating situations that would trigger all of these emotions in an attempt to untangle the mess that the Man created.

The sex act, and attendant violence, was more a recapitulation of the feelings I had as a little, helpless boy. Those first nine years of my sexual life, from age eight to seventeen, were marred by dirty, rough and violent sex with men; and it became an unconscious, compulsively repetitive act; an identification with the aggressor and the only way I knew how to reclaim my sense of control, power and life. These

251

epiphanies, these dawning revelations, were weirdly soothing. I had found a comfortable place to land after years of horror and abuse.

After a few weeks with Robyn, and at her urging, I started going to 'Alcoholics Anonymous', 'Narcotics Anonymous' and 'Sex Addicts Anonymous'. I went back and forth between all three and I started creating a sobriety plan for myself. It was hard for me to work through all of this at the time though, as I often told myself that I wasn't an 'addict.' I had the stubbornness and naiveté to think I could get off any and all of them whenever I wanted. Yes, I was shooting heroin, smoking crack cocaine and having reckless sex, but I reminded myself that I would often go weeks or months without touching anything. My naiveté finally wore down when I had the courage to admit to myself that I couldn't stop any of these vices when my soul felt empty and worthless. It was at these times when you put a drug or a drink in front of me and I simply could not say *"no."*

When it came to sex, that was more complicated, more psychological. On occasion I was having sex every day with different women, there was the sex and violence with men and I was never able to stay loyal in a relationship. However, there were months in between when I didn't have sex at all and didn't want to. It was always a back and forth, up and down pattern with me; and I lost my way time and time. I threw myself into the programs and it took me a few meetings in each of the support groups to open up and share. I had no idea of what to say at first, and I preferred to listen to others as they shared their stories of addiction, trauma and recovery. I learned so much from them and I could relate to everything they were talking about.

First and foremost, I had to admit that I had a problem. I started taking inventory of who I was as a person; my behavior and thoughts, who I did wrong to, who I harmed; writing them down and trying to take responsibility for my actions. There were some very long lists. Second,

I had to accept that I was no different, no better than anyone else in the room. There was no leader, no president; we were all on the same level. It did not matter if you had been sober for twelve years or twelve days. We were all there for the same reasons. We were there to listen, to share and to support one another. That is what I loved most about being in the program.

The subway rides and walks home after therapy, or after one of these meetings, were some of the loneliest of my life. I would listen to music through my iPod and contemplate absolutely everything I had going on. I'd never felt so alone, so cold, during those winter months and so out of the realm of comprehension as to what was actually going on in my life and what I was discovering about myself. There were days and nights when I wasn't sure how much longer I could do this; at times I just wanted to escape to a new part of the world where no one knew who I was or what my story was about and I could start all over again.

Not long after I started therapy, Dani and Tom were invited to a friend's birthday party and asked me to go along. They insisted I join them as I had not really left the house to go anywhere but work, the gym and to therapy. They told me that I needed a night out; I needed to relax and have fun. I agreed to go with them, but wasn't really interested. At the party Dani was hanging with the girls, whilst Tom and I were sitting at the bar, off to the side chatting between ourselves. Halfway through the night Dani came running over to us and, in her beautifully loud and bubbly way, she began telling me that she found the perfect girl for me. I remember insisting that I didn't want to meet her; that it was the last thing I needed. But Dani did not listen. She pointed her out, and she really was beautiful, and she urged me to at least meet her.

A few moments later Dani did bring her over. As beautiful as she was from afar, she was even more so up close; an American born woman from Turkish and Albanian heritage, with dark hair, dark eyes and tender facial features. Her name was Julie; she was born in Buffalo, New York and moved to Manhattan two years before I did. She loved that I was from Australia, saying she always wanted to visit. We spoke for about ten minutes before telling Dani, Tom and myself that she had to go to work and invited us along for a drink. She was the hostess at Greenhouse, a New York night club, or a 'door bitch' as I used to call it. We exchanged numbers and she left. I definitely wanted to see her again, so a short time later the three of us went to the Greenhouse and there she was, standing out front, directing people in and out. She escorted us to the bar and gave us a few drink tickets. I didn't have a drink, but Dani and Tom took advantage of the situation. Julie spoke with us when she could and we got on quite well. I wanted to see her again, even though I wasn't ready to actually start dating someone.

We did start dating and, for the first few weeks, I didn't tell her anything about what was going on with me; I was afraid that she would run away. I would sometimes meet her straight after a therapy session and tell her that I was just in 'a meeting'; I was already starting this relationship by lying. We enjoyed each other's company, visiting before work or on our nights off; we went to the theatre a lot and often just relaxed in her apartment. I introduced her to Sam, but there was always tension between them; jealousy on Julie's part when it came to Sam, and they never really got along well.

I left Locanda Verde, after getting offered a job at The Norwood Club, a members-only club on Fourteenth Street and Eighth Avenue, catering to the Arts and Creative community. It was in an old converted townhouse with a private dining room in the basement; the first floor was the lounge room where meetings and casual dining took place, and the second floor was a formal restaurant. One floor above that was a nightclub and the top floor was a screening room, where members would screen their movies and have conferences.

Julie and I were doing well, seeing each other as often as we could and we were about six weeks into our relationship. We still hadn't had sex but things were getting a lot more serious. She lived in Soho/Chinatown on Grand Street, a great part of the city, with a roommate. Julie and I were in her bedroom watching 'Vanilla Sky', her favorite movie. We were half way through the film and things were getting heated between us; clothes were coming off and we were both wanting to move forward. I felt like I was in a good place mentally to go there with her. As things progressed, I needed a quick second to take a deep breath and steady myself as my thoughts were going everywhere. I tried to get back in control of my emotions. We got back into it, kissing and getting naked, the movie was still playing on her laptop so I slammed that shut.

Again, I needed to take another few seconds to compose myself, something was coming over me and I couldn't control it, my mind was racing, as was my heart, my emotions and hormones. I continually had to look away from her and get my breath back for that quick beat. I'd been wanting to sleep with her since the second I saw her, I had very strong feelings for her and I know she felt the same way about me. I was ready and we were just about to have sex when, suddenly, I burst out crying and I couldn't breathe. I had to get away from her. I jumped off of the bed feeling like I'd been hit in the stomach with a baseball bat. I felt winded. I was paralyzed for that moment in time.

Julie was in shock;

"Are you OK?... Are you hurt?... Did I hurt you?... Did I do something to you?... What happened?"

I kept telling her;

Toy Cars   Nathan Spiteri

"It isn't anything that you did, I don't know what is happening, I don't know what is wrong with me right now... It's not you, please believe me...I'm so sorry...What the fuck is happening to me?"

She tried to comfort me but I put my hand up to stop her. I couldn't look at her. I couldn't touch her. I couldn't be anywhere near her and I couldn't stop crying.
An enormous wave of new emotions washed over me; feelings that I had never felt before. It was like I was frozen, stuck in time and couldn't move, couldn't talk and couldn't function. My head was spinning and I felt like I was going to faint; I felt completely lost. It was something all so powerful and real.

What the fuck is happening?... Is this what (real) love feels like?... Was I letting go and feeling true love for the very first time?... Is this me being free of the past and moving forward with my life?... This is so fucking scary... I can't do this.

I hungered for love, connection and deep intimacy, but they all terrified me at the very same time to the point of immobilizing me. I froze. I lost my shit. I had to get out of there. I got dressed, composed myself, apologized to her and left, leaving her stranded without any answers as to what had just happened. I'm not sure if she realized what was going on with me; if she worked out that I was falling in love with her and that I had never felt these feelings for anyone before in my life. Looking back now, I should have stayed; should have talked about it, pushed through the fear, and we should have made love. That would have been the perfect ending to a perfect night. But nothing about me or my life was perfect and the self-sabotage worked its way back into my head. I wasn't deserving of someone so beautiful, I didn't deserve to find happiness, and I most definitely didn't deserve love. I wanted to do bad things, to hurt myself. I didn't care about all of the good work I was doing in therapy and in recovery. I wanted to throw it all away

256

and go back to a place where I felt most comfortable. I have since come to understand that I hit what's called an 'Upper Limit Threshold'. This is where there is no map for navigating new positive, joyful, loving emotions, so the only thing to do is destroy the moment and bring everything down to a place I knew well; old, well-rehearsed, very familiar, isolating, self-loathing and self-sabotaging patterns. I managed to stay strong and made it home, sat up on the roof, and for the first time since being in New York, I just wanted to go home to Australia.

Tom came up, we had a long chat. He made sure that I was ok, sharing with me that he and Dani loved me and that they would always be there for me. This was a huge wakeup call and powerful reflection for me as I had been forgetting all about my hard work in the program and in therapy. In my next session, I discussed this with Robyn. She asked me;

"How do you truly feel about yourself and about your life?"

After sitting back and really thinking about it, I told her;

"I hate my life and wish that I were dead."

I said and thought that line so many times in my life. We explored happiness and joy, and she asked me if I knew the difference. *"No,"* I said, *"No, I do not."* I had always thought that they were the same. She sat forward, looked lovingly into my eyes and told me that happiness comes from doing something for ourselves, like buying the material things we love, as well as from how others feel about us. Whereas joy *is an elevated state of being* in a specific moment in time. It is a soul-enriching feeling of wellbeing; a sense of contentment and selflessness that comes from deep within.

I thought for a moment, and realized that I had experienced happiness at certain times in my life, but that I had never known joy. Suddenly I remembered the moment I was riding as a passenger in a car in Malta; driving along the coast road with my cousin and my friend, Shane. I had blocked that moment out of my memory during all of these lonely years. But now, with Robyn's help, it was all coming back to me. I was flooded with a sense of deep contentment as I remembered looking out from the passenger side window of that car; staring at the beautiful world around and in front of me. And for that brief, blessed moment in time, I felt pure joy.

We also spoke of self-sabotage and shame, and I came to the realization that I wasn't all bad. I wasn't just a product of the Man's manipulations and grooming. I was capable of feeling many positive feelings that other, *normal*, people felt and experienced in this life. I wasn't that lost little boy anymore.

Chapter 32

Summer was upon us, I was finding some normalcy, structure, and was feeling good. I was also keeping Julie at arm's length, we ignored that incident and were moving forward with our relationship. We finally had sex and were in a good place. I still wasn't good at communicating, explaining moments in time, sharing my emotions and trusting anyone, let alone her. I was still afraid people were going to hurt me or abandon me like the Man did all those years before. If we were going to give this relationship a serious chance and move forward, Julie needed to know everything; it was time for me to explain my past to her.

We were in her bedroom once again and I sat her down, summoned the courage from inside, and shared my story. I told her about the repeated rapes from when I was a little boy; the violence and sex with men, the drugs, alcohol and sex addictions. I told her everything, maybe a little too much and too soon. She was grateful to me for being so vulnerable and honest with her; we were both crying, she expressed how she knew something was off with me and also how proud she was that I trusted her enough to share these raw and brutal truths with her. She said that she was proud and honored to be with me; that she cared for me and was excited to go through this journey with me, supporting me in any way that she could. I told her how happy I was to be with her and how much she meant to me. That night was the first time we made love, not sex, and it was, for me, a new and powerfully meaningful experience. We were definitely forming a deeper, more evolved connection. For the next two weeks, I didn't see too much of her; she was busy with work and had plans with her twin sister and friends. I was fine with that because as much as I wanted to be with her, I also needed time alone, the time I still craved most.

When Julie and I finally did get together, things were different; she was distant and I felt it right away. We talked about it; I asked her what was wrong. She told me that whilst she was honored that I told her everything, she'd had time to think about all of it; to consult with her twin and her friends; and she told me that now she couldn't do it. She said that it was all too much for her and that she couldn't be with me. She was worried about everything; about the violence and the sex with men, the drug use and the possibility of relapses. She broke up with me, stating that I needed to work on myself and to get myself better. I was devastated. I felt deeply confused and totally abandoned. I told myself that I understood her fears, and I truly tried to. However, that didn't lessen any of my heartache and pain.

I kept on with my therapy; it was both lifesaving and life altering. From my very first session I had always been an open book, sharing all that I could about my life with whilst learning and discovering new things about myself in every way possible. My parents and Karl were coming to visit me in September; Robyn and I were talking about a plan on how and when I should tell them. *Would I do it on the phone before they come, or wait until they were here and tell them face to face?*

I decided to wait and share it with them in person. We agreed that I would call Janice and Peter and tell them first on the phone. I always trusted Janice and knew she would give me the right advice on how to tell mum and dad. I stopped with the program; making up excuses that I was too busy with life and therapy and that I had the drinking, drugs and sex *'under control'*. I hadn't touched a drug in over six months and hadn't been sleeping with anyone. I started drinking again, thinking that I had it under control. I needed to get Julie out of my head, so I would go to parties regularly with Tom and Dani. They were great for me during this entire time, they never questioned or disapproved of anything that I did in my past. With them I felt safe.

We went to a 'Sunday Funday' pool party at the Gansevoort Hotel Rooftop (in the Meatpacking district of Manhattan) and the very first two people I bumped into were Julie and her twin sister. It was the first time I'd seen her since we'd broken up. She was actually on her way out of the event, and I felt a relief come over me. There was a girl at the party who wouldn't leave me alone. She was a sexy South American, throwing herself at me, giving me a massage as I jumped in and out of the pool, and inviting me to meet up with her later that night. Previously, I would have thrown myself at her, but I just couldn't do it this time. She came out for dinner with Dani, Tom and myself, asking me (again) to go home with her. Dani and Tom were supportive as they thought it would help me to get over Julie. But I couldn't do it, I wanted Julie.

A few weeks later Julie rang me asking to talk in person. We met and she expressed that she had made a mistake and wanted to get back together with me. I was hesitant as I knew I still had so much work to do on myself, but my heart wanted her back. We started seeing each other again. I got into the mindset that everything was good, I was getting better; I was in therapy and I was discovering more moments of joy and self-acceptance. Subconsciously, however, I knew I shouldn't be in this relationship and that I would eventually hurt her. I tried, but deep inside I knew that I was still living a lie.

Having passed all of my medicals, interviews and having filed the right paperwork, my Green Card finally arrived. I was officially a permanent resident, valid for ten years. I had all the rights of a United States citizen, only I couldn't vote in elections. I would now be able to more aggressively pursue my acting career without any visa issues.

Towards the end of summer, Robyn invited me to join a group therapy session in addition to my individual therapy work. There were four other people in the group. I was excited and agreed to do it based on her assurance that it would bring in new dimensions of healing that would help me to recover and grow. I arrived at the first session a few minutes late, met everyone in the group; together we were four men and one woman. We introduced ourselves one by one. Michael was first up; he was a gentleman in his fifties, an Advertising Executive for a top Advertising Firm in the city; he was gay, HIV positive, and his partner had just died from cancer. Joanne was next, also in her fifties and gay; she was a senior designer for a top fashion house, lost her job in the 2008 financial crisis, she was told that she was *'too old'* and couldn't find another job in the industry after that. She became a bartender and an alcoholic and had to move out of her spacious condo with her partner and rent a little one-bedroom apartment. Next was Russell in his forties, gay and addicted to sex; he loved to sing and to write songs (that was only when he wasn't having sex or masturbating all day.) Lastly, but definitely not least, was Tim, late twenties, gay, depressed and overweight; he spent his life being teased and bullied, he loved to write poetry and short stories, but he wouldn't shower, brush his teeth or use deodorant. My new band of merry misfits.

When the time came to introduce myself, I shared my story. As soon as I mentioned the violence against men, I felt a tremendous amount of anger come from Michael. He called me a 'homophobe' and insisted that I hated gay people. The other members were all in agreement with him, and I felt judged and ambushed. I totally understood where they were coming from. I tried to explain myself but they weren't hearing any of it. This was the very first time that I realised the consequences of my actions, specifically regarding the violence that I had inflicted on gay men. Up until now, I had never been held accountable for this and it hit me hard. I was now beginning to realize the emotional, mental and physical pain that I had caused innocent men.

I wanted to run away and pretend that none of this was happening.

I had never been tested like this before, and I used it all as an opportunity for my growth. I still had a long way to go, and I tried my best to welcome the lessons this was teaching me. But deep inside I felt more shame than I had ever felt before. I was being forced to look at my behavior and the devastating effects it had on others in the world. I had nowhere to hide. At the end of the session, most of the members left without even acknowledging me. I stayed back and had a quick chat with Robyn. She told me;

"I am so proud of you, I could see the struggle in your eyes. You are going to grow a great deal from this experience. Stay with the group, it is going to get a whole lot harder but it will be all so worth it in the end."

I hoped she was right. Over the weeks, the group warmed up to me; they began to understand my actions and were showing more empathy for my efforts toward my recovery.

Chapter 33

Life outside of the group was fine; I continued with my work at Norwood which was slow going in the summer as most of the members were out of the city on vacation. Julie and I were doing well and I was staying at her apartment as often as I could; she rarely came out to mine because she didn't like traveling to Brooklyn. As Sam was leaving for Toronto soon, we were trying to spend as much time together as we could. Most importantly, Robyn and I created a plan of action for telling my parents my story upon their visit to New York. Karl was going to spend a few days in Florida with friends so this would afford me the opportunity to have a more intimate meeting with them. First, I had to tell Janice and Peter. I rang Janice; I had only spoken with her infrequently before this call. I had previously shared with her that I was back in therapy, that I had been suffering from depression and that I had been 'going through some things'. I was pacing; making laps around the whole apartment. With fear in my heart, I rang her. I placed the call on speaker, feeling that this would be easier than holding the phone to my ear. I started;

"...there is something that I need to say to you; can you please be quiet and just listen."

Janice never swears, and at this point she said;

"Oh shit..."

This told me that she was bracing herself for what was about to follow. I then blurted it out... all of it.

264

There was an emptiness on the other end of the phone line; not a word was spoken in return to all that I had shared. When Janice finally summoned the strength to respond, she asked;

"Are you lying?"

In a weak and frightened voice, I replied;

"No"

She was in shock;

"...what do you mean? what the fuck are you even talking about?!"

I then went into detail for her; explaining the who, the what, the when and the where. I will never know the why. This time she knew I was serious; I could hear her crying on the line. The first thing she said to me after her tears subsided a little was;

"Wow, this explains everything about you... I finally get why you were who you were, why you behaved in all the ways you did... Why you did the strange things that you did as a child and also growing up through your teenage and adult years... I get it all... Have you told anyone else?"

A flood of thoughts and emotions engulfed me with her question. I felt scared; how was everyone going to take it all? Would they accept me or would they reject me? Would they believe me? Would they be angry with me? Would they support me?

"...No, not yet, I am going to tell Mum, Dad and Karl when they arrive in New York and I am going to call Peter when we get off this call."

This was so much for us both to take in, we were both overwhelmed and in tears. At this point we were both barely able to get the words out coherently;

"I am so sorry, I am so sorry that this happened to you, that I wasn't there for you.... I am sorry that I let you down and I didn't protect you at the pool that day... I am so sorry; I am so sorry... I am so sorry... why didn't you come to me?... I am so sorry..."

I sat quietly as she cried, and when I felt had enough strength to answer, I said;

"It is not your fault... I don't blame you for anything... I don't need your apology... you have done nothing wrong... there was nothing that you could have done... I just need you to understand me... who I was and why I was the way I was, my behaviors, my actions through all of it... it was not your fault, you have always been the best sister... I love you so much."

The hardest part of that phone call was hanging up. It was near impossible to say goodbye; she didn't want to let me go. It felt like it was the very last time that I was ever going to speak with her; but in reality, it was actually the very first time.

After the call, I was hit by a rush of surreal emotions, like it all didn't just happen. But it did. I know that it did. I felt a heaviness that I had felt for decades begin to lift. I went for a walk around the neighbourhood as I needed some time before calling Peter. The fresh air did me good. I called him about an hour later. Janice had already called and told him, which I was happy about, thinking that now I wouldn't need to go into the full details again, but he wanted to hear it all from me, which I appreciated. I told him everything, except for the sex and violence with men. It still felt so hard for me to share these

266

specific details, I found that all much harder than talking about me as a kid. For me it all came down to a deep sense of shame. He asked if he could do anything for me, and he suggested that I come home to be with the family. Janice had also told him that I was going to tell mum, dad and Karl when they arrived. He told me that he loved me, words we never said to each other before, it was reassuring, refreshing and awakening to hear. In just two phone calls I could already feel myself growing closer to them both; a new found love and respect was finally taking root in our family.

Dani and Tom were going through some hard times; they were moving in different directions and drifting further apart. Dani and I were getting closer, nothing at all romantic. We both had families living on the other side of the world, and we would commiserate about missing home, wanting to go back to see them all again. Tom appeared to be getting a little jealous of our connection; he would talk about how much he missed his family too, how he never got to see them and how hard it was for him. Dani and I felt it odd since Tom's family lived just across the river in New Jersey and he visited them often. We would try to explain this to him, sharing that he really had little idea of what it was like to be so far away from family who all lived on the other side of the world. He would fight us on this insisting that he was in the exact same situation as we were. This may have been what caused an even deeper rift in their relationship.

Mum, Dad and Karl arrived in New York. I was so happy to see them but was nervous and apprehensive all at the same time. I was unsure if I should tell them at the beginning of their trip, the middle or at the end. Robyn guided me to share with them when they first arrived. This way we would have the necessary time to talk about it all whilst they were in town. The first night I took them out for dinner locally at the waterfront in Brooklyn Heights, giving them a great view of lower Manhattan. A day or two later Karl went down to Florida to visit friends so it was now or never. I decided to take them somewhere quiet and relaxed so as to make sure we wouldn't be interrupted every few minutes. I had no idea of what I was going to say or how I was going to say it. We sat down at our table, and a strength appeared from within me. I started by saying;

"...there's something that I need to tell you both..."

Mum, being the caring but nosy mother replied;

"Have you got a girl pregnant?... You owe someone money?... You're in trouble with the police?... You're sick?... People are after you?"

I replied with a sharp *"No"* after each question. I took a deep breath and began;

"Please just listen, this is going to be hard for you to understand, but please listen. I was abused as a kid."

I don't think they understood exactly what I was saying because mum's initial response was;

"Don't be silly, you weren't abused. We never abused you."

That's when I finally told them.

"No, you didn't abuse me. I was raped when I was eight years old at the Queanbeyan Pool."

They were both in a state of shock and didn't say anything. Mum still didn't really understand what was happening.

"...don't be stupid, what are you talking about?"

I repeated myself, this time going into a little more detail until, finally, they understood that I was being serious.

Dad did not say a word, I don't think he knew how or what to say and was in total shock, as was mum. It was, however, all mum at this stage speaking and asking questions (just like Janice and Peter). Mum wanted to know everything; what had happened to her little boy, whom she loved with every fiber of her being. She wanted to know all the who, the what, the when, and the where questions.

I was acutely aware of how they were receiving all of this information; I could see and feel the shock and horror all over them. I tried to answer as gently and as honestly as I could. I watched my dad become enraged; pain first, and then anger, filled his eyes. Dad was always the softer and quieter of my parents, a gentle and loving man; but in this moment he was different. I had never seen my father so protective and powerful.

He commanded me;

"Who is the Man?... I want to kill him."

My mum was blanched.

It was the first time ever that I saw their roles reversed. She was customarily the tougher one, the disciplinarian of the pair. In this moment she became the softest, most loving and gentle woman I'd ever seen. She was crying, stood up instinctively from her seat and came over to me;

"I love you very much.
I am going to protect you and keep you safe.
Come here, I want to give you the biggest hug."

269

I didn't want it; I didn't know how to receive it. I still hated affection and it felt completely uncomfortable. She did it anyway. She gave me the hug of my life and she showered me with love like I had never felt before. I let her have her hug because she needed it, but I just wanted to get away because I still wasn't mentally and emotionally ready to receive. This was all so new to me and I was deeply confused, learning new things and experiencing new emotions every single day.

Just as I did with Janice and Peter, I explained to my parents that it was not their fault and there was nothing either of them could have done. I assured them profusely that I didn't blame them at all, not one bit. Once mum sat back down, and after the initial shock wore off, she said exactly the same thing that Janice did;

"...that explains so much... everything. Now I feel that I understand you."

Just as I didn't say anything to Janice and Peter about the violence and sex with men, nor about the depth of my drug use, I didn't tell my parents either. *Baby steps* I told myself. *We all need baby steps.* I think if I did tell them everything at that time it would have killed them.

The rest of the dinner was very quiet, and it felt very awkward. What possible conversation could we have had after that? As soon as we had finished dinner Mum asked to go straight home. They went to bed shortly thereafter, and I heard my mum crying from the other side of the wall. This is what broke my heart the most; hearing my mum and dad suffering, in despair, in the deepest pain over their child that they loved so dearly.

The next morning, they awoke early and took a day-trip to Washington D.C. to visit the national monuments. This was the best thing for them, as it gave them the much-needed reprieve, a chance to take their minds off it all even for a little bit over the day. A few days later Karl returned from Florida, he and I went for a walk and I told him everything. He was twenty years old; I'm not sure he knew how to take it all or even what to say to me. The first thing he did say back to me was, *"Do you want a hug?"* It was actually very sweet and made me laugh. I told him *"I'm fine, I don't need a hug, everything is going to be OK."* He asked for a few details; however, I could feel he didn't actually want to know too much at all. For the rest of the time they were in New York with me we didn't speak about it. I think my parents needed time to process all that I had shared; the only thing that they did ask about was my therapy, and how my mental state was. I told them about the different therapy programs that I was in and they were pleased that I was taking care of myself in this way. I did take them for dinner with Julie and they seemed to all get along quite well; Dad thought she was beautiful so I got his tick of approval.

Dad also celebrated his birthday whilst they were in New York, so we went to 'Strip House,' a famous New York steak house near Union Square. Tom and Sam joined us; Dani couldn't make it because her parents were actually in town at the same time. Julie had a prior engagement, she met us afterwards and we all went to the top of the Empire State Building, and it was wonderful being able to show them New York at night from high above. It was definitely a full house that week, but it was great to have both sets of parents in town. It wasn't long after this time that Dani's father was diagnosed with cancer and died; he was a lovely man. He and Dani had tremendous love for one another. Dani went home to South Africa to be with her dad during his final days, and didn't plan on a definite date of return. This is when she and Tom split up, leaving Tom and me in the apartment.

Soon after my parents left, it was time for Sam to leave for Toronto; her OPT was up and there was no other way for her to get a working visa or to stay in the United States. She was struggling both financially and emotionally, and she wanted to be closer to her parents and her brother. This also gave me an excuse to go and visit her as often as I could in Canada.

Back in therapy, Robyn and I spoke about my parents' visit and how things went when I shared my story with my family. I explained that it felt frightening telling Janice and Peter, but was also easier because it was over the telephone, rather than in person. I told her that with Karl it was fine, he didn't exactly know how to process the information I shared and he didn't really want to talk about it in detail either. I told her that, after sharing with mum and dad, I was left feeling empty and frustrated that they didn't want to talk about it more whilst they were visiting. I had hoped that we could have talked and shared more deeply; about who I am, who I was in my essence and in my relationship with them as a child. I wanted them to understand so much more about my teen years, and to know me more as an adult. I wanted to make sure that they fully appreciated what had happened to me and the impact that it truly had. I wanted them to know that I wasn't upset with them nor did I ever blame them for anything. At the same time, I recognised that they needed the space and time to process it all. I understood that it must have been completely overwhelming for them and that it must have killed them to hear all I had to say; for it rendered them completely helpless as protectors of me, both now and at that time.

Group therapy was continuing to be a challenge, but I persevered. I was learning as much from the others as they were from me. I could relate to their struggles. Robyn had given us a homework assignment that, unbeknownst to her, changed the entire way I saw myself in relation to everyone else in the group. We were all told to bring something in, (either work related or personal,) that we were proud of. It could be something that we had achieved and that brought us joy or happiness. As soon as I heard this, I felt a panic come over me; *What did I have or achieve that I ever was proud of in this life?*

The week passed, we were back in group and it was time for everyone to share. Michael started; he spoke about the ad campaigns that he had created. He had worked on some of the biggest ads in the country; campaigns we would see every day in magazines and on television. It was very cool to see what campaigns he was a part of. Joanne brought in her sketchbook and portfolio, with all of the designs and labels she had worked on and created. She passed her book around and it was amazing to see the sketches knowing I had seen many of them in real life. Joanne's accomplishments were equally as impressive as Michael's work. Russell went next and, as he spoke, I became increasingly more anxious; my heart rate increased and I was becoming emotional. He talked of his love for music, about writing songs, his singing and the 'gigs' he's had. He pulled out his phone and played some music and started singing a song that he had written. The man had a great voice, he was talented. Tim was next. He brought in a scrap book filled with poems, short stories and songs that he had written. He selected one of his favorites and read it aloud to us. It was beautiful and heartfelt. He was a gifted writer and his poem pulled us in, revealing to us his pain and love, expressing his emotions in words and rhyme.

My turn came. *Fuck! What am I going to talk about?* By the time Tim was finished, I was already crying; I couldn't think very clearly, I was taking slow breaths just to compose myself. I looked up from my chair, took a deep breath and said;

"I have nothing!"
"I have absolutely nothing that I'm proud of or that I've achieved in my life."

I kept repeating the words;

"...I have nothing... I have nothing... I have nothing..."

Robyn said;

"There must have been something, Nathan."

There wasn't. There was absolutely nothing in my life that I had done or experienced that I was proud of. Nothing that I felt any joy or happiness in or that I could talk about and share with everyone.

There are certain moments in life that we will always remember, this was one of those moments for me. It killed me; it broke me in two as I slowly came to realize just how much of a scumbag and piece of shit I had been throughout my life and how many people I truly did hurt. I recognized at this moment how my self-sabotage, my shame and my reckless behavior had impacted and permeated all facets of my being. At this point, I felt completely powerless. It felt like I had just experienced the lowest point of my life and I truly just wanted to be done with it all. *I was nothing*, I didn't want to exist anymore, I wanted to curl up into a ball and die. I had nothing to be proud of and furthermore, my family, friends and loved ones had nothing to be proud of me for either. This was my true rock bottom. I had finally reached it and I couldn't fall any deeper. I couldn't even look at Robyn, or anyone in the group at that point. I felt so ashamed and empty.
Just then, I heard a small voice reach towards me;

"You're here. This is what you should be proud of. This; this moment, this act of being here is the strongest thing you could ever do."

It was Tim. That little, smelly unkempt motherfucker who I never wanted to sit next to had just handed me the most beautiful gift in life, and that broke me even more. Robyn agreed with him, further expressing how hard I've been working on myself to even get to this point. She told me to look up at everyone. I couldn't do it; I didn't want to. Finally, I did look up; I looked into the eyes of each group member and, one by one, I discovered that they were looking back at me with genuine love.

Robyn said;

"You have support... you have support."

She kept repeating it. By the third time it was louder and with more passion;

"YOU HAVE SUPPORT!"

She told me to say the words for myself; this made me break down even more. I needed some time, time to compose myself, to find my breath. The words finally came out of my mouth; inaudibly and only to myself, but I said them. She told me to say them again; this time louder and with conviction, like I believed them, and so that everyone could hear me. I took a deep breath, composed myself, and I said those words like my life depended on them; like I was breaking down every wall that had ever tried to contain me;

"I HAVE SUPPORT!"

I yelled. Everyone definitely heard me this time.

I think that this was the first time that I ever felt a true connection and love toward a group of people. This was both amazing and tragic at the same time, especially considering that I had just recently told my very loving family what had happened to me. That session felt like the longest hour of my life. It was definitely at moments like these when I felt the most vulnerable; when I wanted to do self-harm and harm to others; when I felt most worthless, like I didn't belong anywhere. I was still struggling to accept and receive love, still closed off from the people who mattered the most in my life.

The walk out of the office and the building was slow and weighty. After what I had just been through, I was done. I found myself in a shitty little bar on Fourteenth Street; a bar I knew well that was opposite Norwood. I just wanted to drink myself stupid. I sat on a stool at the empty bar, it was late afternoon, and I drank whisky rocks, one after the other. I wanted drugs but I had deleted all the numbers of dealers I knew so it had to be just alcohol for me. I sat there for hours drinking, hadn't eaten, and got very drunk. An NBA game was on the TV just above my head. A big burly guy was sitting behind me, watching the game, and I kept turning to look at him, thinking he was looking at me. In a paranoid state; I finally demanded;

"What the fuck are you looking at?!"

Without hesitation he replied;

"...turn around and finish your drink!"

I remember calling him a *"fucking cocksucker"* and it all went downhill very rapidly. He asked me what I said and I don't remember my reply, but I'm sure it was offensive.
The man confronted me, calling me something that provoked me. I hit him, didn't hurt him too much and he belted me one, knocking me to the floor. I wanted to get hit, it's what I needed and everything that I deserved. I wanted to feel it again so I faced up to him, telling him;

"Please hit me again."

The guy didn't move an inch and I screamed at him, getting in his face, continuously screaming;

"HIT ME... HIT ME... HIT ME..."

I also called him every name under the sun. He hit me hard and I fell to the floor; bleeding. I got up again, crying, I pushed my head toward him in the hope that he would hit me some more, begging him;

"...again... please... hit me!"

He put his hands up as if to say *"No more."* I felt that he could obviously see the excruciating pain in my eyes and that I wanted this. He was a big guy who could have really hurt me if he wanted to. The bartender came around from behind the bar and walked me out. He knew something was wrong with me. I went home and locked myself in my room away from the world; I couldn't see anyone or talk to anyone, Julie, Tom, no one. As much as I was seeing the difference therapy was making in me, I was also becoming more and more closed off to the rest of the world; unable to understand and express my completely foreign and raw emotions.

I spoke to Robyn about the incident, explaining how much I needed to feel the pain and also how worthless I felt especially after our previous group session. I explained the way I felt about myself was that I wanted to be confronted by a seven foot, five-hundred-pound muscle man and I'd want him to beat me up instantly, and aggressively. I further explained to her how I actually welcomed it, I looked forward to it even, knowing that nothing he could have done to me would ever come close to the depth of pain and suffering that I'd already experienced in my life, so; *"go ahead... give me your best shot."*

277

We came to the conclusion that I couldn't live this way any longer, but I was still having trouble getting out of that mindset. When I was in one of my dark depressive states (and I wasn't locked in my bedroom at home) I would just walk. I would walk the streets of Manhattan and Brooklyn for hours. It would be slow; I would be in my head and I was very methodical. Sometimes I would find myself on a park bench staring as the world went by; watching and trying to analyze couples and individuals as they would walk past me. No matter how completely over my life I was; no matter how down on myself and depressed I was, I would go out of my way to be nice to these strangers, to smile at them and to say *"Hello."* They would never know what I was thinking or how I was hurting. Sometimes I soothed myself in the knowledge that;

...no matter what I am going through and how I am feeling, there is always someone (out there) who is worse off than me... I need to put all of this into a proper perspective somehow...

Chapter 34

That Christmas and New Year I stayed in New York instead of going home to see my family. I knew I would be back there for Kelly's wedding in February. Julie and I were invited, so I was taking her back to Australia with me. We spent a quiet Christmas together, just the two of us. It was actually very nice; we both worked for New Year's, there was always great money to be made and Norwood always put on amazing parties this time of year. On the second of January we flew down to Cancun for four nights to get away, stayed at a great resort, and explored as much of Mexico as we could. It was relaxing, it was easy, it was everything that we both needed. Kelly asked me to pick up the wedding ring she had ordered from 'Tiffany & Co.' for her husband-to-be; it was cheaper to buy it here in America, so I agreed to do it for her. Julie had told me that she thought and felt it was a bad idea and not to do it. I told her it was fine and nothing was going to go wrong.

During this time, Tom and I were starting to drift apart, having little arguments and fights. The ring arrived in its all-too- familiar little blue Tiffany's box and I hid it in the very back of my underwear drawer for safe keeping. Julie, Tom and I were the only people in NY who knew I had it. But several days later, after having spent the night at Julie's apartment while Tom entertained friends in our place, I returned home to notice my bedroom had been ransacked. I ran straight over to my underwear drawer and discovered that the blue box wasn't in the little blue Tiffany's bag. I eventually found the ring box but the ring was gone. I looked everywhere for it, literally stripping my bedroom bare, but I couldn't find it. I searched the whole apartment, the living room, kitchen, bathroom. I searched Tom's room as well - that is where I found the little instruction card that was originally placed inside the blue box explaining how to clean the ring. I called Tom and asked him if he touched the ring or if he knew where it might be, hoping it was safe with him. He said he had no idea where it was or what I was even talking about, before telling me that he had people over the night before. I told him that I found the instruction card on his bed and he suggested that we had been broken into and someone stole it, putting the card on his bed so it looked like he took it. I mentioned that the lock to the building door was untouched, as was the lock to our apartment door; and that nothing else was touched at all. Our two laptops were still there, his camera, a Rolex watch, all sitting out in the living room in full view.

Absolutely nothing in the apartment was touched besides my underwear drawer and the ring that only three people knew about, and it definitely wasn't myself or Julie. There was a school across the road so he blamed the school kids, saying they broke in, which was even more ridiculous. I kept telling him that nothing else in the apartment was touched but he couldn't comprehend that. He then followed up by saying that he was worried for his safety in the apartment and was in fear for his life. That's when I lost it and told him to

"...grow the fuck up and don't be so precious. You must know where it is, or can you please ask the people that you had over last night and find out if any of them have touched it."

That's when he told me that I was being aggressive, that he didn't like the tone I was using with him and that he was scared for his safety once again. I said, *"go fuck yourself,"* and hung up the phone. He didn't come home for the rest of the week until the day I was leaving for Australia. Slightly suspicious, I thought.

I had to order a whole new ring and spent close to two and a half thousand dollars on it. I told Kelly what had happened and that I would take care of it, I didn't ask her for money because it was my responsibility and I fucked up. There was a police station across the road. Tom had left a used glass in the sink, so I picked it up from the inside, made sure not to touch the outside of the glass or his fingerprints, and I put it in a zip lock bag. I then grabbed the ring box and little, blue Tiffany's box from the inside, put them in another Ziplock bag and went to the police station. I told an officer what had happened and asked if he could fingerprint the box and the glass to see if Tom had touched it. The officer laughed and was very impressed with my forensic work but said it was too late because when I originally discovered the ring gone, I touched the outside of both boxes a few times looking for the ring, thus rendering the evidence tampered with. He offered to call Tom to give him a little scare, so I gave the officer his number, but never heard anything else about the situation again. I was quite proud though in my attempt to discover who the thief was.

I picked the ring up two days before leaving and guarded it with my life. Julie and I made it to Australia, ring in hand. We spent two nights in Sydney before going back to see family in Canberra. We were supposed to stay with Kelly but we couldn't find the key she had supposedly left hidden for us, so we got a hotel in Bondi on the beach instead. We met with Kelly the first night for dinner, giving her the ring and explaining what happened. A few days later when we were back in Queanbeyan, I heard from Kelly, telling me that they were only having friends at the wedding and no partners. I asked if she could make an exception for Julie because we did fly all the way from New York for her wedding, but she said there would be no way to make it happen, because if she invites Julie, she would have to invite all other partners. Julie and I agreed that I should go to the wedding and that she would be fine because a group of my friends and my siblings were going to be in Sydney with us for the weekend. It was nice being home and introducing Julie to everyone, they all loved her and she liked them. We went back up to Sydney for the wedding and it was raining heavily all day. I didn't go to the service, just the reception.

I was seated at the back table with the single folks and every other table was taken up by the bride and groom's friends and all their partners, I couldn't believe it! I spoke to a friend at the wedding who told me that Kelly thought my story about the stolen ring was a lie; that I was actually trying to get money out of her. I also learned that Kelly removed the key from the hiding spot at her house so I couldn't stay with her. I was so fucking pissed off, Kelly was supposedly a close friend of mine and I would never have thought to do something like that to her, or to anyone else for that matter. I didn't want to be there; I felt misunderstood and used, and these were familiar emotions to me. I discovered that this would be the first of many times that I would have to be discerning about the way I was treated by friends and strangers.

The next week Julie and I went to our beach house for a few days with my family, who took time off from work. We spent every day taking Julie to different beaches and towns near our house and had a great relaxing time. It was easy with Julie; she didn't care too much to go exploring the country and was happy to relax by the beach; I felt trusted and loved.

I always looked at losing the ring, and Julie not being invited to the wedding, as two of many bits of karma coming back to bite me in the arse. It's what I deserved for the hurt, the lies and the cheating I inflicted upon others. Karma was ever present in my life; I was just too stupid and naive to realize it was happening and rearing its ugly head. For so many years I had my head up my own arse, far too blind to see what was standing right in front of me, all the good in my life and all of the pain I was causing myself and so many other people.

We got back to New York. Group therapy was done and I decided to take some time off from my individual work with Robyn. I moved out of my apartment with Tom and moved in with Julie. It worked out well because her lease was up and her housemate moved out with her boyfriend. I loved living on Grand Street, and I loved living with Julie. I was content with the life that we set up together. I was back working at Norwood; Julie was still in nightlife but looking to get out. I was auditioning a lot and I received plenty of short and student film opportunities, as well as independent feature films. I was learning a lot being on set, working with people from all walks of life and was incorporating all I had learnt in school and life experiences into my craft. I was back studying with different acting coaches, hustling where I could, introducing myself to agents and casting directors. I was doing everything I could to push my career forward. I was happy.

Julie, however, was putting pressure on me to give up the dream of acting and to get a 'normal' job. We had been together for about two years and cracks were starting to show, mostly from my doing. I wasn't sharing myself with her; who I really was and what I was feeling. I never shared the details of my life with her, it wasn't a part of who I was nor was it in my vocabulary. I didn't want her to know anything about me; I didn't want anyone to know anything about me, and on the other side of that, I didn't care to know who others were and what made them tick. I was closed off and I had no idea how to communicate. Julie kept things to herself too; she was an introvert like me, so between the two of us, we never really asked many questions and pretended that all was fine.

Nevertheless, Julie wanted a long-term commitment. She said that she was ready to get married and start a family. I wanted to be with her;

283

that wasn't the issue. For me, the issue was that I was still an eight-year-old boy trying to find himself, work out who he was and what he was going to do with his life. Whenever we watched a movie or tv show where there was a wedding scene, or with a couple who got engaged, she would look at me wanting the same. She never had to say anything, she didn't need to; I knew everything she was saying by just looking into her eyes. Once our lease was up, I moved out as I wasn't ready to commit; there was no way I could give her what she wanted. We dated 'on and off' from that point and it was the beginning of the end.

I moved into a basement apartment in Bedford Stuyvesant (Bedstuy), Brooklyn, on Bedford and DeKalb Avenues, with two brothers that I worked with from Norwood and another friend. One month into living there, a huge storm caused the roof to cave in and collapse. The kitchen and living areas were flooded as well as one of the bedrooms. Because it was such an old building, when the roof collapsed, muddy water, dust, dead rats and rat shit became our uninvited houseguests. It was absolutely disgusting and filthy, the living conditions were more than intolerable. We rang the landlord; he didn't want to fix any of the damage, he simply wanted to kick us out. We called an emergency number for situations like this, a worker came out to inspect the situation;

"This is one of the worst living situations I have seen. The landlord needs to fix it. If he doesn't you can all legally stay in the apartment, rent free, for six months before you can be kicked out."

We patched up the roof ourselves, cleaned and sterilized every crevice of the place, and legally stayed for those six months before leaving for good. I moved back in with Julie, into a little studio apartment on Orchard Street in the Lower East Side. We were *good*, or at least we were pretending to be. She kept telling me that I was secretive and

284

emotionally blocked, yet still put pressure on me to get married. We both wanted it to work, but were both drifting away from each other at the same time. I decided to go home to Australia for Christmas so I could get some space to decide what to do. Julie gave me an ultimatum, stating that if I didn't give her an engagement ring before I left, she was going to break up with me. I didn't give her that ring, and she did indeed break it off the day I left.

Whilst in Australia, I decided that I wanted to be with her and bought her an engagement ring. The night I returned to New York I asked her to marry me. She declined, stating that it was too late and that I was only doing it because it was what she wanted. My head was spinning. I did as she wanted and tried to make her happy. I didn't know what to do, so I created a story that I had always planned to get her a ring in Australia, but it didn't work. I asked her to hold onto the ring to think about it, and I left.

We agreed to go into couple's therapy as a last resort. I asked Robyn if we could work with her; she said she didn't deal with couples but put me in touch with another therapist, a colleague of hers, named Karen. I loved Karen, she was a tiny, five foot nothing beast of a woman; very similar to Anne in Australia. She could see the bullshit in people and said exactly what was on her mind. Couple's therapy was a frustrating time for me; it was Julie's first-time experiencing therapy and I felt like she wasn't fully invested, nor taking it as seriously as I was. She seemed already checked out; not fully truthful or present. We committed to ten sessions; Julie lasted for half of them, and it was then that our relationship was finally done. I kept going to Karen and continued to see her after the ten sessions were up. I worked with her for about two years, took a break to go home to Australia and, when I returned to New York I learned that she had retired and since passed away, God bless her.

One of the most healing parts of my therapy with Karen involved doing EMDR (Eye Movement Desensitization & Reprocessing) Therapy. EMDR is a powerful and relatively new psychotherapy technique which has been very successful in helping people who suffer from trauma, sexual and physical abuse, anxiety, disturbing memories, post-traumatic stress and many other emotional problems. EMDR uses bilateral stimulation, right/left eye movement, or tactical stimulation, which repeatedly activates the opposite sides of the brain, releasing emotional experiences that are *'trapped'* in the body. This helps the neurophysiological system, the basis of the mind/body connection, to free itself of emotional and neurochemical blockages. As a person's graphic memories are processed by the brain through EMDR, an emotional release allows for the beginning of a resolution of the trauma in the psyche. EMDR allowed me to go deep within my psyche to explore dissociated parts of myself and disavowed aspects of my past. I was able to openly reconcile more of what I went through, how I felt about my relationships with myself, the Man, my family, previous partners and my life in general.

There were two things I will never forget from my work with Karen; lessons that I will value for my entire lifetime. The first lesson came in the form of a question that changed my life. She asked;

> *"If you could go back in time as the man you are today and talk to your eight-year-old self, what would you tell him?"*

The question stymied me; I didn't know what to say. I sat there thinking for an interminable amount of time. Karen pressed me for an answer, telling me to really think about it. She would not let up. She was great like that; she was tough and would tell me when I wasn't *'in the fight'* with her and was giving up too easily. Finally, the answer hit me. I sat up on her couch, wired by the weight of it all, and cried out;

"IT WASN'T YOUR FAULT!"

If I could go back and speak to the eight-year-old boy inside of me, I would tell him, with all the love and wisdom of my heart, that it wasn't his fault.

This discovery, this life changing revelation, changed the way I looked at myself. As soon as I spoke those words, as soon as I said them (cried them) out loud, I felt the immediate release of an impenetrable weight lift from my shoulders. It was a release of shame, self-sabotage, pressure and secret self-hate, all things I erroneously carried with me for a lifetime; and it was replaced by an expansive feeling of freedom, self-discovery and possibility. I felt like a new person; I had broken the chains that bound me; shattered the anchor that caused me to drown in my own self-pity. I saw more clearly, effortlessly and with understanding, that these emotions, my emotions, all stemmed from the grooming and manipulation that I had received as a child. Everything the Man had said to me in those dark and faithless years led me to this very moment; to this final point of *'letting go'*. I was discovering new and necessary things about myself; having breakthroughs and learning more about who I was and how I wanted to live my life.

The second lesson I learned from my work with Karen came in the form of a homework assignment, and it too changed my life. Karen suggested I write a letter to the Man, expressing freely and with honesty all that I felt inside. I was to see it as an open, empty canvas upon which I could write all that I needed to say to achieve closure with him; and then to do with the letter whatever I pleased. I could burn it, keep it, give it to my mother, father, or someone else special in my life. There was no rush to write this letter and to do it when the moment felt right to me. I was to give myself permission to choose the time I felt ready for that closure; ready to move forward with my life.

287

I was both excited and terrified by this task; I had no idea when that time would be or what I would even write. But I knew that, someday, I would be ready.

During a quiet summer afternoon towards the end of my time working at Norwood, I was behind the bar and a new member had come in for a drink. His name was Stanley and, when we got to talking, he mentioned that he was a trauma and sex therapist. My eyes lit up; his presence there felt like a gift from God; as if he had come into my life at that moment for a reason. I told him aspects of my life and asked if we could meet up to chat some more and possibly work together. Stanley agreed; he was interested in knowing more about me. We met and agreed to work together in therapy. He worked out of his apartment which had an attached courtyard, so when the weather was nice, we would sit outside and chat. We spoke extensively about sex, relationships and sexuality. I learned not to put a label on who I was; '*straight, gay, bi*' but rather to just live my life, to explore and be in touch with my sexuality and to be attracted to whomever I wanted. This was another 'weight-lifting 'moment for me, as I was finally starting to accept that I could be whoever I was and whoever I wanted to be sexually.

I was finally starting to feel free.

We spoke a lot about healthy masculinity versus toxic masculinity; about how men today are still suppressing their emotions, not able to communicate, to cry or even reveal uncomfortable feelings or stories of their past and their present, without fear of being considered weak, small and lesser than. We also unpacked how toxic masculinity, and unresolved traumas in general, can bring about power over control dynamics and the impacts that these create.

We discussed that there is still a stigma attached to men who are in-touch with their emotions; with their authentic, 'inner 'selves versus their fake, 'outer' selves. With Stanley, I discovered the true definition of 'masculine' and 'masculinity'. Through it all, I discovered that I was more of a man, and certainly more masculine, than most men in the world today, because I was not afraid to cry, to open up and talk about my past and present, to communicate and share my feelings and my sexuality. I learned new ways to communicate more fully and with sincerity; in addition, I became capable of actually saying *"I'm sorry,"* and believing it. I was finding new ways to express how I really felt and admit to my wrong-doings. I learned how to take ownership of my actions; both my bad, as well as my good actions. I owned my past, every bit of it; who I was then, and who I now am. Through it all, I had a dawning awareness of what I finally wanted from my life; feeling a deeper understanding and appreciation towards the things that brought me healthy love and honest joy. This is masculinity!

Chapter 35

I was still unable to remember, and sometimes struggled to talk about, specific events from my past. It was through Stanley that the next chapter of my life began; my writing life. Every week he asked me to write things down from my childhood in as much detail as I could; my relationship with the Man, my family, the cruise lounges and gay clubs, the violence and the drugs, my relationship with Olivia in Belgium, Julie, friendships and sexual encounters. Literally everything I could remember. We would break them down and discuss them together the following week. After months of working with Stanley I had written page upon page; chapters and stories worth of memories. I was working through them all, discovering so much about myself; I began to share them with friends who knew me well. Stanley, as well as several others, told me that I needed to '*do something*' with these stories. It was then that I realised that I wanted to create content and art. I realised that by sharing my discoveries I could help others process, heal and grow from their traumatic experiences. Through this exercise in therapy, I rediscovered my love for writing. I took a screenwriting course and I started writing a movie script about my life. It was an intense process, I found it cathartic, but it was also retraumatizing at the same time. When I revisited specific memories, I was overwhelmed and often triggered, reliving them all over again as I gave them life on the open canvas. The empty pages became my trusted healer and companion, I discovered lessons that had been waiting there for me to find as they laid bare along the broken roads I had travelled. The script took several years to write and it has had many incarnations and rewrites. I would write it then leave it alone for months because I needed to get far away from it. Sometimes I was compelled and on fire, and sometimes I wanted nothing to do with it.

Once I became more comfortable with who I was, at ease with my discoveries and more at home in my skin, there was an ease in my writing, in my emotional preparation and mental well-being. I found it easier to arrive at a place where I could say *"OK, enough is enough."* I could write and rewrite this forever, but I've done all I can to it and it's now with the gods; out of my hands and into the hands of trusting others and my own path. I continued my therapy with Stanley until he moved to the West Coast to be closer to his daughter and grandchildren; the lessons he taught me will stay with me always.

Over the next few years, I continued with my therapy, moving forward with my healing, recovery, and being in and out of sobriety. I would go for months without drinking, then *'fall off the wagon'* and drink for months at a time, only to repeat the same cycle again. I learned that relapse is an insidious process which occurs long before the first drink is taken. It was a cycle I couldn't get out of, through no fault of AA, therapy or any other recovery program that I was in. I believe in all of them; they saved my life. However, it was my own will power, or lack thereof, that stood in my way. As much as I wanted to be clean and sober, I found that I could not be.

Years on, I moved through mixed feelings towards alcohol. I have found a better, healthier relationship with all of it. It doesn't own me and I am not using it to escape anything. There are times when I might enjoy a drink and there are times when I find it boring, it does absolutely nothing for me and I want nothing to do with it. I haven't touched drugs for well over one year. I realized that *I loved the way drugs made me feel; but more importantly, I loved the way drugs didn't make me feel.* I needed to stop numbing my feelings, my body, my emotions, my senses, my thoughts and my surroundings. I made a decision that to be able to live my life as free, to be my true and authentic self, I needed to be free from all controlling vices that inhibited my genuine existence of living life in joy, love, and truth.

The biggest issue that has plagued me over all of my years is my handling of relationships; romantic, as well as friendship. I sometimes still wonder whether I know how to do it. I am getting better though, every day. I have always been able to maintain great relationships with my best mates in Australia; possibly because I don't see them as often, and when I do see them, it's like it was yesterday that we were last together. I love those boys. Here in New York, I only have two or three true friends and, in a city of millions of people, I sometimes feel like the loneliest person in the world. I have many acquaintances, but true friends can be hard to find. I don't blame anyone other than myself; I prefer my own company, and I can still struggle at times with trust, communication and opening myself up to new people. What I noticed is that sometimes, I can become friends with someone, let him or her in for a few weeks, and then build a wall and push them away. This is also happening less and less as I catch myself when I do it and make a different choice. It is easier for me to make friends with women over men; I feel more comfortable with women, I trust them more, it is easier to let them in, to open up and talk with them. Whilst all my best friends in Australia are male, they are all from my early school days, from before everything happened. I have been choosing different behaviors and making more of an effort.

Romantically, I have been in and out of many relationships; they have been where I had struggled the most. I had followed the same patterns; I would let a woman in, dote over her, thinking she is the greatest gift that I have ever found. Then not long after (as I could sometimes also do in friendships), I put a wall up. All of my romantic relationships had told me that I can be secretive. I think this was because I found it challenging to communicate with vulnerability. I discovered that I

292

would share everything about my past, but I found it confronting to share anything about how I truly felt in the present moment. I'm not afraid that I will be cheated on; I'm not a jealous person at all. Rather, I can still fear that, if I open up, and let love in, people will abandon me; like all those years ago when the Man abandoned me. Thus, I subconsciously sabotage the relationship. Although I have come a long way in therapy, discovered so much about myself, lifted so much weight off of my shoulders, I still sometimes hold onto the self-sabotage. This *'I don't deserve anything good'* script still casts a shadow over me. This is an ongoing place of growth and healing for me.

Chapter 36

Many women have come and gone and I have learned many things from them all, but there has been one constant in my life over the years. We met at the end of my relationship with Julie and we both weren't looking for anything serious. She was a successful lawyer on Wall Street and didn't see me fitting into her life as anything but a very casual fling. She would admit to herself that she was arrogant in her assessment, and for me, she was someone to help me get over Julie and move forward. She has been my lover, my girlfriend, my enemy and my friend over the years. We have loved each other and we have hated each other; or more so, she has hated me, been disappointed in me, many times over, for what I put her through, which still hurts so much. Despite going through cycles of not speaking, as much as I've let her down and disappointed her (on multiple occasions) over the years, she has absolutely always been there for me. I did not see the good in her in the beginning, which in hindsight was one of my biggest mistakes, because most women would not have stuck with me and supported me through thick and thin, the good times and the very bad and ugly times like she did. We have gone months without talking, when she or I were dating other people, but we were never out of each other's thoughts. She has been the biggest thorn in my side, the biggest pain in my arse, we hate to love each other and love to hate each other, but to be honest I wouldn't want it any other way. She has always been the first to call me out on my bullshit, tell me when I am wrong, making me sit back, take stock of my actions and the consequences that they have on myself and others. Instead of walking away, she did have an abundance of empathy and always felt the need to take me under her wing and try to fix me. We created a very unhealthy codependent connection as the relationship was filled with lies, manipulation and Coward's Bargains on both sides. She is the closest thing I have felt to love. We laugh, we cry and we share everything with one another; but because of the way our relationship first began, I never gave it a chance or took it too seriously. Now, she is one of my best friends, someone I can always call on when in need, and vice versa. I love her dearly. For the rest of our lives we will always be friends, love and hate each other all at the same time. She has been there for me through some of my darkest hours, as well as through some of my brighter days. I hurt her many times through my lies, cheating and manipulation. The way I treated her was the exact same way I treated every girl I was romantically involved with, and the thought of this pains me dearly. I know I have been a major disappointment as a boyfriend, a lover, and even as a friend to multiple women. In being with her and knowing her, I have learned so much about myself and grown a lot as a person; she has definitely been one of my biggest influences.

For many years I wasn't a good human being; not at all and I know it. I now know that I was selfish and that I didn't give a fuck about anyone else but myself. I was a product of my childhood, a little boy who had absolutely no idea of the chaos that I was actually trapped in. This chaos created more chaos, repatterning itself into an all-consuming avalanche of disease that kept feeding itself. I never had an innocent childhood which impacted me developmentally - as a result I did not have the chance to develop a robust or healthy sense of self. However, I now know that the subconscious, repetitive destructive cycles and violent acts were employed by my fractured sense of self and driven by my unhealthy ego. All of this was far beyond my conscious understanding and even beyond the reach of my will, all working together in desperate attempts to survive all that I had endured. I knew at the time of my infractions that I was doing wrong, but I couldn't stop, nor could I change my mindset. I was trapped in a cyclone, spiraling downward with no end point in sight. I had not yet done the work needed, nor implemented the steps necessary, to break the unbidden, unanswered questions from my traumatic youth.

The best way I could describe myself in relationships was that I avoided intimacy at all costs, thus I have never really learned what true love is. I was inherently attracted to insecure attachment types given my avoidant trauma-patterns. My partners avoided asking for what they needed in fear that I would not deliver. I, of course, could not deliver. The more I pushed my partner away, the more she felt the need to fight for the relationship. It became a tug-of-war of sorts, years of push-and-pull, a merry-go-round, until the partner had finally had enough. I would then feel the need for the closeness again and would, on occasion, 'love bomb' her, asking to be taken back, begging for another chance. I would then convince myself (and her), that I had done the work necessary to be in an adult relationship, but I would invariably *'act out'* again; and the merry-go-round would keep revolving. The things a woman craved from me the most (love, reliability, consistency, communication, trust and intimacy) were the things I couldn't, wouldn't, give. The more she craved, the more enmeshed and suffocated I felt and, once again, I would need to get away. I had many tactics for avoiding intimacy; excessively watching TV, working out at the gym, agreeing to run errands for other people, date other women, anything but be in the present moment with her. My partner would figure out that something was wrong and cross-examine me, which is when I'd call her crazy or try to 'gaslight' her. I'd then walk out on her rather than deal honestly with the issues in front of me. She'd rage at me until she finally got exhausted. I would then romanticize what we had, miss her, and the cycle would start again.

After speaking with ex-partners, they told me that they would shut down to the point where they stopped bothering to connect with me or to communicate on any meaningful level because they felt I was unpredictable. They were worn down by my telling them that I loved them, being warm and connected on one visit, then acting aloof and cold on the next. I would complain about them being there, make snide remarks, tell them that I missed them and suddenly change my mind and say that I didn't want them around. That is where the 'gaslighting' would come in, as I would try to make them doubt themselves by saying to them *"I was just joking...you're being overly sensitive... you are being crazy... it's all in your head... what are you talking about?!"* They felt torn; not wanting to be around me anymore while also feeling that what we had was beautiful, rare and worth saving.

I am relieved to know that this behavior has shifted and I have since been told how I've *'grown up immensely'*, learning to communicate with others in loving, caring and emotionally mature ways. I've become more self-effacing; I know when I'm doing wrong and I immediately apologize. I am no longer shutting down emotionally. It's amazing how much bad I have written here, and still, I ache to be better. I believe that the bad experiences are what we learn and grow from; that deep regret contains the seeds of repair; and that there is a wealth of wisdom inside of, and weaved through, our pain. The journey has been extremely hard, pushing me to the edges of my sanity, shattering me into millions of little pieces. It has also been rich, fucking crazy, fun, dangerous, wild, illuminating, character building, educational and enlightening. Like every one of us, my path toward self-awareness and self-love requires that I fully own my past; the person I was and am. This is my truth. My only way to heal.

Today

Chapter 37

By this stage I was well into my therapy journey and spent many years focusing on getting myself better. Fast forward a few years, I was in New York and I woke up one morning with an inability to move. I had not gone out the night before; didn't drink, do drugs, sex, nothing. It was the worst pain of my life; I was on the floor for four days and I couldn't move. I remember the feeling of only wanting my mother; wanting to be home and for her to take care of me. In all of my pain I discovered that I was growing emotionally, as I was finally able to recognize the love, she always had for me. I returned to Australia for Christmas and to have back surgery after rupturing my L5-S1 disc at the end of 2017.

During my recovery, the entire family travelled to Malta to be with Auntie Lina, dad's sister. Lina was dying of cancer, so for one month (over Easter), we got to experience our first trip together as a whole immediate family. While there were moments of sadness, it was a truly bonding experience for all of us.

After Lina died, I returned to New York, only to learn that my sister's husband, Charlie, had experienced a recurrence of his cancer. He had been in remission and was on the way up. Charlie fought for his life with determination and courage, making sure that Janice and their little son would always be cared for. He died in late August. I returned to Australia the night before his funeral. The morning of, I visited the morgue to see his body with Janice, one last time. It would be my last goodbye. I remember staring at his peaceful body saying to Janice;

"If I could swap places with him right now, for you and your son, I would do it in a heartbeat."

Life isn't fair; Charlie had so much life left to live; he deserved to live, so much more than I did. He was the sweetest man that I had ever met, a loving father to his one-and-a-half-year-old boy, a remarkable husband, a man full of love and good intentions. He certainly made us all laugh, sometimes *with* him and other times *at* him. Seeing him lying there profoundly changed something within me. It made me realize just how precious life actually is; how small and vulnerable we all are in the face of this expansive universe, and how quickly life can be taken away. No matter how much love, money, ego or fame we acquire, there are processes in this life that are so much bigger than us all, processes that we will never quite understand and never be able to stop despite our best efforts. I realized then that I had to change my life around or I was going to end up in a similar box. I looked at the smile on his face, and suddenly realized that people not only teach us in life, but they also teach us in death.

My heart was broken for the very first time; for Charlie, for my sister and her son; for his family, and for mine. I walked out of the room, leaving Janice to say her final goodbye to the love of her life. It was then that I realized that he is the man that I want to be like; I want to follow in his footsteps and lead by his example. He had one of the biggest funerals Canberra had ever seen with people spilling out of the church and onto the streets. A real testament to the man he was, so humble and loving, a man with absolutely no arrogance whatsoever. This was a man who had influenced the lives of everyone who's path he came across. I stayed in Canberra for three weeks, living with Janice and her little man, supporting them as they moved through the beginning of their grief process. Between Peter's two little children and Janice's little boy, I have three miracles in my life. They are everything to me; everything I have and everything I do is now for them. I want them to be proud of their uncle; to be able to look up to me and live their life following in my example.

Several days after the funeral, I met up with Bree, my childhood friend who now works as a journalist for 'The Canberra Times', the biggest newspaper in Canberra. She had heard about my story and she wanted to write an article to help raise awareness about child abuse. We got together at a little cafe in Fyshwick, how ironic. Fyshwick has changed a lot in the past twenty years; becoming more commercial, however still mostly industrial. She asked me questions about my life and I told her everything she wanted to know. She told me that she would show me the article before printing to make sure she gave the story the justice and attention it deserved. I told my parents about it and mum asked if it could be an anonymous article; hoping that my name and photo would be omitted. I spoke to Bree about this and she said that my name and photo had to be included so that the article would carry the weight needed to raise awareness of this very real event: A true life story about a Queanbeyan boy who endured terrible abuse but is now living and pursuing his dreams in New York. The article held even more weight at the time of release as there was a lot of talk in Australia about child sexual abuse from the Catholic Church, schools and other organizations. In fact, the Prime Minister of Australia was just about to offer a public apology to all abuse survivors in the country, thus Bree was extra keen to make sure the article was published with accuracy and intimacy. My sole purpose in doing the interview was to raise awareness of, and start the conversation about, child sexual abuse. It is still a taboo subject, with too many people turning a blind eye to the very real horrors that occur all-too often to innocent children.

In addition, its relevance aptly fits in our world today; a world that is filled with toxic masculinity, stigma and shame that surrounds sexuality. I told myself;

If by releasing this article, I could help save one person's life; stop a child or an adult from killing themselves, or from going down the road of drugs, violence and sex like I did, then I will have done my job.

This was all I wished to achieve from sharing my story in the paper.

There was one more very important thing I had to do during my visit to Australia. It was time for me to write that letter. It was the right time with everything that was going on and I was mentally and emotionally prepared to complete the task. I went to my parents' house; I searched everywhere for the little tow truck that the Man had given me all those years ago, and finally found it in the rumpus room. It looked exactly the same except that it was a little scratched up from my nephews having played with it. If I had known where it was earlier, I would have never let them touch it. I went into my childhood bedroom and sat on the floor. The room looked exactly the same to me, with the very furniture I used as a boy. I sat at the little desk where I used to do all of my homework, and I wrote that letter. I told him;

"I am finally free... you don't own me anymore... you don't have any power over me... and none of it is my fault."

There were plenty other things said in this letter that are between the Man and I. I sat with the letter for a day or two, not exactly certain what it was I wanted to do with it; if I wanted to give it to anyone in my family. Finally, I thought it was best kept between the two of us. It was a letter only for him; my message to him, my final goodbye to him. It was for no one else.

It was a beautiful day; the sun was shining and I took the letter down to Queanbeyan Park and sat under a canopy of tall trees. I sat in the moment, taking a deep breath, sitting with my thoughts and feelings. I let them hit me on my body, seeing where they landed and how they affected me. After sitting with them for some time I let them go and felt comfortable and safe with where I was.

I sat in the park for a while, reflecting upon my thoughts. I felt at peace with my past and with my situation at that moment. I found that in writing the letter I was able to piece it all together; place all the unwelcomed violence, and the confusion that followed, onto a page that healed me as I wrote it. I said a few words to myself and to the Man, placed the letter on the ground with the tow-truck sitting on top of it. I grabbed some twigs and kindling, placed them under the letter and around the truck to make sure it stayed alight for a while and for the truck to at least burn some. I grabbed a lighter from my pocket and lit the kindling. I sat there and watched the letter and car burn for a few minutes before getting up and leaving them there to melt away and for the ashes to burn up, float and disappear into the heavens, in the town where it all began. It was time to move forward with my life; no more looking back, using my past as a crutch and an excuse for the way I live my life.

Chapter 38

The last few weeks at home with my family were many things; deep heartache, pain, growth, peace, love and closure. It was now time to go back to New York. Bree and I were in constant communication, she sent me the article to read over and edit. In between the first edit and my final approval, Bree spoke to Janice for her perspective on everything that happened. Reading what Janice shared deeply affected me. I had totally forgotten what I had said at my birthday party regarding my suicidal ideations. She also included that she was not able to help me when I was a young boy. I cried at the impact that my revelations had on those whom I love so dearly. I finally knew how I wanted to live my life. All of the lessons that I learned through my therapy, group work, in AA and other self-help programs were all making sense to me now. Everything was coming together; I had clarity, motivation and purpose in my life. The therapist I saw whilst home in Canberra helped a great deal as did the therapist I worked with when I returned back to New York. I needed someone to talk to; my life was about to explode; I was starting to feel the pressure and stress of it all building up. I needed someone to tell me that I was doing the right thing.

The weekend that the article was scheduled to be released had finally arrived. It was Halloween weekend 2018, also my mother's birthday. Happy Birthday mum! The article was printed in 'The Sunday Times', the biggest selling day of the week for the newspaper. For the whole week leading up to the release I prepared myself for what was about to happen; how my life was going to change forever. Everyone in Queanbeyan and Canberra, and thousands around Australia and the world, were going to know what happened; know my story, who I was, what I went through, and why I was doing all of this. For better or worse, I knew that people were going to look at me differently. I was still ambivalent as to whether I was doing the right thing. Thoughts rolled around constantly;

Should I be putting myself out there like this to be ridiculed and made fun of?... What am I doing?... I can't do this!... How is my family going to react?... How are they going to feel?... What are they going to think?... What are people going to think?... There goes my privacy, fuck this is stupid!... I should never have done this.

This was followed by my healthier, more confident voice;

Calm down, I actually know that this is the right thing to do... It is going to help thousands of people... We need to speak out about this as a society... It's all so fucking twisted... Of course I am doing the right thing, as much as this is about me, it's actually about something so much bigger... The right people will love me for it... Fuck it, it's done now!!

In an effort to help me maintain my calm, a very close friend in New York had invited me to his house in Ocean Grove, on the New Jersey shore. I so needed to be with friends at this time, I needed to have some fun and get my mind off everything. On Saturday afternoon (which was Sunday morning in Australia), I found myself pacing up and down the hallways of Colin's house, riddled with apprehension and anxiety head to toe.

At about four o'clock Saturday afternoon, which was about six Sunday morning in Canberra, I received my first message on Facebook. Then they all started rolling in like an avalanche. I was receiving texts on every platform; phone, emails, Instagram and Facebook. I couldn't and didn't want to read them, so I turned my phone off for the evening. I didn't want to know about any of it; I semi-successfully distracted myself by attending a huge Halloween party with friends. The following morning, upon turning on my phone, I discovered that I had received close to one hundred messages from strangers, from my best and oldest friends in Australia, some of whom never knew my story. I heard from friends that I hadn't spoken to in over twenty years, all offering their love, their support, as well as expressing their shock around not knowing or ever seeing the changes and signs in me as a child. A few actually had a similar response to that of my mum and sister; *"Well, knowing this now explains everything."* and *"It is all so clear now."*

The messages that hit me the most were from people I knew who had admitted to having experienced similar traumas in Queanbeyan, some also saying that their abuse happened at the same pool, while others stated their abuse occurred in different places around the town. Dozens of people from Canberra and all over Australia reached out to me, strangers I had never met before, expressing;

"You have saved my life... You are a voice for me... You have given me the power to finally talk about what happened to me... Your article and your truth has given me the courage to finally talk to my family and my loved ones... You have given me the power to get the help that I need... You have given me the strength to confront my abuser...You are so brave and courageous for speaking out."

I was completely overwhelmed.

I was engulfed by a huge range of emotions and, for the first time in my life, I felt proud of something I had done. I wanted to go back to group therapy to tell everyone that I finally had something to be proud of. I rang my parents and my siblings; I was worried about the feedback or backlash they were going to receive. They said that I was on the front page of the newspaper, followed up by a huge center article with a full-page picture of me. There was no hiding. They said they had received nothing but beautiful and supportive messages from people. I didn't care if I was going to receive any negative feedback myself, I just didn't want my family to be punished in any way for any of this. The article was also released (on line) in many different papers throughout Australia that came under the Fairfax Media umbrella, the organization that owns 'The Canberra Times'. I was told that it received close to one million hits on-line after the first few weeks of publication, so we know the message got out there.

To this day, I still receive messages from all around the world, from grateful people telling me that I saved their lives by sharing. Two of the most impactful messages I received were from separate ladies both in the Middle East and both telling me that they were raped and that they couldn't talk about it in their country. They added that I was the first person they had ever told. One of the ladies said that a similar story had come out in her city and the victim was murdered by her husband as the incident had *'brought shame upon the family'*. The husband walked free.

I began to see this was all so much greater than me, my article and my story;

...This was all worth it... This is all too much and heavy... I need to somehow help these women... I need to get them someone to talk to... They are at a high risk of suicide or murder... This is my purpose.

I helped them to both engage with online therapy. Additionally, many men from India have reached out to me saying that they, too, cannot talk to anyone openly about this in their country. I find it unbelievable

306

that life today still works this way in so many countries around the world and so many people are struggling with this.
Yes, I understand that I'm doing a great thing by speaking out, standing strong and helping as many people as I can, but the truth of it is, it is also very heavy to carry alone.

I strongly believe that we all need to speak out powerfully about it all and also support each other to do so whether it be through family, friends, social groups and support networks. I've needed to make sure that I have the right people and support networks around me to protect, support and help me cope with all of this added pressure. I am often bombarded with questions from strangers asking how they can *'fix'* their lives. I respond by sharing that I don't have the answers for them; I am not a therapist or someone who is professionally trained to offer specific psychotherapeutic advice. I can, however, encourage people, guide and coach them towards sharing their truth. The most powerful way for me to do this is by sharing my journey, sharing my truth and my search for closure and my quest for peace. Their journey will be their own. I remind each of them that they have their own personal path to travel, and I hope they take what they can from my article, my messages on social media, and now this book and go on their own journey knowing that they are being cheered on and supported.

Karma really is a powerful thing; something I never before believed in, appreciated, nor even really understood. I have been told that *"hurt people hurt people."* What I have seen clearly and continue to appreciate is that before taking responsibility, seeking out the help I needed, owning my behaviors, karma would show up in many ways at numerous times, blatantly smacking me in the face or kicking my arse. As I've cleaned up my life and done the right thing, karma has given back to me in abundance. I've met some amazing people in the past two years, some with whom I've had many powerful and meaningful connections, both romantically and through friendships. Through the healing process, my mind and my heart are open now; I welcome new relationships and new exciting opportunities, and they are coming in abundance. From all of this I have aligned myself with many charities and organizations in both Australia and the United States, most notably as a Global Ambassador for the Child Liberation Foundation; a nonprofit organization whose aim it is to eradicate the world of Child Sex Trafficking. Millions of children are trafficked and enslaved worldwide each year and the average age of these children is thirteen. My purpose involves traveling to many countries to help save kids who have been sold into sex trafficking and slavery. I am already working as an Ambassador to the global 'No More' campaign and the 'Australia Says No More' campaign. The mission is to unite a diverse global community to end domestic violence, sexual assault and abuse. An organisation I am proud to be associated with is' Menslink '(a Canberra only based organization) helping young men between the ages of ten to twenty-five get through tough times with the least amount of damage to themselves and those around them. Menslink provides free mentoring, counseling and education programs across the Canberra Region. Another great Australian organisation is 'SAMSN', (Survivors and Mates Support Network). It is one of the country's leading associations for male survivors of child sexual abuse. I feel honoured to be providing my support to them as well.

Through all of this, a wonderful byproduct is that I have rediscovered my passion for the arts, creating content, and acting. It has led me to writing scripts that will (hopefully) allow me to bring many stories to the screen and stage. I have noticed in my own life how positive karma continues to unfold - as I continue to do my inner work and step through the barriers with courageous vulnerability, new opportunities for life expansion emerge. I am being offered many acting opportunities (still my favourite thing to do), starting a podcast, and studying with talented and amazing teachers. I have met a fantastic woman, who has provided me with the opportunity and the liberty to write this book and to share my story the way I wanted: my words, my voice and my truth. My first words to the publisher were the same words I've always had from the very beginning of this journey;

"It is about and always has been about saving lives, starting the conversation, educating the world and finally giving back."

In June of 2019, I was invited to be the keynote speaker at the seventh annual 'Paths to Healing' conference in Madison, Wisconsin, addressing the issues of adult survivors of child sexual assault, with a focus on male victims. It was my first major public speaking appearance. I spoke for a little over an hour; shared the story of my rape and subsequent descent into depression and heavy drug use. It was such a powerful day as I learned so much through speaking openly and honestly to people who were on their own paths to healing and needed to hear what I had to share. It was amazing to see how my sharing held keys for them. It was at this conference where I met a man who had a message for *me* that would challenge my view of a major part of my life story. Upon finishing my speech, this gentleman asked me if I knew the reason why the Man had abandoned me. That question always stumped me; I didn't have an answer. He explained that a potential and probable reason he disappeared from my life was because I was growing up; I wasn't that little boy anymore. I was going through puberty and turning into a man, getting hair on my body. He went on to explain to me that the Man was possibly moving onto his next victim. His words hit me hard; they were insightful, honest and eye-opening. This allowed me to further understand my relationship with the Man, while also providing me with the closure I needed to continue moving forward in my life.

I sat in on a counselor giving a talk and one of the most insightful lessons I learnt from her was a piece on educating our children from a very young age. We need to explain to them that their penis and vagina are called just that. We shouldn't give it a nickname, adults shouldn't be making jokes and playing with them. We should be telling our children that their penis and vagina belong to them and no one else; no one should be touching it, playing with it, talking about it, or touching them anywhere else on their body. If someone does touch them, abuse or talk to them inappropriately, they need to know that they can say *"NO,"* they can tell someone, they won't get into trouble and they **will** be believed. We need to co-create a culture of safety. As much as we need to educate our children, we first need to educate ourselves as adults and as a society.

We only have this one life to live. We are here for a short amount of time, I choose to live mine to the fullest extent possible, and with a smile on my face. I have taken a step back, given myself time, allowing myself to have patience and to breathe. I finally know who I am as a person and what is important to me. I choose peace, love and true joy. This is what it's all about for me now, I crave the beautiful and yet simple things that I have never really experienced before; perhaps a little beach shack, a beautiful partner who I can grow old with, laugh and cry with, and create a family with. This is all I need.

I have reached the point in my life where I am able to forgive myself. This has been the most important, as well as the hardest, thing I have ever had to do. The work, the education, the growth and understanding of who I was, what I went through and who I am now, has all allowed me to finally move forward powerfully. A key part in all of this was processing and moving through all the anger and hatred that I had toward myself, towards others and towards the world. In forgiving myself, I have allowed myself to continue forgiving the Man, layer by layer, something that I need to do if I ultimately choose peace, love and freedom in my life.

I recently discovered that the Man is dead and, like millions of other men and women around the world, I will never have a chance to confront my abuser in person, to sit with him, to talk to him and ask him the many questions that have always been with me. However, I was always of the mindset that if I ever had the chance to speak to the Man one last time, I would ask him;

"Why me?... Why did you choose me that day at the swimming pool?... Did you actually ever love and care for me?... How many other boys did you do it to?... Did it happen to you when you were a child?... Do you actually have any remorse?... Do you even care or are you at all sorry?"

I'm still not sure if I actually want to ask him any of this, for, at this point, I'm not sure if I even need to know the answers.
Once done getting everything I needed from him, I fantasize that I would take a baseball bat and kill him. I would beat that very last bit of life out of him, not (entirely) because of what he did to me (I am continuously experiencing more peace with this) but also so that he could never hurt another child and human being ever again. At other times I imagine that I would just walk away, leaving him to live out his days in his own personal and emotional hell; leaving him to remember the hurt, pain and devastation he inflicted upon innocent others over the years.
People often ask me if I have any regrets about the things I did, and if I would change anything. My answer is this;

"Yes, of course I have regrets, I regret the violence, the reckless acts of rage that resulted in hurting people. I regret hurting myself, both physically and mentally. I regret the self-loathing, the faithlessness; the pain, the sorrow, the manipulation, the cheating and the lies. However, I would not change a thing. Yes, it has been a journey filled with total chaos, and all of the decades of turmoil and chaos has

311

brought me to exactly where I am today. If I changed one little bit of it, I don't believe I would be sitting here in this body and with this mindset, writing these words and sharing my story with you. I may even be dead, or even in jail or on the streets, in a gutter somewhere with AIDS or HIV. I may still be hurting others, continuing the decline into a self-loathing drug addict."

I would also say;

"What happened to me, happened for a reason. One of the main reasons is for me to be brave and to stand tall. To give life to others through the sharing of my story. It happened to me so that I can educate the world about child sex abuse and its catastrophic consequences. It happened so that I can make a difference, to save a life. It is now time for me to give life back to myself. This is my story; it is different from everyone else's. I'm not here to compare, to say mine is worse or better than yours. I'm here to share, so that it may highlight the very real dangers of not speaking up, and not getting the help needed, as soon as possible. I share this with you so that others in my situation, perhaps someone like you (or someone you know) will know that I believe you and others will believe you."

"YOU ARE NOT ALONE."
"YOU ARE NEVER ALONE."

Many people in their ignorance have told me to *"get over it,"* to *"move on with life"* and to *"stop living in the past."* What they don't appreciate is that there are some things in life that we will never simply just *'get over'.* What happened to me is now part of who I am. It is ingrained into me; it's a part of my DNA. I tell myself, and I tell you as well;

"While we may never 'get over' certain traumas, we can 'get through' them.
I have learned from my past; I have resolved to move forward, integrating these lessons into my new life, so that I may create a better world for myself and for others."

Life is simple, and we could live it that way. But so many of us complicate our lives with unhealthy ego, hubris and untamed desires. We fail to silence the noise, the primitive voices in our head that ceaselessly pull us back into old patterns of behavior; behaviors that no longer serve us well and the constant need for quantity over quality.

The last thing I want to say is that I am aware that I am not 'all better'; that I am not fully recovered. I know that the injustices of my past still haunt me; that there are forces I must fight and manage for the rest of my life. I am not a perfect person; I still struggle with depression as well as with Post Traumatic Stress Disorder. I live it, I feel it and I breath it, sometimes on a daily basis. I ask myself often, *Am I healed?* I answer by reminding my younger, more frightened self, that healing is an ever-growing process; a forever journey. I have my ups and downs, I continue to live, to grow, to heal and to discover new things every day. I have faith that not every love will end in hurt. I now believe that healthy love supports and cherishes growth and asks only that we become wiser and stronger versions of ourselves. This is my life now and I know I am strong. I am powerful and I am a proud voice for the thousands who don't have one; *"I am no longer a victim; I am a survivor."* And I will continue to survive; to evolve, to educate, to love and to thrive.

It is time to stand up, to have the conversation, educate ourselves and the world and be proud of who we all are. Irrespective of our past and what we may have been through; we are all survivors; we are no longer victims and we are here.

313

Freedom is of the mind, not of the body. Speaking and living my truth is a powerful thing, and my truth is my power and my ultimate freedom.

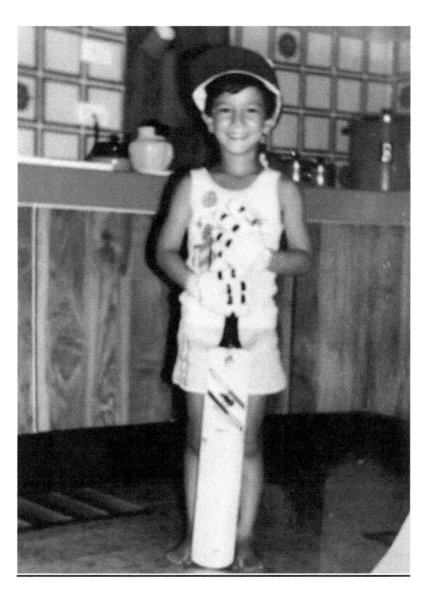

<u>Young Nathan</u>

ACKNOWLEDGMENTS

Special thanks to the following people, who have helped with the creation of this book in some way:

Mum and Dad, my siblings, my whole family, Sally-Anne Ward, Samantha Coyle, Karen Ayre, Shammah Dhall, Norman Fried, Colin Heywood, Joseph Evangelisti, Beatriz Cavalieri, Melanie Jai, Conan Uphill, Robert Farrell, Bernie Da Silva, Gianni Guglielmin, Matthew Cachia, Shane Quinn, Edmond Cachia, Bree Winchester, Elise Idiens, Robyn Handburg, Karen D'Amore, Stanley Siegel, Aussies Say No More Campaign, Child Liberation Foundation, Survivors and Mates Support Network, Menslink, Kirsten Geary, Brad Calcaterra, Matthew Corozine, Haley Richardson, Carol Rosenfeld, James Andrew, Elizabeth Mandarano, Alix Cross, Boris Glamocanin, Jasmine Forecast, George Kay, Arrnott Olssen, Mal and Mel and Mel and Mal.

Forgive me if there is anyone that I overlooked.

Toy Cars   Nathan Spiteri